FROM THE HIDEWOOD

MIDWEST  REFLECTIONS

Memoirs and personal histories of the people of the Upper Midwest

Eggs in the Coffee, Sheep in the Corn
My 17 Years as a Farm Wife
Marjorie Myers Douglas

Dancing the Cows Home
A Wisconsin Girlhood
Sara De Luca

Halfway Home
A Granddaughter's Biography
Mary Logue

FROM THE HIDEWOOD

Memories of a Dakota Neighborhood

ROBERT AMERSON

MINNESOTA HISTORICAL SOCIETY PRESS
ST. PAUL

Midwest Reflections
Memoirs and personal histories of the people of the Upper Midwest

Manufactured in the United States of America
10 9 8 7 6 5 4 3 2 1

International Standard Book Number 0-87351-333-9 (cloth)
0-87351-334-7 (paper)

♾ The paper used in this publication meets the minimum requirements of the American National Standard for Information Sciences—Permanence for Printed Library Materials, ANSI Z39.48-1984.

Peggy O'Neil, words and music by Harry Pease, Ed G. Nelson, Gilbert Dodge
© 1921 (renewed) EMI Feist Catalog Inc.
All rights reserved   Used by permission
Warner Bros. Publications U.S. Inc., Miami, Fla. 33014
Pennies from Heaven, by John Burke and Arthur Johnston
© 1936 (renewed) Chappell & Co.
All rights reserved   Used by permission
Warner Bros. Publications U.S. Inc., Miami, Fla. 33014
You Gotta Be a Football Hero, by Buddy Fields, Al Lewis, Al Sherman
© 1933 (renewed) EMI Feist Catalog Inc.
All rights reserved   Used by permission
Warner Bros. Publications U.S. Inc., Miami, Fla. 33014

Library of Congress Cataloging-in-Publication Data

Amerson, Robert, 1925-
    From the Hidewood : memories of a Dakota neighborhood /
    Robert C. Amerson
        p. cm.
    ISBN 0-87351-333-9 (cloth). — ISBN 0-87351-334-7 (paper)
    1. Country life—South Dakota—Deuel County. 2. Deuel County
(S.D.)—Social life and customs. 3. Amerson, Robert, 1925–   Childhood
and youth. I. Title.
    F657.D4A48 1996
    978.3'2503—dc20   96-6356
                                                                 CIP

The map on page viii and all sketches were drawn by the author.

To the memory of
Bernice Casjens Amerson
and other strong farm women
whose determination, during
the hard times of Depression
and drought, made such a
difference to so many

contents

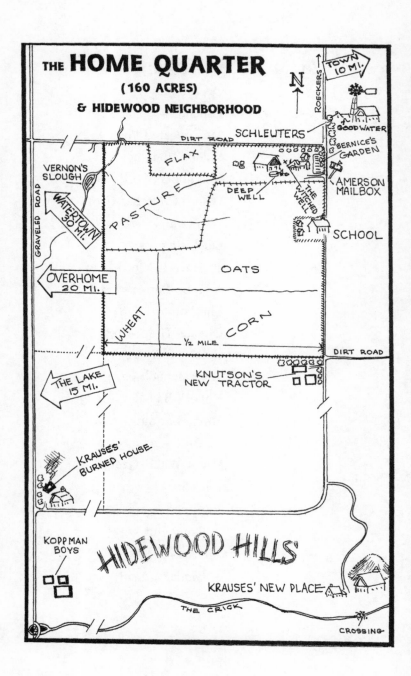

preface

The Hidewood Hills is the remote, rural neighborhood in eastern South Dakota's Deuel County where I was raised. Now, fifty-three years after I left home, I am drawn again and again to my memories of that old farm community. I cannot escape the feeling that something of value can be rediscovered there.

It may be that the uniquely *American* nature of that time and place are especially poignant to me because I spent many years living in other countries, at our embassies on U.S. Foreign Service assignments. But I know I am not alone in my thoughts about "old-fashioned values"—the very phrase is a cliché. Many people of my generation feel nostalgia for our childhoods, despite the genuine hard times wrought by dust storms and the Depression. We like to think that life was simpler then, and that the values of the traditional family farm and the small town still represented mainstream America. It gives us great pleasure to recount for children and grandchildren the unfamiliar aspects of the lives we lived—a way of life that has vanished as surely as have the one-room schoolhouses, country doctors, threshing crews, slop buckets, and outhouses with half-moons on the doors.

But simpler was not always better, and certainly not easier. Laundering overalls and diapers on a washboard was simple enough, but today's washers and dryers have to be considered preferable. Horses could pull a plow, but tractors got the job done faster. In truth, nobody wants to return to all that was the past.

Still, there was something there that should not be lost. Is it possible to hang on to the best of our family-farm experience? Or to try to re-create it, in these times when so much has changed? We might want to look more closely at the way we were, to see just how much of the past is worth preserving. That has been my main purpose in assembling these recollections.

The eastern edge of South Dakota marks roughly where the plains begin—maybe where the West begins, as many folks there like to say. Some men wear cowboy hats and high-heeled boots when they go into town, although most people agree that the real cattle country starts out west of the river. The river, the Missouri, bisects South Dakota on its way south. All this eastern end, next to Minnesota, is in-between country, part ranching but mainly farming, and some of it good farming, especially in the rich flatlands of the Big Sioux River valley.

The neighborhood known as the Hidewood is an in-between spot in this in-between country. Some of the land is flat, especially the broad bottomlands along the Hidewood Creek (pronounced "crick," in these parts), but the topography is mostly hilly, and newly plowed hillside soil is likely to show clay and rocks. Like the Missouri River that divides the state, the creek splits Hidewood Township before it runs into the Big Sioux. In the early years, a lack of bridges limited interchange, social or workaday, as farmers naturally spent more time with neighbors they could see. Our neighborhood "on this side of the crick," a pocket of some four or five square miles, thus felt somewhat apart—between zones of richer land next to lakes and rivers and some ten miles from the nearest towns.

Its remoteness meant it developed late. Homesteaders quite logically staked claims first on richer land, closer to railroad terminals and growing settlements. As a result, farmers near the towns would enjoy electric power decades before Rural Electrification Administration lines entered the Hidewood following World War II. This sense of isolation in the neighborhood seemed to impart a unique spirit to its inhabitants.

Native Americans and explorers knew this prairie country for its grass—grass that had seemingly been there forever, its deep, tough root system providing stability and a cover of sameness to the soil. But beneath the tall grasses lay what would draw white invaders to the middle of the continent: land, land they could take for farming, land offered *free* after the Homestead Act of 1862. Any man or woman over twenty-one who was head of a household and was or intended to become an American citizen could locate an unencumbered quarter section, 160 acres, and stake a claim. Ownership followed after five years of working the soil and payment of a mere fourteen-dollar fee. Homesteaders settled first in Illinois, Iowa, Wisconsin, and Minnesota, which offered black loam soils and good timber; then, as Old Country newcomers joined relatives or acquaintances, these states became heavily populated. By the 1870s, Dakota Territory began to look better to land-seeking immigrants. They saw a golden opportunity, and takers numbered in the thousands.

One of them was my grandfather. In 1876, a robust, Norwegian carpenter-farmer recently turned twenty, he got off the boat in New York and headed first for Galesville, Wisconsin, where dozens of other emigrants from his home village had already settled. Passenger lists on the British ship out of Liverpool changed his name from Johannes Amundsen to John Emerson; he liked his new American identity enough to keep it, except to change the spelling to Amerson. Whatever his name, he knew who he was and where he had to go—west, where there was still land to be had. He left the friendly Wisconsin settlement and boarded a train that chugged across Minnesota to where the wide-open plains of Dakota began. He stopped at Watertown to investigate the area, and near a settlement called Castlewood, he found work at Keator's Ranch, run by an enterprising operator bent on expansion. There many new arrivals gathered until they could figure out what to do next. After a year or so, John took action. First he married Agnette Kristiansen (or Agnes, as she called herself in America), another Norwegian immigrant he had met working at the ranch. Then he filed his own home-stead claim near Lake Poinsett in Hamlin County, where fellow Scandinavians were settling, and built for himself and his wife their first sod shanty on a prairie hillside.

John and Agnes produced a daughter and five sons, the fourth of whom, Clarence, became my father. After an early Norwegian-Lutheran marriage that ended in tragedy, Clarence wed Bernice Casjens (whose name was pronounced "*Bern*-iss"), a young woman of German-Dutch heritage whose U.S.-born parents had migrated up from crowded Iowa and eventually found their own land near Hayti, Hamlin's county seat. The youthful second wife inevitably felt excluded in the "Norskie" community. Clarence and his growing family moved away and soon became a part of the Hidewood neighborhood.

Other denizens of the Hidewood could claim more direct descent from the area's first pioneers. Fred Roecker, one of the Hidewood's earliest settlers, homesteaded his tree claim in 1884. As he and his son began to break the sod, others filtered in to start working adjacent land. Most of them bore German names—Konold, Weisel, Schleuter, Kluckman, Goldbeck, Koppman, and Krause; scattered families of Scandinavian or Dutch origin arrived later. (The Germans would come to be called Dutch, corrupted from Deutsch, while the Dutch would commonly be known as Hollanders.) The Hidewood's pioneers, like those of so many other communities, endured great hardships to establish the neighborhood that their sons and daughters continued to build.

All the characters in these interconnected tales are real, and the events portrayed took place in approximately the sequence depicted. Each chapter explores a different aspect of family and neighborhood experiences over an eight-year period, leading up to the time of full U.S. involvement in World War II. As a boy (from about nine to seventeen years of age, in the elapsed time of these stories), I participated, one way or another, in most of the events described, and so I have relied heavily on personal memory. I have also compared my recollections with those of my several siblings and four of my aunts and uncles. Perhaps most important, I am fortunate to have reviewed often with my mother, who died at eighty-nine in 1993, various delicate aspects of her own central role and how she felt about these events at the time they were occurring. Where pertinent, I have researched the printed record, such as courthouse files or newspapers of the time. Interviews with former teachers of our one-room school provided additional insights into the neighborhood, as have conversations with a few old neighbors still living in the area.

Because I have woven strands from many sources into the fabric, and because greater understanding has come to each of us with the passage of years, this is more than an "I remember when" account. Rather, I have sought to re-create the mood back in that particular moment in time. These stories say this is the way it felt and sounded and looked—at least to me and my family. The varying points of view in each individual situation represent the person most involved. In the opening story, for instance, I—as nine-year-old Sonny—was on hand during the months examined, but this is really the story of how the devastating circumstances of 1934 affected my mother, Bernice, already under severe strain in her personal life. The viewpoint is hers; dialogue and unspoken thoughts have been carefully chosen to represent what we know to have been characteristic of her. And so with all the stories in this collection.

A writer cannot hope, with a few neighborhood memories, to represent fully any given region or time period. But if each of these stories fairly reflects a piece of the true mosaic, perhaps together they can help us to understand and make use of our own past.

OVERHOME

Bernice
1934

Following the men in the loaded truck, she steered the Model T over splotches of dark ice that lingered in the unused driveway. Ahead on the frozen ground, the truck's dual wheels crunched dried mud and kicked up thin dust that continued its random swirls after they stopped in front of the empty house. Nobody had lived on this place for years. The house seemed even more forbidding than she remembered from the quick look the previous week: so many broken windowpanes, one door sagging half-open, dull paint flaking from the weathered siding. The outbuildings were no better, the old barn a faded, dirty pink, shingles missing from the granary roof. Around the yard, dry brown stems from last year's weeds stuck through patches of gray snow where the late-winter sun still had not made a difference. Why did March have to be the month when people moved? It seemed the wrong time to start out on anything.

Bernice switched off the Ford's rattling motor and looked around at the children: Sonny, nearly nine, with her in the front seat; Clarice, twelve, in back minding the bundled-up baby and the two little girls. All five sat in silence; even the baby's blue eyes seemed focused out the side window, taking in the new place.

"It may not look like much now," she said, "but we'll fix it all up nice." She knew her attempt at cheerfulness sounded unconvincing.

Up ahead the tall, lean figure of Clarence appeared around the side of the truck. He glanced back, as if to make sure his family had actually followed him all the way. He held one side of his blue denim jacket collar against the chilling wind and strode up the rickety porch steps to push open the sagging door. When he turned to signal Johnny, their always-helpful neighbor, to start backing the truck, Bernice could see the familiar smile that seemed to light her husband's craggy Scandinavian face when friends were around. She felt the old envy begin to stir within her, but she could not let it bother her today. She yanked at her door handle and summoned determination. "Come on," she urged the children, as if inviting them to play a new game, "lots to do, and you can all help!"

The two men grunted at lifting the heavy furniture, and the boy imitated them, carrying lighter chairs and cardboard boxes. Bernice attacked the layer of dry grime crusted on darkly warped floorboards and even on the paint-chipped wainscoting. She paused only to give directions: "The writing desk? Oh, in that corner. Sonny, that box can go in the east room for now. Clarice, put the baby in the highchair, and the girls can help you unpack pots and pans in the pantry."

After an hour they were surrounded in the kitchen by items immediately needed, and the rest of the load was sorted and out of the way to await later attention. People would soon be getting hungry, she knew. She added a few more sticks to the cookstove fire and spread the oilcloth on the kitchen table. Passing the west window, she couldn't help pausing to look in the direction from which they had traveled that day—looking toward home. There, beyond these Hidewood Hills, beneath where the pale orange afternoon sun hung low, within that purple horizon lay everything that had been familiar to her until this moment.

"Overhome," as she always called her folks' place since leaving there, was twenty miles to the west near Hayti. Most of her brothers and sisters still lived there, barely hanging on, with Maw and Paw already gone. Within that purple haze, too, were the two farms she had known as wife and mother. Now I have moved again, she thought—in the wrong direction, still farther away from Overhome warmth.

She became aware that the two men stood behind her at the window. "Don't look like snow, anyhow," Clarence said.

"Yeh," Johnny agreed, his high, nasal tone so different from Clarence's deeper voice, "and boy, you do get a long view up here in the high country. Must be twenty, thirty miles, past the Sioux river bottom, even."

"A long way, all right," she said.

Johnny began to button up his jacket. "Yeh, well, guess I better be gettin' back there, time for chores."

Bernice insisted that they "stop and have somethin' t'eat first." She set out the loaf of her bread, the ring of bologna, and the can of pork and beans they'd brought along, and, kids and all, they sat around the big table, perched upon whatever was handy—chairs, boxes, cream cans. With a fire crackling in the cookstove, it seemed almost a spontaneous, festive picnic. They even joked when they sampled the bitter water from the only well; Clarence said that before long he'd have some warm milk to bring in. He and Johnny talked about problems shared during the past week hauling livestock and machinery to the new place. The three grown-ups went over some of the good times they'd had together in the other neighborhood.

When Johnny rose to leave, Bernice put shyness aside and warmly pumped his hand. She knew they were going to miss that familiar bald head, those laugh-crinkled eyes. "We'll never have another good neighbor like you," she heard herself saying, though she felt embarrassed about it right afterward. Then their old neighbor drove away, Clarence went out do the chores, and Bernice, alone with the children, began the long task of getting settled.

In the darkness that night, with the family bedded down on mattresses scattered on bare boards of dining room and the downstairs bedroom, she reviewed her work plans for early morning. Scrub kitchen floor and walls with soap and hot water; set up the cast-iron heater in the dining room; assemble the bed frames upstairs. Next week, fix the front room; maybe next summer, after the landlord's carpenters come for basic repair work, some painting and new wallpaper to make this a decent home. From details of specific and practical tasks her flowing thoughts continued on their own, stimulated by impressions that would mark this day—just two weeks before her thirtieth birthday—as a kind of personal milestone. There had also been others.

She remembered the day back at Overhome, twelve years earlier, when she had heard from a friend about the housekeeper job with a widower named Clarence Amerson over in the Norwegian community. "Maybe it is time for me to get away from home, to work out," she'd said to Maw that day. As the oldest girl among ten brothers and sisters, she had always been Maw's main helper, attending to the needs of the younger children as they came along, constantly cleaning and cooking and sewing. Before she'd finished grade school, she'd had to drop out in order to help at home, thus making it possible for the younger ones not only to complete the eight grades but—for the girls—even to go on to high school. She was getting restless. "I'm eighteen years old now," she had declared that day. "I should start living my own life, don't you think so, Maw?" Her mother had not seemed pleased at the idea, at first scowling without response. "If you want," finally came the dry reply.

She remembered the first time she saw Clarence, whose young wife had died only weeks earlier of some kind of fever after the birth of their second child. Tall, dark, gentle and soft-spoken, already in his thirties, Clarence seemed all the more attractive because of his desperate need of assistance. A neighbor woman was temporarily keeping the baby, Clarice, and as he sat in his untidy kitchen to talk with Bernice about employment, his three-year-old Marie had clung pathetically to his overall pantlegs. "She wants to come along, wherever I go," he'd explained, apologetic. "Kinda hard sometimes, out in the cold, cleanin' barns and everything, you know." Bernice had had to blink away tears as she murmured, "Oh yes, it must be very hard"; she'd agreed to take the job.

The work had been easy enough. More difficult was being away from home, the feeling of isolation, "alone among the Norskies," so different from her own less-rigid German-Dutch family. Impossible to overlook, or forget, the signs of actual hostility those first months. Having only rarely seen the inside of a house of worship, one Sunday she experimentally accompanied Clarence to his Lutheran church. But the intense minister had let it be known from the pulpit that non-Lutherans were not welcome at his services. Stern matrons of the Ladies Aid had criticized her openly for such offenses as bobbing her hair or chewing gum in public, reminding her regularly how they had all cherished the wonderful Gunda, Clarence's poor, dead Norwegian wife. She'd begun to feel a resentment growing within her against these closed-minded Norwegian Lutherans, against religion. Against—dared she even think it?—a God who would permit pain administered in His name.

But she had found a few friends. How wonderful it had
been to have Nathalie, a girl her own age, staying with grand-
parents just down the road. Spunky, fun-loving Nathalie and
her spit curl dark and glamorous against the creamy com-
plexion of her powdered forehead. Nathalie, a pal to share
gossip or secrets with. For Bernice the secrets to share had
soon become momentous, as gradually, inevitably, she and
Clarence, in physical proximity, began to view each other in
a new light.

She admired the way he went about his work in quiet
decency. Unlike so many of the neighborhood's hard-drinking
young men, Clarence did not use whiskey or tobacco. Nor
did he swear or talk dirty. His interests, outside his horses and
cows, included an occasional Sunday baseball game. And she
knew he was musical. His fiddle case rested in a closet she'd
straightened out; she'd also heard about the Amerson brothers playing for dances. He had not yet taken the fiddle out to
play, but every once in a while she'd hear him humming old-
time tunes as he went about his farmyard chores. Though he
never actually said so, she could tell that he appreciated how
well she was mothering the baby and little Marie—in fact,
taking good care of all of them.

He began to show that he liked having her around.
Sometimes in the evening after supper, the two of them
would sit at the kitchen table in the yellow light of the
kerosene lamp, and although neither of them felt comfortable in small talk, they would exchange thoughts about the
children, or the weather, or the neighbors and crops. Perhaps
neither felt the need to reveal too much while letting the
other know it was nice to be together. The intimations were
there. All the while she could feel growing between them the
tingling sensation of physical attraction. One evening after
supper, close together on the davenport, both of them tense
with denial of desire, she had let him know they would have

to be married before she could do what he wanted, and gentle Clarence had held her close and agreed.

She had confided in her new friend, who came right to the point. "I was afraid this was going to happen," Nathalie said, twirling a finger around one of her spiral spit curls.

"Afraid? Why?"

"Bernice, I've said it a hundred times: you're young, you're pretty, wait awhile! We've never been anywhere—we could go away together, to the Cities, to California!"

"But how could I—"

"If you don't do it now you'll be stuck out here, raisin' kids the rest of your life."

"But he needs me!"

"Does he love you? Did he tell you that he *loves* you?"

"He wants to marry me, that's enough. I couldn't leave now."

Nathalie gave her a long and sober look. "Well, I spose you're right. You might have had a more romantic courtship," she said, flicking a spit curl sassily, "but I gotta admit, he is a pretty spiffy fella."

Bernice had had her own misgivings about the matter-of-fact proposal, hardly the kind of romancing envisioned in girlish dreams. She knew, too, that there would always be the hovering shadow of his first wife, his first love. Maybe she would, as Nathalie had said, be stuck out here raising kids. But all those things are not so bad, she'd convinced herself, when you have a spiffy fella and a good provider, too. And so the next day she and Clarence had made plans for their wedding—though not, she insisted, among his Lutheran co-parishioners. The ceremony took place in October 1923 in an unfamiliar church miles away in Watertown, the area's largest town, where no one would comment on a wedding with just the two of them, without advance notice or invitations.

Lying in the dark of the new and strange room, Bernice recalled other milestones: their own children, the boy coming while they were still in the Norwegian neighborhood, the three girls—Elaine, Mavis, and Jeanie—after they'd moved a few miles away to the showplace rented farm on the rich flatlands near Estelline. And the shock late last winter when the owner had suddenly decided he wanted to farm there himself, which forced them on short notice to find something else. Finally, nearly in desperation, they had heard about a quarter section up in the Hidewood, some twenty miles farther northeast. It was disagreeable to have to give up good bottomland for unknown rocky hills and for Bernice to exchange the big, white home, hardwood floors and all, for the abandoned, decaying shell perched atop those barren hills. But there was little choice. They would have to make the best of it.

The best of it, she thought now, aware of the chill in this March night, will probably be that schoolhouse, only thirty rods away, a big improvement over the kids' having to walk two miles. They can even run home for dinner during the noon hour. And there are probably lots of other good things about this place we'll find out about as we go along. As she relaxed toward sleep, she repeated to herself her simple conclusion: We'll work hard and we'll make a go of it.

She did not know then what obstacles she would have to face in the next few weeks.

No fall plowing had been done, so Clarence spared no effort in his race against the seasons. As soon as the frost was out of the ground, he got his five-horse team on the gangplow and into the field, working them from dawn to dark. He obtained a seed loan from the Production Credit Association in Watertown. Then came more long days when from the porch she could mark his progress, the horses' dark shapes raising dust off in the distance, moving slowly back and forth across the sloping earth of the prepared fields. Some days she took him his forenoon and afternoon lunch herself, and right after he downed the last of the warm tea from the pint fruit jar he would be off again, attentively riding the wide grain drill whose working parts emitted a chorus of squeaks, as if from frightened barn swallows held prisoner inside the warped seed box. He got his oats in only a week later than his neighbors did. Then there were more days of walking in the dust cloud behind the broad drag, and he would come home nights with his face and legs caked black with field dirt. By corn-planting time in early May, he had nearly caught up with the seasonal schedule.

During these weeks there never seemed to be time for the two of them, by themselves. When he was not in the fields, he might be out doing chores in the darkness of both morning and night. On Sundays he avoided normal fieldwork, as tradition required, but he spent hours repairing broken harness straps or fixing fence or carrying plowed-up stones off a field. At night fatigue and the nearness of others in this smaller house imposed silence over what might have been the intimacy of their bedroom.

Bernice missed the good times. Times for fun, like dancing together at the house party they'd organized before leaving the other place. Times when the two of them could talk leisurely about things. One night in mid-May she managed to get the kids upstairs early, and they sat alone at the kitchen table, looking over separate sections of the newspaper. Clarence had already pulled his dusty work socks half-off, cooling his feet. She broke the silence with her question: "How'd the planting go today?"

He looked up from the spread page. "What?"

"Did you have enough seed corn to finish that field?"

"Oh yah." His eyes returned to the newspaper. "Used up the last of that bushel from Broksiecks."

"Well, maybe you can take it a little easier now."

"Ahhh. Work ain't goin' t'get done, unless y'do it."

"A person can't work all the time, neither, day an' night like this."

He did not respond, but after a while he folded the newspaper and leaned over to pull at his socks and put his shoes back on. He picked up the kerosene lantern and went out into the dark night, mumbling—it seemed more to himself than to her—that "the sow might come in before morning." Bernice could not be sure what had made him get up and leave, the newspaper report on hog prices or simply his desire to be left alone, to avoid having to talk about things. She supposed he was having his own problems about leaving the old neighborhoods behind.

She herself was still adjusting to new surroundings, she realized. Mrs. Schleuter—"Sleeter," they pronounced it— the closest neighbor up the road, had her two daughters stop by to pick up the kids on their first day of school. Nice of her, and she had come to get acquainted that same day. But though kind and thoughtful they might be, Vera Schleuter and the other women of the neighborhood seemed so different the way they *belonged* here, relaxed and self-confident. I can never be like them, Bernice knew in her heart.

She knew something else about herself, too—that the death of her mother a year earlier still bothered her. "Maybe I should never have left home when I did," she told herself aloud one day, soapy diaper suspended over her washboard. Maw had been so poorly, and all those little kids around to take care of. "Maybe that's why she died so young." She worried about the five orphaned youngsters still Overhome, their other elder brothers and sisters now in Iowa and Oregon. She often pictured the five of them, doing their best at the home place at least until the youngest could finish school: Harry, whom they all called "Bub," barely twenty, hardly old enough to try to be the man of the place; energetic Irene, eighteen, staying around to help out; Margie and Ruby, still in high school; and the baby, Bert—well, he *is* fourteen now, she reminded herself. She tried to get over to see them every once in a while. Every time she could see that they all missed Maw, too, something terrible. Maw dead. So often these weeks she found herself stopping in the middle of work, thinking about Maw: the tired look just before she died; the smell of funeral carnations; the clammy feel of Maw's cold hand touched one last time in the open coffin.

As always, work awaited to divert her thoughts, to offer the hope of better times. Surely she was doing her share, every day all day. Three meals to prepare for the seven of them, the regular baking, dishes to wash (she missed the assistance of older stepdaughter Marie, now staying with another family in order to attend high school in Hayti, but thank heaven that Clarice and the little girls could be of some help). Then there was the cream separator to take apart and clean, disk by tedious disk, every morning. Because water from the farm well was too hard, drinking water had to be hauled in cream cans from neighbors' wells. Soft rainwater for the wash needed to be dipped up from the deep cistern under the floor in the east room and carried to the cookstove for warming. She had not yet succeeded in acquiring even a used hand-powered washing machine, and twice weekly her reddened knuckles stung and her back throbbed after hours bent over washboard and tubs.

To get by, they would need cash from selling cream and eggs and, later, chickens. With the first signs of spring, she worked in the chicken coop to improve the laying nests, and she culled the cluck hens from the layers among her Leghorns and set them on nests of eggs to raise chicks. While Clarence sowed in the fields, she planted nearly an acre of garden—vegetables to feed the family later in the summer and to put up for the winter. There were long weeks during that spring when she often feared that she might not have strength enough for the task. At such times she felt her spirit at its lowest ebb, and a menacing mood of tension and vague despair seemed to be growing within her. Still she kept on, trying not to think about it too much, plunging into the work that had to be done, hoping to find solace.

Her garden did not fail her. She willingly spent hours in the fading light of dusk weeding, watering, nurturing, clasping at the promise in the green shoots of each row. Other momentary breaks came in the work routine. With the warmer weather arrived the two carpenters promised by Herman Kreins, who represented the landlord-insurance company. While this meant more work for the daily noon dinner, their progress provided encouraging landmarks: smooth plaster drying on the kitchen ceiling, a new outside cellar door, concrete walls in the damp cellar with shelf space for all the canning she would do in the fall. Dresses and bonnets she sewed for the girls allowed her to return to pleasures known since childhood, dressing up dolls and babies.

Every month or so, true to her hopes, some of the Overhome kids came over on a Sunday, and this was always a comfort. In May one afternoon, she opened up the *Daily Argus Leader* and read with utter fascination about five identical girl babies being born to a family up in Canada—quintuplets, they were called—and the gray doctor with a kind face who talked about the fantastic delivery. For several days running, she marveled at the idea of having five baby girls all alike. She carefully clipped the stories and photos, folding the soft paper into the scrapbook drawer of the writing desk, where she also kept her other collection of clippings—most of them two years old now—about the Lindbergh baby's kidnapping.

While distractions such as these took her attention, the

effect would not last. Soon she would be back at the wash-board enduring the odor of manure-stained overalls and hoping that she could keep going until the harvest was in.

The hot winds of summer brought more adversity. No rain came, and Clarence grew ever more grimly silent as he watched his stunted oats fail to fill out kernels, his corn leaves burn and shrivel. Only the sharp-spined Russian thistles seemed to prosper in the drought, sprouting their bushy green everywhere, in fields where they stole precious moisture from dying crops and along untended fence lines, bristling and sturdy like reserve ranks of enemy forces. The *Argus Leader* printed reports of dust storms down south, in Oklahoma and Kansas, and soon the Dakota skies, too, began to darken with enormous clouds of soil particles that could no longer adhere to the earth and rose instead on the dry wind. A day came when the sun was obscured at noon, and dust drifted like a darkened blizzard around fenceposts and outbuildings, obliging Clarence, when he had to be outside, to breathe through his bandanna or shirtsleeves crooked to protect his face. In the house Bernice and the girls, armed with strips of cloth torn from an old floursack, tried to keep the marauding darkness from filtering in through cracks along windows or doors. Birds in the trees, disoriented by the absence of daylight, fell silent and motionless; animals in the pastures turned their rumps into the stinging wind and huddled together; children cleaned the black from their nostrils and eyes, coughed and wheezed and felt strangely depressed.

"Crop failure"—she could remember her father's fearful use of these dreaded words—became a common utterance. For farmers in the Hidewood, it meant there would be little to harvest. Clarence mowed some of the dwarfed oats to store as hay against the coming winter months, and he had to borrow more money to truck in from less damaged areas additional hay sold as timothy but really half pigeon grass and thistle. In the cornfields the stunted stalks could be salvaged only as fodder. No grain or corn could be gleaned from the fields to fatten hogs or even to keep chickens until full maturity.

The realization gradually imposed itself with numbing finality: after months of unceasing labor, the reward was crop failure. Bernice felt somehow betrayed, and she brooded about the unfairness.

"Even the cream checks are getting smaller," she complained to Clarence one day at the dinner table.

"Cows can't make much milk outa Russian thistle."

"Not enough money even for what we need in town. Kids are going to need clothes for school."

"What they got might have t'be good enough."

His words made her anger spill over. "Good enough! If that ain't just like you! Any decent manager would know we can't keep goin' on like this."

Once again, his response was silence as he quickly finished his plate and disappeared outside. Then she berated herself, for she knew it solved nothing when she nagged at him that way. Sometimes she just couldn't stop these crazed rantings, and it seemed to be getting worse.

Going about the heavy routine of her daily work, she found herself at times so hemmed in by frustration that she cared little whether the children might be listening and watching, wide-eyed and somber, as she gave vent to her anger and mouthed her swirling emotions, declaiming aloud to no one at all. She was in this kind of dark mood, doing the endless washing one summer day, when Sonny ran back from the mailbox waving a letter.

"It's addressed to you, Ma—from California!"

Nathalie. She could feel a quiet excitement as she dried her hands and turned away from the washtubs to sit on the porch steps. How welcome, she thought, this chance to sit down with my old pal! Her hands actually trembled, she noticed with a short laugh, as she tore open the envelope and began reading: "Dear Bernice, Just a line to say hello, not much news. . . ." Nathalie, always a better talker than letter writer, scrawled brief references about her husband working at the bank, their son singing with a chorus at school, the peacefulness of their life in Los Angeles. She ended with a sentence that Bernice read over and over: "I just wish you could be here with me to enjoy the view right here in our backyard, where the flowers bloom year around and grass is always green, but guess I better stop here and turn on the water hose for our orange trees if we want to pick our own fruit later on. As ever, . . ."

She folded the letter back into its torn envelope. The picture of Nathalie, lounging in some kind of paradise, faded from her mind as she became aware again of the stench of diapers and cow manure wafting from the murky washtub. She regarded the mounds of dirty clothes that her family of seven seemed to produce every few days, and she looked across the fence at the sterile, caked-dry fields. Rushing anger replaced the pleasure of opening Nathalie's letter. "Maybe you meant well," she told her absent friend, "but maybe you're rubbing it in, too. Maybe you're saying, 'I told you so.'"

During the next few days she found it harder than ever to keep going. Clarence seemed more withdrawn, too, going through the routine of his outside work. Left alone in the fantasy of her fevered mind, she began to compare her circumstances with visions of Nathalie's paradise, and the festering resentment built up inside her. "Why did I have to get stuck out here like this?" The question returned constantly, in various forms, and the unspoken answer increasingly seemed to point to her husband. He started it. He was to blame. "Be good to my kids and I'll give you a home," he had told her as a condition of employment; it seemed a mockery now. She called back to mind the morning, a few weeks after the wedding when, walking by the barn, she had overheard Clarence explain his new marriage to an old Norskie neighbor, maybe just kidding, maybe telling the truth: "I just had to have somebody to take care of the kids."

Worst of all, a scene she had mainly succeeded in blocking from her consciousness returned to torment her. She pictured again her new husband, the day she returned early from a stroll down the road with the children to visit Nathalie. Peering stealthily into the dim light of the attic, she had found him bent over the old immigrant trunk that had belonged to his first wife, fondling her stored wedding dress, tears running down his handsome face.

Now Bernice could not prevent these awful memories from once again invading her being. The old wounds, inflicted so long ago, became running sores of bitterness. She'd never been accepted. That stiff-backed minister even had denied her the right to hold her own baby during Sonny's baptism because she was not a confirmed Lutheran. There were dark days when everything Norwegian might be cursed as evil, disdained as worthless. Sometimes, working in the empty kitchen, she ranted alone, just to let off steam. Sometimes when Clarence sat by himself at the late-supper table, she would find some excuse to attack him with pent-up fury. "'Be good to my kids and I'll give you a home!'" she would taunt. "Oh, I know I'm not your precious Norskie *Gunda!* Gunda, *Gunda!*" She knew she should not say such things, especially with the kids around to hear. Her jealous outbursts always made Clarice so frightened she would disappear from her sight; and one time Sonny watched her with calm insolence from the doorway before he followed his father outside. But she could not help herself. Her feelings had to pour out sometimes. After she calmed down, she always felt some regret for her excessive anger, and she regretted also that her husband always escaped to the barn rather than having it out with her then and there. It might have been better from the beginning, she knew, instead of having problems fester inside, to have taken time to talk about all that. But of course they never had.

By late September, her solitary mutterings sometimes took on a more menacing tone as she gave voice to inner impulses, threatening to "take the kids and get out of here." She felt a kinship with those tiny dust particles that couldn't take it anymore, and at times she envisioned herself rising on the sultry wind to be carried somewhere, anywhere. Her hopelessness seemed to encourage wild imaginings of actual escape plans—packing suitcases, selling chickens to buy bus tickets, eating oranges under a phantom palm tree. The nearly unbearable inner turbulence subsided sometimes but would return if some little thing went wrong. Then would come days of calm, when she saw that she would somehow have to make drastic changes in her life—or risk a nervous breakdown.

On a warm October Sunday, the Overhome kids drove in before noon to spend the day. Bernice had been hoping they might show up and had killed three of her largest spring fries for dinner "just in case," as she said to Sonny, who handed her the young roosters at the chopping block. Around the crowded table the boys, Bub and Bert, got everybody laughing again with their witty remarks—how wonderful, hearing that laughter!—and after the meal, Clarence took Bub out to look at the hogs. Bert had a rifle along, and Sonny and Clarice walked down to the pasture with him to shoot gophers. Bernice's three little girls went to add something new to their playhouse under the cottonwoods. Leona and Zena, the eldest of Bernice's five sisters, were living in Iowa, but she had the three youngest ones to herself around the kitchen table, all of them in a mood of relaxed conversation:

Irene, more mature than others at eighteen, always lively; red-haired Margie, at the age when looks are everything; and frail, introspective, bespectacled Ruby, like Margie ready to finish high school.

"See where they arrested the Lindbergh kidnapper," Bernice put in at one point.

"Oh yeah," Irene jumped up from the table. "That reminds me!" She knew of her sister's interest in the case and had brought along an illustrated magazine article for the scrapbook. Bernice quickly leafed through it with concentrated interest. "'Bruno Richard Hauptmann, German immigrant,'" she read aloud from the headline.

"I'm glad they caught the so-and-so," Irene said.

"Makes us Dutchmen look kinda bad, though, don't it?" Bernice meant it only as a joke, but her sisters merely looked confused, and she realized how exaggerated her feeling had become about being German. What's important about a kidnapper is whether he's guilty, not where he comes from.

The others did not seem to notice her discomfort. Margie began talking about a big banquet she and Ruby wanted to attend at school. "And neither one of us has a dress for it. You know what they call it, an evening gown?"

"Hmm," Bernice, smiling inwardly, regarded the redheaded teenager who loved movie magazines. "Shouldn't be a problem. You get the material, and I'll make 'em for both of you."

"Really?" The young faces shone bright.

There was more good talk among the sisters, and when it was time to break up, Irene looked directly into Bernice's eyes with an unusual air of candid intimacy. "You know, Big Sister," she said, "being here at your place is kind of like . . . coming home, I guess!"

All of them looked at her and nodded agreement. Bernice nodded with them. "It's nice for me, too, when you come. Just ain't been the same since Maw died, for any of us."

"You're kind of our mother now," little Ruby said, tears beginning to glisten behind her round glasses.

"And our mother will make us new dresses!" from Margie, who preferred gaiety to soulfulness.

"Well, anyway, Bernice," Irene summed up, "you're the only one of us who's married and who stays put on a place of your own. So I guess all of us will always want to come to your house to feel at home."

"You are one of our blessings, Bernice!" Ruby intoned. "We must count our blessings, name them one by one, like in the hymn." Ruby had taken to religion more than anyone else in the family, especially since her mother's funeral.

Big Sister shifted slightly in her chair, pleased but uncomfortable at the unaccustomed open sentimentality. "It *is* pretty good, all right. We all have each other, the ten of us."

The serious young girl, her small face shining around the oversized eyeglasses, found it hard to stop. "And we thank the Lord that we are all healthy, and that your kids are so nice, too, and strong and no sickness. Think of it, the families that get polio or diphtheria."

"Come on, slowpoke," Irene called from the door. "Bub an' Bert are in the car already. We got chores to do, too."

Bernice accompanied her sisters outside. It made her feel proud when she saw that Clarence was still with the boys, leaning his arms against the car to talk farming. The little girls ran back from their playhouse to join in, and all seven of them were waving hands as the Overhome kids drove out the dusty driveway. During the next few hours, as they washed up the dishes and did the evening chores and prepared for bed, Bernice found that many words and thoughts of the day's conversation kept running through her head. It had been a good visit.

Before rocking the baby to sleep, she picked up the

magazine clipping Irene had left. In the light of the kerosene lamp on the kitchen table, she studied every photograph and caption, reviewing the kidnapping of the Lindbergh baby two years before, the ransom money paid, the anguished search, the mutilated little body found nearby, and the arrest of the accused kidnapper. Once again she felt horror at a child stolen and murdered; her focus on the photographs became blurred. In the dining room she pulled open the drawer of the tall writing desk to add the article to her scrapbook, alongside recent newspaper photos of the beautiful newborn Dionne quintuplets. Death and life, she thought, we are all part of it. When things go right, the older ones fade away and the next generation takes over. Standing there at the high desk, the clippings spread before her, she tried to imagine what it must be like to see the dead body of your baby, even to have a child suffer crippling illness. She pictured herself at that moment in a new light, more brightly illuminating than before. Here I am, she thought, surrounded by brothers and sisters and my own healthy kids, who all need me. And by a good man, a husband who really needs me, too. Not everybody is lucky enough to have all that.

She took longer than usual rocking the baby. Those ideas about getting away to California or someplace—I must have been a little bit crazy, she told herself, even to think such things. My place is here. This is Overhome now.

She knew it would not be easy. Maybe she would not be able to take those awful, tormenting spells if they returned. But she felt a new resolve. She would do her best. She hummed softly as she rocked, and discovered that the melody came from Ruby's old hymn: "Count your blessings, Name them one by one, You will be surprised at what the Lord hath done." The baby slept in her arms, but she hummed through the chorus one more time.

FENCING

Clarence
1934

A quiet Sunday morning in August. The scorching weather had cooled, following a shower too puny to do much more than settle the dust. And far too late to save the harvest. Morning chores and breakfast over, Clarence bent over the timbered sill of the horsebarn door, mending harness. The barn stood empty; his horses could take Sunday off, to roll and graze.

He selected a copper rivet and washer from the small carton half-spilled on the flat sill and worked the rivet through the hole he had punched in the dry leather. He forced the washer onto it with opened pliers, then clinched the yielding copper and held his work at arm's length. His straw-hatted head wagged.

"Aah, this dang bridle's about shot, too," he muttered.

So much around the place still needed repair. Things seemed out of kilter this year—first having to move, then the weather, the grain drill breaking down right at seeding, the old harness straps that continually had to be patched together. He had hoped this would be the year when he might look around auction sales for a pair of good harness; it would be nice, he thought, to get the colts dressed up, break them in right as a team. Well, no chance now. Have to keep at it, wait for better times, about all you can do.

When he finished the job he paused, leaning against the doorway to stare once again at the fields that had betrayed him. In all his years of farming, he had never seen a drought like it. Seeds hardly sprouted last spring in the dry-cracked soil; anything that dared to grow got blasted with hot winds day after day until green withered and brown spread. Soon came the dust, first drifting in the corn rows like dirty snow, then picked up by those angry winds from the south and whipped to the sky in false clouds. Now those pitiful fields out there: stunted cornstalks that would never produce even nubbins. The oats he had mowed for hay weeks earlier. He would have to salvage what he could and get a loan to buy feed grain for the winter stock. His gaze wandered to the browned pasture. Not much left in there either, he thought, no wonder the cows try to break out, to get at whatever they can find on the other side. He took a deep breath and let it out slowly. Better get at fixing that fence.

No one in sight around the yard. He peered through the screen door into the kitchen, where his wife at the stove poured hot rinsing water over the cream separator disks. He hesitated, hoping he would not find her in the mood of angry silence that seemed to come over her lately when the drought's dry winds blew. Sometimes it could get worse, the way she talked.

"I could use some help fencin'," he called in. "That kid is never around when you need him."

"Well, I don't know," her voice came back, sounding normal. He relaxed. Drying hands on a floursack dish towel, she came to the door and shouted past him: "Sonny?

SONNY-Y-Y!" No response. "Come to think of it," she added then, "I seen him sittin' in the car, about an hour ago."

That is where he found his towheaded nine-year-old son, slumped in the front seat of the Model T in front of the garage, reading something. The boy did not welcome the interruption.

"Aw, Pa, do I have to? Now?"

He regarded his son with half-amused patience and repeated the light-hearted admonition he sometimes used when Sonny tried to get out of work: "You'd starve to death in a bakery."

"But gee whiz, I'm just about done with this Big Little Book Ma brought from Watertown yesterday. It's about Popeye, you know the funny-papers guy who gets strong when he eats spinach?" The boy, agitated, displayed the fat book's colorful cover. "Listen to this part. Some crooks have picked a fight with him and he just gulped down a can of spinach: 'Popeye waded in, his arms pumping like a windmill, and—'"

"Heh! We could use that fella over at the well." He held the car door open. "Naw, you come on now. We got work to do. That book can wait."

The boy followed him with reluctance across the barren yard toward the granary, where fencing tools waited, while Clarence considered the matter of sons. A man—a farmer, especially—needs at least one son. His own father had sired five of them. Five young men to carry on the work and one daughter to marry another farmer. Now what I got is just the opposite, he thought: I have five daughters that I hardly ever see—and there came the familiar stab in his gut that recurred every time he let his mind focus on his two elder daughters or on their mother, Gunda, his young love fresh from Norway, dead now these twelve years. He should be over grieving for her by now, he knew, and maybe he was, but something about that whole subject complicated everything still. Trouble was, those two girls served as walking reminders of what used to be, and in these days of tough times he didn't even dare talk directly with either of them for fear their new ma might feel jealous about it, think he played favorites. So he tended to concentrate on his work, letting the wife and daughter business take care of itself.

The boy, now, was something else. No complications with his ma, anyway. But Clarence had to recognize that for some reason he did not spend as much time with his son as some neighbors seemed to with their boys. For one thing, he was not sure you could make a farmer out of this kid.

He bent to pick up a galvanized pail and handed it to Sonny.

"Here," he said, "you can carry this bucket of staples and the crowbar." He draped the wire-stretcher ropes over his own shoulder and balanced the long post auger in the other hand; he felt the weight of the hammer in the overalls loop on the left, the pliers snugly at home in the right-leg pocket. All set, in uniform, for fence-fixing.

"This crowbar is kinda heavy," from the boy, hefting his load.

"You can do it. You'll have to carry some of this stuff, too, when we get to the chokecherry trees. I cut a couple of posts out there I'll take along."

"Wait a minute, Pa," the boy said, holding gleaming, U-shaped metal between thumb and two fingers. The boy had opened the twenty-five-cent bag of new staples that nestled on top of the bent and rusty used ones in the bucket. "I'll show you something." He squared off away from the bright red granary door. "This should be really neat, with a brand-new staple." With wrist-flicking action, he threw his projectile; it stuck dutifully, magically, in the granary door. "See? Bert showed me how to do it. I can make 'em stick pert-near every time!"

"Well, I wondered where them holes in the door were comin' from," Clarence scolded. "These buildings just been painted this summer, you know that. Make holes and the wood'll start rottin' away again. Don't go throwin' staples or anything else at the buildings, now." Irritated at such foolishness, he turned and headed for the gate leading to the barnyard and pasture beyond.

The boy followed, chastised and silenced. When they reached the cluster of chokecherry trees, he ran ahead and reached among the sparse lower branches to pluck at the small fruit that had somehow managed to ripen in spite of the drought. His face puckered at the taste of the first chokecherries, and others showed dark red in his extended palm.

"Want some, Pa?"

"Naw, not now. Your ma's goin' to pick some later for jelly. Here, you carry the wire stretcher; I'll have to take these posts."

The two of them trudged on together toward the pasture, Clarence now balancing the two heavy chokecherry trunks on his shoulder, and the boy with the wire-stretcher ropes around his collar like a thick scarf. The weight seemed to make him feel that he was almost doing a man's work, and he became talkative again.

"Rye-or-air," he began, then spat out a mouthful of chokecherry pits and started again. "Right over there," pointing with the arm that held the staples bucket, "is where I got that gopher last Sunday, when Bert was here with the rifle. Big flicker-tail. First shot, too."

Clarence pictured Bert, Bernice's scrawny, redheaded kid brother, just fourteen. Kind of car-crazy, that kid, the way he rolled buggy-wheel rims and old tires around, pretending they were Fords and Pierce-Arrows, and spent his scarce money on those Tootsietoy cars from the dime store. Gets Sonny all involved in such play, too. Sticking staples in the granary door, and now that old single-shot Stevens to play with, could be dangerous.

"I hope you was careful out here with that gun," he said. "Some of them bullets can carry a mile, they say. Horses and cattle out here in the pasture."

"Aw, those are the long rifles. We only shot shorts. We was careful."

After a few more steps, the inevitable question came: "Pa, when do you think we can get a rifle of our own?"

"Those things cost money. Be a while yet."

They trudged on and finally came to the spot where some of the cows yesterday had pushed against the fence, reaching for better grass. Two of the old wooden posts had broken off, and all three strands of barbed wire sagged low, an open invitation for those looking for a way out. Two of the cows had jumped: Old Holstein—always a jumper, that morning he'd had to wire a heavy yoke for her to drag around by the neck to keep her sensible—Old Holstein had cleared the fence yesterday, but the other, Blackie, slung low in the bag, had come home with a bad cut on a front teat. Where the fence sagged lowest, Clarence dropped his cargo, then used one of the chokecherry posts to pry the three barbed wires away from the fence line.

"Here," he beckoned his son, "you hold the wires away a few minutes and give me space to dig the post holes. Watch out the post don't slip, those barbs are sharp."

He hurried, twisting the T-bar of the auger, then dumping first dry grass roots and dusty topsoil onto a little mound in the browned grass grazed short. The second augerful showed lighter streaks of clay, and the third came up completely tan. The boy was still in a conversational mood.

"Pa, why do they make barbed wire, anyway? The barbs are sharp, but they don't keep the cows from leaning against the fence, and then when they try to jump they might get cut. So why barbed wire?"

"Well, I guess some of 'em are too dumb, or maybe too smart, to pay attention to the barbs. Until it's too late."

"I was reading in the *Successful Farmer* about what they call electric fence. Gives the cows a shock when they touch it, and they learn to stay away. Just runs off a battery. Wouldn't that be better?"

"Yah, might be nice, all right. But it'll be a while before we can afford anything like that. Now, you keep those wires out of the way, and I'll stick that other new post in here."

Jabbing with the end of the hammer handle, he tamped the gray and brown earth back into the hole around the chokecherry post. The boy was still talking.

"I really like reading. You find out about lots of things, like tractors, electric fences, . . ."

And how reading can get you out of work, Clarence smiled to himself; but he said, "Or the way eating spinach can make you a strong fighter, huh?"

The boy giggled. "That, too. Big Little Books are fun, though. I bet Miss Terry will have good things to read to us in school next month."

"You really liked her, didn't you, your very first teacher, back in the other school?"

"Oh, yeah. I'm glad we're going to have her again. Pa, didn't you ever like to read, when you was a kid?"

"Well, we didn't have many books around then." Clarence pictured the old schoolhouse on its corner acre of prairie that he and his brothers had walked four miles to every winter, until they got old enough to help with the farm work.

"Did you listen to the radio?"

He laughed at that one. "No, there was no radio, those days."

"Play any games?"

"Oh, you know, like you—tag, pump-pump-pullaway, at school. Baseball, sometimes, Sundays in the summer. And we made our own things to play with. Like darts."

"Darts? What's that?"

He hadn't thought in years about all this. "Well, we used to make wooden darts, like arrows, sort of, couple of feet long. Go way up in the air, so high you could barely see 'em, and then they'd come straight down and stick in the ground. Okay."

Clarence brusquely cut off the conversation and stood; he needed to test the new post. A little crooked, but firm. He released the boy from holding back the wires, and they carried their equipment down the fence line to the other broken post. Along the way he inspected the growth underfoot, away from the pasture side. Those cows were right to try to get at this stuff, he thought. Some peppergrass and thistle, but enough good grass to make another cutting worthwhile for hay. It would all help.

"We get home," he said, starting to auger the second hole, "we'll have to sharpen the mower sickle. I'll need you to turn the grindstone." He expected the boy to complain at this additional tedious task, so often repeated during the summer, but there was silence for a while. Then the small voice, tensed to even higher pitch, burst at him again.

"Pa, how come you always work so much now? After you got to be a man, couldn't you ever take time to play anymore?"

Clarence could not respond right away. Honest questions, and he was not sure he had honest answers. "Well," he offered tentatively, "when there's work to be done, you got to do it."

"Grown-ups never take time for any fun at all."

Clarence regarded the boy sharply, feeling vaguely offended. The twisting auger paused while he made the point: "Oh, I don't know about that. When I was a young fella, we always knew how to have a good time, too, along with the work. Buggy rides, ball games, dances, lots of things like that."

"Even when you was a grown-up man?" The boy sounded dubious.

"Sure, a man don't have to work all the time."

His son now looked back at him, silent and thoughtful. Clarence twisted the auger twice more, and as he dumped clay onto the mound, his own words came back at him: *a man don't have to work all the time.* But that is just what I been doing, he had to admit to himself, all this year since we moved here. All work and no play. How long has it been since I played the fiddle, had a glass of beer in town, listened to the radio just for fun? I even passed up a chance to play ball at the school picnic, stayed in the field planting corn instead. For what? You try to be a good provider to your family, and when the rain won't come, you think you can make it right by working a little harder.

The two of them talked less as they finished the fencing. Clarence loosened the stapled wires all the way up to the corner post two hundred yards distant, then fastened the stretcher to the solidly based corner post, and together they pulled each strand taut. He stopped at each post to hammer staples in tight to hold the wire again. A reinserted broken post seemed really too short, but better than no post at all; the two new tree-cut posts provided sufficient sturdiness and height. "She's a good job, Pa," Sonny offered, imitating man-talk as they picked up their tools.

By the time they walked back through the gate at the water tank, the notion had settled in Clarence's head, and when the boy asked whether he should get the grindstone ready, this was the surprise reply: "Ah, we don't have to do that yet. Maybe we can have some fun first."

The little blue eyes regarded him, intrigued, suspicious.

Clarence continued matter-of-factly: "Over behind the granary there's a pile of old shingles the carpenters threw away
this summer when they fixed the buildings. Go find two,
three good ones." Why hadn't the idea of this old pastime
come back to him long before?

They sat together in the sun at the open granary door.
Clarence used his jackknife to whittle at the shingles, the
thickest part of the wood forming each dart's heavier pointed shaft, which he widened to a featherlike tail where the
wood was thin. Just the way Far, who'd learned his carpentry
in the Old Country, had taught his sons so long ago. At the
balance point, he cut an angled notch. The boy found a yard-
long piece of cord string, and they tied one end of it to a stick
of equal length, leaving the other end knotted to fit into the
notched dart.

The two of them took their three darts and the shooter
stick out into the oats stubble, where they would have plenty of room. Demonstrating for Sonny, Clarence held the stick
in his right hand, kept the dart in his left tight against the
string, swung both arms toward the sky a couple of times for
practice without letting go, then SWISH! With a mighty
swoop the first dart sped up and up, nearly out of sight, seemingly staying up there forever before turning back to earth
straight down, sticking proud and erect in the oats stubble.
The boy's sounds of excitement matched his own satisfaction.
A farmer can do some things on his own, he told himself. This
had been a good day for making repairs.

AN EDUCATED PERSON

Bernice and Miss Terry
1934–1935

For Bernice, the best thing about the new place had always been the schoolhouse.

"Just thirty rods down the road," Clarence had told her after his first look at the Hidewood, trying to make her feel better about having to move, before she'd seen anything here.

Later, driving together into this new farm, she'd felt the pleasure of a promise fulfilled when Clarence pointed out the schoolhouse, standing white as chalk just across the gray field. It seemed so clean and uncluttered, and near enough so she could see the kids playing by the dark red barn in the school-yard. While inspecting the dilapidated porch steps of their new home, she'd heard a melodious gong coming from behind them: the big bell atop the school roof. That close! Her kids would be able to make it to school in five minutes, even run home for dinner over the noon hour. On their last place, she'd worried through six years about the kids' two-mile walk to school. Wintertime, it was dark before Marie and Clarice and undersized Sonny got home, sometimes half-frozen when the weather turned bad. No wonder they'd caught so many colds.

Gradually, in the weeks after their move, the schoolhouse began to take on additional meaning for Bernice, signifying something larger and more personal than mere convenience. In the course of her daily work, every time she stepped outside onto those rickety wooden porch steps, she'd pause and go through her own private ceremony, staring across the way. Yes, still there, as that big bell reminded her now four times a day. Imagine, she'd think to herself, the luxury of just sitting and reading and learning inside there, all day long. All spring, the regular sight and sounds of the school somehow lifted her spirits. It seemed to offer something to hang on to through the unceasing drudgery of settling in and cooking and washing and tending the little ones—while needed rain stayed away, week after dust-blown week, and crop failure threatened.

The very nearness of the schoolyard made it a tempting place for the kids to explore. One warm summer day at dusk, Sonny and Clarice hurried into the house carrying a brown case by its handle. "It's the school phonograph, Ma!" In the semidark, excitement glowed from the boy's face, framed by bleached blond hair. Bernice at first shook her head—"You can't just take property out of the schoolhouse, unlocked or not"—but she eventually gave in to their begging. "It's not really stealing, only borrowing. Just this once. Oh c'mon Ma, let us listen to these records." Well, she reasoned, I guess it can't do any harm to let them have a little fun—we don't have a phonograph or even a radio that works now.

The kids took turns. One wound the crank and another lowered the needle onto the spinning disk, and from the little mesh square flowed tunes from another world. Clarice and Sonny even sang along, as if they understood the words. "You got to be a football hero, to get along with the beautiful girls," according to one number. They marched around the kitchen, showing off, shouting "Youth! Courage! Loyalty!" right along with a song labeled the "Young Citizens' League March." It was something. Before they sneaked the phonograph back to the schoolhouse that night, she made them understand this would be the only time, but in fact she let them get away with it twice more that summer. She justified such questionable behavior by thinking of her children's need for some kind of entertainment. And she got no helpful opinion from Clarence, who just sat there at the kitchen table, behind his newspaper in the yellow lamplight, distantly amused. But deep down she knew that her own curiosity about the schoolhouse's secrets influenced her permissive mood.

All through the summer, at odd moments when she could find enough peaceful isolation to hear herself think, the realization grew within her: in some special way that she had not figured out yet, the little white schoolhouse held more importance for her than any school building in any neighborhood ever had before. "I can feel it in my bones," she murmured over and over, and she vowed to find out more. Sometime soon, when the time is right.

Bernice knew that part of her fascination for the schoolhouse came from her own experience, or, more accurately, her *lack* of experience. She'd gone through only seven grades at the prairie schoolhouse near Sisseton, before she started helping Maw full-time. When the folks moved to Overhome, they were right on the Hayti school's bus line, and all the younger girls went on to high school. Not the four brothers, of course; few farm boys ever went on for a real education. But five out of six sisters getting into high school wasn't bad.

And last year, before Clarence found this farm to rent in the Hidewood, she'd arranged for stepdaughter Marie to work for board and room at a farm home and start high school in Hayti. Bernice took pride in her family's educational achievements, and she tried not to let resentment creep in. Somebody always has to sacrifice to give others a chance. But it left an emptiness within her, and she yearned for something more—at least for a chance to figure out what giving up an education had made her miss. Town things. Books and poems. Learning how to feel more comfortable among strangers. Maybe even taking a look at those football heroes and beautiful girls.

One day in August Clarence brought home news that caused a sensation around the supper table. He had just made the run to Schleuters' to haul home a can of drinking water. He'd learned from Vera Schleuter—her husband, Julius, was on the school board—the name of the new teacher, and it was a name they all knew.

"Bessie Terry? Miss Terry? Oh boy!" The reaction from Sonny predictably came through loudest. Bessie Terry had been his first teacher, for two years, back at the other school. Clarice, always so shy and guarded when her father was in the house, nodded her own enthusiasm. Bernice herself said little, but inside, something clicked. This meant a very good teacher again for her children, including Elaine, nearly six, who would start this fall. Maybe also, her inner voice told her, this is the signal. Time to take action. Yes, I can feel it in my bones.

That evening after the supper dishes were done and the rest of the family had busied themselves away from the kitchen, she slipped outside with a basin of water to the porch steps. After a hot afternoon weeding in the garden, she need-ed to bathe her feet. The cool water—and the quiet—felt lux-urious, and in this mood of self-indulgence, she once again turned her gaze to the schoolhouse. Rays from the setting sun gave a warm glow to the white image, its three shadowed win-dows evoking so many questions about what remained unknown to her. And on top, the heavy bell silhouetted in its stubby tower. In these summer months she had missed its ringing, summoning children to learning the way a church bell calls true believers to worship.

Now Bessie Terry, by some generous twist of fate, would be following them to the Hidewood to be teacher again. A really good teacher, so many ideas, someone a person could talk with. She would know all about schools, had even gone to college. And she must remember me, Bernice thought. Four summers ago, she had taken Sonny with her to Bessie's parents' home near Estelline to ask the teacher's permission to let the boy—"Robert," he would have to be called in school—start first grade, though he was barely five. It had worked out well. Both years. Sonny—and Marie and Clarice, too—had come home with stories of Miss Terry's imaginative learning projects. Bernice recognized that she did not know this woman well—hardly at all, in fact. But Bessie Terry was the only educated person she had ever really talked with, woman to woman, about education. And she would soon be teaching right in that schoolhouse, just across the field. Bernice had never felt at ease when it came to dealing with other people. But somehow, she would have to find a way to pick up that conversation again.

Bessie Terry was twenty-five, a self-styled "old maid schoolteacher" with six years' experience. She had driven her parents' car the fifteen miles to meet with the Hidewood school board and look over the school. She had mixed feelings about what she found.

The countryside, so different from the Big Sioux River bottomland where she'd grown up, seemed less friendly than she'd expected. She supposed some allowance had to be made for the summer drought that had dried up cornfields, stunted smallgrain, and browned the pastures. But the neighborhood looked so vulnerable to weather, the land more hilly and rocky than back home, farms farther apart, fewer trees. "Plainview, District No. 41," they called the school. It stood in plain view, all right, on a high point where you could see ten to twenty miles in three directions. Nice view of the sunsets, but wait until skinny me has to lean into the winter wind. Thoughts of the cold made her feel as vulnerable as the rock-studded Hidewood Hills, showing too many bones.

Her talk with the board men had gone well, and she'd made a point of memorizing the correct spelling and pronunciation of their names: George Roecker (Raker), president; Julius Schleuter (Sleeter); and Harry Koppman. The prospect of room and board with gracious Vera Schleuter was appealing. The family lived about a half-mile from the school, and their little "teacher's bedroom" upstairs seemed adequate. Both parents and children were long accustomed to having the teacher living with them, and they would surely make her feel welcome. A quick look at the schoolhouse itself had brought no surprises. The standard one room, maybe a little smaller than some, with entry-hall coal bin and coat hooks. Dangling from the ceiling was something new for her: the pull-rope that rang the iron bell up there. She had tugged it once and liked that attention-getting sound of institutional authority. Just being inside a one-room school again had brought back good feelings about the joys of shaping young minds—but it also evoked memories of hardships that always came with teaching in a place like this. She had to think about money, as well. Eight months at only fifty dollars a month, and twenty of that would go for room and board five days a week with the Schleuters. Would she ever be able to save enough to pay for more college? She thought again about the cold, about the loneliness. But with all the talk of Depression and drought, not everyone could even find work these days.

Here at least was a job, a *teaching* job. She signed.

The day school opened, her brother, Johnny, drove her in his Model A coupe to the Schleuter farm. He had agreed to repeat this delivery schedule weekly, dropping her off early Monday mornings and picking her up again Fridays after school unless the roads got too bad. Bessie took a few minutes to unpack hanging clothes from her suitcase. She turned down coffee but accepted a packed lunch from Vera Schleuter, who bustled around the breakfast table. Then, carrying her jam-packed bag of teaching ideas, Bessie began her brisk walk in the September sun down the half-mile of graveled road to her new job. She wanted some time alone in the schoolroom to get her desk in order—and her thoughts, too—before the youngsters showed up. She had memorized most of the fourteen names from the list and hoped to match faces from the very first impression: nothing like quick identification to show who's in charge. Abreast of the tall roadside cottonwoods, she peered across a big garden to the Amerson place but spotted no movement around the yard except for their old cattle dog, who barked briefly as she passed the mailbox. She felt glad to be able to count on two familiar faces there, two good kids in school, and she began to recite names aloud: "Clarice, grade seven; Robert, four. And their first-grader, Elaine, I think. Then the two Schleuter girls, Lois, eighth, and Darlene, sixth. There! That's five out of the fourteen already!"

She slowed her pace to take in every detail of what would be her workplace for the next eight months, assuming she could endure it. The old, dark barn squatting in the far corner of the one-acre yard—how many of these kids still come to school on horseback? The two white outhouses, nestled under box elder trees. A modest belfry, the pull-rope looped around its wheel alongside the big bell itself. She mounted the open, two-step concrete landing. The unlocked door needed a shove. Into the entry hall, newly painted in light tan. Two inner doors to the schoolroom, one right and one left. Inside, she decided she would keep the teacher's desk where it was, between the doorways and facing three sections of desks with attached folding seats, some of them double. Coal stove in the back, and in one corner a tall metal cabinet that served as the school library; on the lower shelf she found a portable phonograph and a box containing sticks, a triangle, bells, a drum, and kazoos for the "rhythm band." To accompany the band, a real pump organ up front. She grimaced and wished she'd taken those lessons as a kid. Behind her desk and at the side wall above the sand table, the blackboards were not real slate, but they would do. Strung out above them, in white writing on black paper panels, the whole Palmer-method handwritten alphabet, small letters and capitals. It would come in handy for regular penmanship exercises.

Everything looked tidy, thoughtfully cared for. The three board members' wives had done the job, working two days the previous week to paint and wallpaper, oil the darkened and aromatic wood floor, wash the three windows inside and out, and launder, starch, and iron the curtains. Bessie Terry leaned back in her chair and took a deep breath. "Ahhh," she proclaimed to the empty room, "I just *love* the smell of a schoolhouse on the first day!"

Eight hours later, the next day's teaching outlines stowed in her heavy book bag, she pulled the outside door closed and began her return walk. All in all, it had been a good day. She reviewed faces once again and considered possible problems discernible in those first impressions. Eyes down, half-mesmerized by the regular pace of her sensible shoes crunching gravel, inner focus absorbed in thought, she had almost passed the cottonwoods again before becoming aware of someone standing at the garden fence, facing her across the shallow ditch.

No call came from the woman, and the afternoon sun behind her made it hard to see. But Bessie knew it must be Mrs. Amerson.

"Well, hello!" Bessie lifted her free hand in greeting and turned to descend through the roadside grass, still green in the ditch. Now she recalled more specific details about this mother, today in print dress and sweater, tentative eyes squinting behind the rimless glasses, short brown curls askew in the breeze. Bessie had not seen much of her since that visit to the house to get Robert started in first grade, but she recalled well this woman's interest in schooling. And now they had in common their newness in this distant community.

Bernice nodded her own greeting. "I was just out here to check the tomatoes. Might have a frost tonight." For Bernice, the lanky teacher looked the same as before, all skin and bones underneath the wool jacket, and a big crooked-toothed smile that lit up her whole face.

"Glad to see you, Mrs. Amerson! It's nice to find old friends around a new school, believe me."

"Nice for us, too."

"Clarice and Robert are off to a good start again. And your little Elaine—what a sweetie of a first-grader."

"Well, it's nice for us, too."

So began a series of occasional encounters between the two women. The garden fence offered a logical meeting site until the first heavy frost forced Bernice to harvest her remaining tomatoes. Then sometimes she would have a letter ready to mail, and along about four in the afternoon she'd keep an eye toward the schoolhouse. She'd set off as soon as she caught sight of the teacher, and by the time she'd put the letter and its three pennies inside the roadside mailbox and raised the flag, the familiar slender figure with book bag in hand had almost arrived.

At first their conversations were limited to the obvious topics—weather conditions, the progress of Bernice's three children in school, news about people they both knew back in the old neighborhood. Then, little by little, confidences grew. Bernice felt that each of these talks gave her small insights into the life of an educated person. She bided her time. More personal questions could be asked later on.

Bessie, in turn, found in Bernice an eager listener for the stream of ideas and comments that always seemed ready to tumble out. Not that the Schleuters weren't good talking company, too—they all loved a gabfest. But Julius was on the board, after all, and there at the house younger ears might be listening for what the teacher might reveal. She had to be discreet. These isolated chats with Bernice, on the other hand, gave her precious moments of liberation from daily constrictions. Like sneaking a forbidden cigarette with a pal, back in high school. Out here by herself, she missed the companionship of a special classmate who understood her, or a college roommate to share secrets with at midnight. Well, she told herself, she had known when she signed the contract that a country schoolteacher has to make do.

"We started a project yesterday that'll give us some fun next spring," Bessie reported, beaming, during a mailbox meeting one day late in the fall.

"What's that?"

"Grasshopper eggs!"

Bernice didn't think she'd heard right. "Grasshopper eggs?"

"That's right." Bessie described how she had had the kids explore in Clarence's picked cornfield, pulling up the two or

three stalks in each hill until they found what she was looking for: below ground level, insect eggs clinging to the root
structure. "We put 'em in a jar on the sand table. Now the
kids are wondering when they're going to hatch."

Sometimes Bessie's ideas sounded a little silly, but
Bernice found herself intrigued. "How'd you know where to
look?"

"Oh, I guess I read about grasshoppers someplace, the
way they lay their eggs. Just thought we'd go out and see for
ourselves." Bessie's smile widened, watching her friend's
reaction.

"Gol, we've seen hoppers by the thousands this year—
but I never heard of anybody *hatchin'* 'em before!" Bernice
didn't have occasion to laugh in public very often; then she
got serious again. For her, eggs came out of the chicken
house by the pailful every evening for selling or eating—or,
if for hatching, carefully laid in the cluck hens' nests. "What
do those eggs look like, anyway?"

"Tell you what, I'll bring them by tomorrow. You can take
a look for yourself."

The next afternoon, standing by the mailbox again,
Bernice held in her hands a two-quart Mason jar that the
teacher, with a little show of pride, had extracted from her
bulging bag. Sunlight through the clear, curved glass illuminated dozens of brown ovals, like miniature grains of wheat
amid the dangle of dried cornstalk roots. "Imagine," she said,
"incubating eggs in the cornfield during the winter. Ain't that
something!"

Bernice got the whole family to attend the basket social
on Halloween, and it gave her her first look inside the schoolhouse. Sitting at a regular desk almost made her feel back
in the seventh grade again, though the room looked quite dif-

ferent from the one she'd left nearly twenty years earlier.
Bessie and the kids had created a party atmosphere. Orange
and black cutouts of pumpkins and witches festooned the
windows, and tissue-paper streamers hung in graceful arcs
from the ceiling. The ladies' "baskets"—decorated shoe
boxes, most of them—added to the festive mood, placed one
at a time upon the teacher's desk by their arriving owners.
Bessie got Vera Schleuter to play the pump organ. The sand
table on its green stilts in a front corner showed art and science projects. Bernice spotted the Mason jar.

A social highlight came when the bidding began. George
Roecker, sporting a dark suit jacket over his striped overalls,
stood up and announced to the neighborhood that "By golly,
I'm gonna have supper with the teacher!" He made quite a
show of it, looking for all the world like some chubby angel
of the Hidewood, his round face and gold tooth shining in the
bright light of the borrowed gas lamp as he jumped the bid
ever higher.

In the mixed crowd, neither Bernice nor Bessie would
try to continue personal talks, so at their next roadside
encounter Bernice had to tease the teacher a little. "Old
George Roecker must think you're pretty swell! Five dollars
for that basket!" Bessie tilted her scarfed head back into the
chilly breeze and laughed, enjoying a rare occasion when she
could be kidded about male attentions. But she knew that
this kind of innocent fun was probably the closest any of the
neighborhood men would ever come to kicking over the
traces. The basket social, good for the neighborhood and
profitable for the school, left her with the reminder once
again that old maid country schoolteachers might as well forget about any romance in their lives. But this thought she
kept to herself.

She had plenty of other topics she could talk about, while
the good weather held and their outdoor conversations

remained reasonably comfortable. Armistice Day got her going about the War, twenty years ago now, so many boys lost in the trenches. "And now over in Germany, their new leader, some kind of dictator, makes you wonder if the Great War really did make the world safe for democracy." Bernice only nodded. Bessie spoke of her Friday morning current-events programs, in which for opening exercises, instead of reading to them from *Pollyanna,* she had the older kids bring in newspaper clippings. "I'm trying to get them to think about what's going on elsewhere, the great changes taking place, new things—telephones, radios, cars, and tractors. The world these kids will face will be a lot different from the one when we were young, eh? Not even the Hidewood can stay isolated forever." Sometimes, Bessie knew, she probably sounded too preachy.

But she felt free to discuss individual pupils in the school, and she shared her special concerns about two of them. Little Billy, shy and nearsighted, having a hard time learning to read. Lewis, the burly eighth-grader whose attitude actually made her nervous at times. "Not that he does anything really bad. Not yet, anyway. It's the way he looks at me— always trying to show me he doesn't have to follow the rules."

"Oh?"

"Like when I ask everyone to stand for the Pledge of Allegiance, he's always the last one to get to his feet. Just to 'show me.' Then afterwards he keeps standing there, with that little smile, and I have to ask him to be seated. He's getting too old for school, I guess."

"Maybe he's just trying to flirt, like George Roecker," Bernice said. Bessie had no reply. She'd heard from too many other country schoolteachers how overgrown boys could lose control of their glandular urges.

By mid-December, winter weather had begun in earnest. The roads remained passable enough for most families to get to the school for the Christmas program, which turned out rather well, Bessie thought. For one thing, she managed to give every pupil a speaking part in the performances; even little Billy, overcoming his reluctance, got into the spirit of it. But then the two-week vacation at her folks' cozy home made returning to work in the bleak Hidewood that much harder to take. Unrelenting below-zero temperatures and frequent blizzard conditions imposed a feeling of depression that only got worse with the routine of each passing day. Rise in the dark, breakfast at the Schleuter table, by 7:30 bundled up in her black wool scarf and big "farmer overshoes," as she called them, for the walk to school. Plod out the driveway, hear the whistling in the bare trees, then onto the exposed road with that raw, bitter northwest wind penetrating scarf, overcoat, overshoes, everything. Tears distorted her vision, making it hard to see where to place her heavy feet; drifted snow had filled the ditches level with the graded road, and those same drifts obliterated any car trails. So she stumbled along somewhere between the two lines of half-buried fence-posts, trying not to stray into the deeper banks of the ditches, where one might break through the crust and sink up to the knees.

By the time she reached the schoolground, cheeks and hands and feet were usually numb; she worried about frost-bite and accepted the inevitability of chilblains. At the snowswept steps she would turn the doorknob with clumsy mittens, offering a prayer of gratitude that the door had no lock. Inside, the schoolroom was nearly the same tempera-ture as outside, those mornings. She would build a fire with kindling and coal, but an hour later, when the kids got there, they would all still have to huddle around the stove and then leave their coats on until recess time.

In these moods of depression, feeling sorry for herself, she started making mental lists of hardships. No electricity or lamps of any kind to brighten the gloom of gray winter days, so only the kids near the windows can really see to work at their desks. No well on the schoolground means each pupil has to bring drinking water in a lunch pail—and in a thermos, or it will freeze on the way and break a plain glass jar. Hard to teach personal hygiene when these kids can't even wash hands after trips to the miserably cold outhouses. She wondered how much some of them heard at home about the need for cleanliness and brushing teeth. She wanted to create a whole new program to teach them basic health, but she just could not gather the necessary will or energy. Half the school seemed to be out with colds or the flu, and she herself could not avoid days of sickness. It was a bad time.

Late in February, in the middle of one afternoon, an imperious rap on the schoolhouse door startled the whole school. Apprehensive, Bessie discovered framed in the doorway a large woman in a long, black coat, booming hearty greetings. Of course: it was County Superintendent Maria Holen, famous for her surprise visits. After a few minutes of observation time during sixth grade geography, Bessie chased the kids outside for recess to give her and Miss Holen some privacy. She told the superintendent about her approaches to various problems, showed her the sand-table projects, and spoke of plans to grow flowers from seed placed in half-eggshells and to make an all-school expedition around Hidewood Creek for nature study, come spring. All the while, in the back of her mind the decision formed, and before the big woman returned to her car, Bessie asked her for a town teaching job for next year. Miss Holen nodded a couple of times into her double chin. "Well," rasped that sonorous tenor tone, "we'll see what we can do." It wasn't a promise, but she didn't say no, either.

During the next weeks, Bessie did her best to concentrate on the good things about her work at Plainview No. 41.

She nurtured the genuine affection she felt for the young-sters, and when the weather was decent after a fresh snow-fall, she might play fox and geese with them in the yard or watch the older boys on what they called "the rafters" in the barn. They swung like Tarzans from the two-by-six cross-beams about nine feet above the floor. She tried not to think of possible injuries, should one of them fall from that height. She read aloud from *The Little Shepherd of Kingdom Come,* to give them a sense of adventure while learning about the Civil War. When fourth-grader Robert asked about Sir Galahad in the wall picture, she showed him the book, and he soon became immersed in the lore of King Arthur. She picked out pieces for recitation and prepared several of the pupils for competition at the speaking contest scheduled for the county seat. The occasionally intimidating eighth-grad-er, Lewis, became more submissive after she managed to convince him that she herself had been enough of a rebel in her time to enable her to anticipate his shenanigans. He even offered her a ride on his horse—as a peace offering, she thought. After little Billy got new glasses, she teamed him up with his third-grade sister to learn reading, and it was work-ing. All of them seemed to respond to the art projects—paint-ing black silhouettes on glass and backing the pictures with crushed tinfoil, or dipping old jam jars from home into float-ing oil paints to make colorful gifts for their parents.

Sometimes she would think about the talks last fall with Bernice, and increasingly she felt vaguely guilty. Winter weather seemed to make such easy, informal sociability impossible. But it was more than that, she knew. She just was not in the mood anymore. These winter months she had become so totally absorbed in working conditions and her professional future—basic concerns for a schoolteacher with an uncertain personal life ahead. Perhaps she had been naive, overly enthusiastic about the idea of a friendly ear to confide in during those mailbox talks. The fact was that she, teacher Bessie Terry, and Bernice Amerson, farmwife and mother, traveled on separate roads to whatever the future held for each of them. Still, they did share interests—in kids, in education—valid for this year at least. Bessie did not want to think of herself as a flighty, fair-weather friend. One of these days they would have to talk again.

Bernice had her own problems that winter, their first in the new place. The cast-iron, wood-burning heater was hardly adequate for the drafty old house, and they had to close off the east room downstairs. Snowdrifts and subzero days and the kids' colds complicated her daily chores. She had not expected regular contacts with Bessie during the winter months, and she kept up with school matters through her three kids every day. But when the melting began, and especially after passing the March 15 anniversary of their move onto the place, she began to think again about her talks with the schoolteacher. The schoolhouse itself had lost some of its mystery—she glanced only occasionally in that direction now—but the sound of the bell, when she heard it these days, sometimes stirred her imagination anew. Twice she tried to intercept the teacher on her way home, but one afternoon she had started late, and Bessie only waved without stopping as she passed the driveway; and another time, there at the mailbox, the teacher said she had to hurry back to Schleuters, early supper waiting.

Bernice felt rebuffed, high-hatted. She tried to think of reasons for the cold shoulder. She wondered whether she had hurt Bessie's feelings that time when she'd teased her about the men flirting. If we are to have no more talks, she thought, maybe it's not meant for me to find out much about education. Maybe it was all just a foolish notion, anyway. Whatever had changed, Bernice certainly was not going to put herself in a position where the teacher could turn up her nose at her again. She made a point of being out of sight between four and five those afternoons, so she wouldn't even have to figure out whether to wave at the familiar figure passing by.

In late April, Bernice heard from Vera Schleuter that though the board had asked her to stay another year, Bessie would be leaving. A few days before the school picnic, Sonny brought home from school a sealed envelope and dropped it on the kitchen table, alongside her batch of biscuits fresh from the oven. "Mmmm-ah," he mumbled, halfway into a buttered biscuit, "it's from Miss Terry. She told me to give it to you." The note asked, "Could we meet by the mailbox again today or tomorrow?" Today was sunny; tomorrow might bring rain. By a quarter past four she was in her garden, planning just where rows of carrots would be planted, and before long she heard the call from across the fence.

Strangely, it was almost as if the interlude of months had disappeared. Bessie referred to the hard winter, and somehow that was explanation enough. Then she picked up right from their last talk months before, spoke of school activities, of their nature study at Hidewood Creek, of achievements by the Amerson children, of progress with problems. Bernice again mostly listened, her hand resting atop the fencepost, farmer-style. They chatted for fifteen minutes before Bessie approached the subject obviously uppermost in her mind.

"Bernice, I have news I must tell you."

"Oh? What's that?"

"I have a chance to teach in Toronto next year, over in the far corner of the county." She pointed to the southeast. "But in town."

Bernice nodded. "I heard you was offered a job."

"Ah. But I think I'll take it. You know, I've loved teaching here. But I guess I can't take the cold weather anymore."

"Well, can't blame you. This one year—you sure done a lot for these kids."

"Oh, never enough." Bessie looked off to the side, frowning. "Each of us has a role to play, wherever we are. Here, I can only hope I've opened up some windows, prepared them for more learning later. I know a few of these girls will go on to high school." The teacher looked directly at Bernice again. "I hope some of the boys might, too."

"That's harder for boys. Mostly they have to stay home and help farm."

"I know. But Bernice . . ." Bessie moved nearer and placed her hand upon Bernice's on the fencepost. "You've already shown you know high school's important: you got Marie started over in Hayti. Clarice will get started, too, I bet. And when Robert's turn comes, you'll find a way. Boy or no boy, you'll find a way!" Bernice felt a squeeze on her hand, and then the teacher bent to retrieve her leather book bag.

"I won't say good-bye yet, 'cause you'll be coming to the picnic next week. But I have something here to show you."

Bernice recognized the curved glass of the Mason jar, and once again in the sunlight she peered at the dangling cornstalk roots—this time alive with dozens of tiny, hopping insects.

"You should have seen little Billy the day they hatched," Bessie was laughing. "He pressed his nose to the jar and he said, 'I never seen no little bitty hoppers before!'"

Bernice nodded, fascinated by the life inside the jar. "Well, neither have I, far as that goes. They hatch under the ground in the spring? They all come from eggs, like this? What happens to the old ones who lay the eggs?"

"Die off in the fall, I guess. The sacrifice of one generation is repaid in the next. Nature's way." Bessie's gentle voice seemed filled with understanding. "But you know all about that."

Afterward, closing the garden gate again, the teacher's words came back to Bernice with new meaning. Nature's way.

She *did* know about that. Her natural instincts all along had been to give up small, personal things in order to make way for the young ones. Especially a new generation hatched from your own eggs. Each of us has a role to play. I knew about that. I *knew* that! Maybe, she laughed to herself, I am an educated person after all.

CELEBRATION

Sonny
1935

That morning as soon as he heard Pa moving around downstairs Sonny jumped out of bed, and he was already in the kitchen pulling on his socks when Pa emerged, one overall suspender still unhitched, heavy work shoes in his hand, and a surprised look on his ruddy face. Pa was not used to having help from his ten-year-old son before breakfast, and certainly not before milking time. No telling what might happen on the Fourth of July.

The boy was soon out the door, calling back "I'll get the cows," and with only one hand on the top rail, he cleared the wooden gate at the water tank and half-galloped toward the pasture, waving at the sky with his new cap pistol: "Whoopee ti-yi-yo!" The old collie, Pup, glad to be stirred awake by such playful company, offered a yipping bark of his own and hurried to frolic alongside.

He was Tom Mix mounted on Tony, loping down the pasture trail, and his sharp cowhand eyes narrowed as he carefully surveyed the scene. The sun was already up in a clear sky; it was going to be another warm one. Dew still glistening in the grass darkened his scuffed shoes. As he and Pup moved along, grasshoppers crackled and whizzed away, a half-dozen of them in the air at the same time, fanning out and tracing arcs in the sunlight before disappearing again in the damp green. Sonny spotted the black-brown-white shapes of the cattle down in the draw, half of them lying down, some up and grazing. He noted, here and there, tawny fat gophers that warily watched their approach, scurried toward mounds of clay, and flicked bushy tails once or twice before darting downward. For one of them, keeping Pup well back, he glided in stealth close enough to draw a bead with his cap pistol. At the sharp crack in the pasture stillness, the curious rodent disappeared, and old Pup backed away in offended alarm. Sonny discovered that the gun could give him new power over the nearby cows, too: those that had been lazily lying there chewing their cuds lurched to standing position, and all of them regarded him with respectful suspicion. Thus aroused, even without having to sic Pup on them, they were easy to get started toward the barn, their filled bags swaying as they hurried ahead.

"Boy," he said aloud, "if I can make them move with this cap gun—what couldn't I do with a firecracker!" It made him feel good to picture the nearly full, green package of those loud, powerful beauties back in the house, awaiting him and today's celebration. Pa had let him use up three last night to show how to do it, throwing two of them when the wick started sizzling—before the thing could go off in your hand—and exploding the third under a tin can with a flashing bang that sent it soaring, suddenly bloated, through the air. Firecrackers could make things happen, and he had twenty-one of them to take along to the lake.

The Fourth, he was thinking as he angled along the worn cow path behind the herd, is the best day of the year. Better than any Sunday: even if Pa didn't work in the fields on Sundays, he always had plenty of jobs around the place that he needed help with. And the Fourth was better than going to town on Saturday nights, too, he told himself.

He scowled and kicked at a clump of grass. It still made him mad, just thinking about last Saturday night. They'd finished chores early, and by seven the Model T was rolling toward the graveled county road to Clear Lake, Ma in front with the baby on her lap and Clarice, Sonny, Elaine, and Snooky (as Mavis was always called) packed in back with the egg case and cream can. After they dropped the cream at Tom Farrell's station, they found a good place to park right on the main street in front of Jake's Harness Shop. Pa carried the eggs to the New Store, and after Ma ordered the groceries there, she and the three little girls got back in the car and just watched the people go by. Sonny wandered around the street for a while but couldn't find anybody he knew, so came back to the car. He climbed up to the driver's seat and put both hands on the steering wheel. He knew how to drive the Ford. Pa would let him do it again sometime when they were alone.

"Where's Pa at, anyway?" he asked.

"He took that piece from the mower to have it welded over at the blacksmith's," his mother said.

"Can't we go home pretty soon?"

"Have to wait for the cream check, to pay for the rest of the trading. It'll be a while yet. You can go walk around."

"Nobody to go with."

"You usually walk around with Craig." Craig Koppman was his only classmate at school.

"Well, they're not here tonight. I guess they went to Estelline."

A pause, and then his mother looked off to the right and laughed. "Here come Clarice and the Schleuter girls again," she said. "They've paraded by here about ten times."

"Yeah, they sound like old hens, the way they cackle at the boys." He knew that he was jealous of his sister's having friends to be with. Ma shifted the sleeping baby to her other arm. Elaine and Snooky stood behind her in the back seat, their cheeks bulging noisily, a small brown bag clasped between them.

"Want a piece of candy?" his mother asked.

The hard sweet tasted good, but he still felt cooped up in the car, and Ma could tell. "Go on, you look by yourself awhile longer," she urged. He wandered along the sidewalk, past Ralph's café and the pool hall and the drugstore, but the search for familiar faces was in vain. After a few minutes, he returned to loiter on the car's front bumper and kept on watching the passing people.

Once in a while he recognized men or women from the Hidewood, but mostly they were strangers. Farmers like Pa, in their clean striped overalls and dress-up straw hats, carried packages from the hardware store or harness straps to be repaired at Jake's. Women wearing flowered print dresses, toting babies and bags of groceries, stopped to visit with one another. Except for Clarice and the Schleuters, he didn't know any of the girls who, in pairs or gangs, all giggly together, strutted and said their foolish things to passing boys. And other boys, having a good time together, too. It wasn't fair, he thought, that he was the one who had to be alone. He thought about those who had brothers to be with all the time. Somebody to play catch with, somebody to do things with. At home all he had was girls—the two older sisters, the three little ones—and there he was, left out in the middle. At school he had Craig and James—*those* lucky brothers even had regular baseball gloves—but he'd hardly seen them since school let out for the summer.

Sitting there on the bumper, Sonny watched a group of

four older boys stroll up the sidewalk in exaggerated leisure, talking and laughing loudly together. They were town kids, he knew: that casual familiarity with each other, their expressions of assured superiority, brilliantined hair that was carefully combed every day. They stood to look in the window of the harness shop, where old Jake bent over his stitching machine. One of them said something in a secretive whisper and leaned over to elbow-poke a companion; they all broke into laughter again as they turned and headed past him. The tallest one looked his way then and crossed toward him, the others hanging back. Miraculously, the tall boy was smiling and speaking.

"Hi there."

Sonny found voice enough to murmur back a hoarse "Hi."

"Say, uh, could you do us a favor?" His brown eyes shone with friendliness.

They were asking him to do a favor for *them.* "Sure, what?"

"Well, we need a left-handed monkey wrench, see, but we're afraid t'ask, so you go into the harness shop here and ask Jake if we can use his left-handed monkey wrench, okay?"

He could feel his stomach tighten around the emptiness inside. So that's what they were up to, just making fun of the kid from the country. Sonny had heard the one about the left-handed monkey wrench from his uncle Bub, always joking; these guys knew the joke, too, and thought they could get him to fall for it. He couldn't think of anything to say, so he simply stared back until one of the three boys standing back called out: "Aw, c'mon, Willard, you blew it. Shoulda used the striped paint." Another added, "This'n's too old, anyway. We need a littler one—like that." They all followed the direction of his glance, and as Sonny watched, one of them moved to intercept a small, shaggy-haired boy in overalls. The little kid, confused but willing, actually went in to put the striped-paint question to old Jake. The gang huddled to peer through the window and then, laughing again, disappeared down the street. Sonny stood at Ma's open car window. "Did you see that?" he growled, "I hate those kids!"

"Well, you don't have to be like them," she said, "but you don't have to be a country hick, either."

Remembering the incident, and freshly filled with humiliation and anger, Sonny kicked at another sod clump at the edge of the cow path and unlimbered swear words he dared use aloud only when alone. "Sonsabitches," he muttered. Why do town kids have to be that way, getting their good times by poking fun at country rubes? He knew that his mother was right: "You don't have to be like them." But it was hard not to feel envy for the easy life of town boys, playing together every day of the year—and never any of these cows to milk, either.

Pa had the barn door open, and six milking cows started in—all except Old Holstein, always contrary, who wanted to go toward the water tank first. Sonny ran to head her off and pulled his cap pistol from his belt: it took two caps aimed right between the eyes to turn her around.

They pulled their T-shaped milking stools from the wall of the cow barn. "Pa, how soon you think we can go to the lake?"

"Well, guess we better do the milkin' first, anyway," his father said, in a joking way rare in their work talk. "Then there's the rest of the chores t'do."

Chores. Always those chores, no escape. Twice every day, the cows to milk. He remembered how he had pestered Pa to let him start learning, two or three years ago—remembered how first he and Pa had compared hands: his own had seemed so small alongside Pa's broad palm and thick, callused fingers. Then he finally got to squeeze the long, easy teats of Blackie and Old Holstein. Even now, as the foam rose in his milk pail, he could remember the satisfaction of hearing that metallic ringing of his first squirts on the bottom of the gallon-sized syrup can he'd held then between his small knees. It had made him feel more like a man. Now, milking every day, the fun had gone out of it; it was just repeated work. So many chores that never ended, like turning the heavy handle of the cream separator in the pantry, taking skim milk back out to the calves, climbing up in the haymow to throw down something the cows and horses could eat, looking out for the sharp spines of Russian thistles that lurked in each forkful. Pigs and chickens to feed and water. Eggs to get, barn to clean. And when the sun goes down, start the whole thing over. The darn chores. Those lucky town kids.

But today was the Fourth, and doing chores did not seem too high a price to pay for a carefree celebration at the lake. He pitched in energetically, even volunteering to take care of the henhouse chores by himself while his mother fixed potato salad and packed fried chicken and wienies for their planned picnic. Even so, by the time Pa had finished his regular work and then started to patch a tire on the car, it was midmorning. The girls, scrubbed and pretty in their summer dresses, were ready to go long before anyone else was, and Sonny soon had on his new polo shirt and blue pants, the cap pistol stuck in the belt and the package of firecrackers comfortably filling a pocket.

"Go tell your father to hurry up," Ma said, taking off her apron. "We want to get a parking place near the picnic tables." Finally Pa got himself shaved and into his white shirt and suit pants and oxfords—you could hardly tell he was a farmer—and they were off. The dishpan heaped with bowls and buns and lemonade jars took less space in the back seat than

Saturday night's cream can and egg case. Pa drove even more slowly than usual, and Sonny wondered whether it was because he was worried about the tires or simply because he wanted plenty of time to look at the growing fields along the way. He kept making observations: "Sure looks better'n last year," and "There's some corn made it knee-high by the Fourth."

Patience came hard. "Come on, Pa, can't we go any faster?" Sonny had to blurt out as they neared the top of one especially long hill on the graveled road. "Ah, we'll get there," his father's easygoing response drifted back with the warm air flowing from the open car window. He leaned back against the seat; on his blue pantlegs, the firecrackers and five coins bulged through from his pockets, and he touched them with his fingertips. At the other back-seat window, Clarice kept taking out a little mirror from a white purse to investigate various angles of her eyes and lips. The two little girls were being careful to follow their mother's repeated urgings to "keep those organdy dresses and white anklets clean, now." He was checking the roll of caps in his pistol when excited Elaine screeched, "There's the lake!"

Beyond where her small finger pointed, over on the left through clumps of trees and small hills, the receded waters of Lake Poinsett glistened, bluer than the sky. Only minutes later, as they came over the steep little hill, the Fourth was suddenly there below them: the big casino for roller-skating and dancing stood at the edge of what used to be the lakeshore—now, after last year's drought, a half-mile from the water. And he could see, partially hidden among the roadside trees, the flag of the familiar merry-go-round and the small flashing banners marking stands for bingo or hamburgers or games.

They parked between two trees, and Ma hurried to set the dishpan on one of the last empty picnic tables, like Columbus planting the flag in the New World. Along the way back she stopped to greet some family she knew, encamped nearby. For a while, Sonny stood next to the car, absorbing the dazzling sights and sounds. Dozens—hundreds—of people, just taking it easy, the men in their light shirts and straw hats standing in clusters while the dolled-up women tended food and small children and hooted and had a good time among themselves. He sniffed the aroma of celebration— popcorn, frying hotdogs, cigar smoke, burnt powder—drifting in from the midway area accompanied by the merry-go-round's rhythmic pipe-organ chords and clanging cymbals. Cap guns and varied firecrackers exploded at random all around. He pulled his pistol from his belt and fired once, twice. It was barely noticeable in the din. He got the matches from Pa, extracted the wick of one precious boomer from the entanglement in the green package, laid it against a tree trunk, and backed hurriedly away as the sizzling spark signaled danger: bang! The flash and the loudness only feet away excited him, and he looked around to share the moment; no one else paid any attention. A few cars away another firecracker went off, louder than his own had been. He heard his mother calling for "everybody to come and eat now." He put the stick matches away in a separate pocket.

No other Hidewood neighbors seemed to be there. But by the time they had finished their picnic, two of Pa's brothers and an old boyhood friend had stopped by the table, and the four of them lit cigars and ambled across the road to watch the baseball game. Ma hovered around the table, talking with people she used to know, while keeping an eye on the three little girls playing on the swings and teeter-totter. Some of her own brothers and sisters from Overhome would be arriving later. And Marie was due soon, along with the family from Hayti she worked for. "Clarice," she suggested, "why don't you run over to those tables toward the merry-go-round, see if Marie's here yet?"

Free to wander, Sonny stood with hands in pockets, feeling once again for the assurance and promise there: the smooth, waxy paper pack of firecrackers in one and in the other the quarter Pa had given him jingling with the saved dime, nickel, and two pennies. He contemplated the pleasures that forty-two cents could bring—the rides, the games, the pop.

His first decision was easy. Irresistibly, he was drawn toward the pulsating music and the brightly painted ponies rising and swooping, smooth and graceful, endlessly circling in blaring harmony. The ride made him dizzy with sensation, and he nearly got in line to spend a second nickel, then decided he'd better wait. He moved through the milling crowds toward the casino and the strains of quieter melodies coming from inside. For a long time he watched the roller skaters glide—so smoothly and without effort, the muffled roar of hundreds of hard little wheels on the huge wooden floor blending into the background music. After a while he wandered back to the midway and used another nickel on a strawberry ice cream cone. After the last pink was pushed to the very tip and savored, he stopped to try his luck at the penny-toss stand. His first chucked coin rolled completely off the platform; the second nearly ended up in a little twenty-five-cent square, but it touched a line. He watched as the aproned operator—without stopping his nasal call, "Hey, hey, toss a penny, win a dollah, got a winner here!"—exchanged coins with customers with one hand, with the other worked a long-handled broom to sweep the board clean again. Another boy at the other side of the stand tossed his penny. Suddenly Sonny felt a thrill. That familiar face belonged to Wayne, who had been his sole classmate in the third grade, before the move last year. Anticipating the pleasure of a surprise reunion, he hurried around to the other side and tapped the boy on a shoulder.

"Hiya, Wayne! How's my old pal?"

The boy turned around and looked confused for a moment. When he finally did show recognition, it wasn't with the same look of close friendship remembered from times past. There was another boy with him, whom he called Doug, a town boy from Estelline. Neither Wayne nor Doug seemed to be very interested in doing anything until Sonny showed them the pack of firecrackers. Then their enthusiasm grew quickly, and they had all kinds of suggestions on how to make the most exciting explosions. Ten minutes later, the firecrackers gone, their mood of boredom seemed to return. Walking back toward the casino, they kicked at the sand, and then the three of them sat on the edge of the boardwalk. Wayne leaned back on his elbows and looked at Sonny.

"You're sure you ain't got no more firecrackers?"

"All gone. Few more caps, is all." Sonny touched the pistol still in his belt.

"No money neither, t'buy some?"

He hesitated only briefly before sort of shaking his head; if you didn't actually say anything, maybe it wouldn't be considered a real lie.

The town boy stretched lazily. "Maybe I oughta look for my old man," he said, "an' try t'talk him out of another dime or two." Wayne said he thought that was a good idea, but nobody moved.

It was then that Sonny became aware of something new. At first there was only the sound—a distant, distinct, fluttering roar over the roller-skating noise, over the shouts of hawkers at the stands, absorbing the popping firecrackers and growing in intensity with each second until suddenly it was a powerful engine sound that burst into a yellow vision flashing in the sky above them. He had never seen an airplane flying low—so low that he could make out the pilot's white scarf trailing from the rear cockpit, his goggles and helmet,

the gloved hand waving at the crowds below. Then it was out
of sight again, hidden behind the big tree alongside the casino. Sonny ran down the grassy sand embankment to the edge
of the old lake bottom, where nothing obscured the open sky,
and there it was again, the afternoon sun glinting on its double wings, banking and turning toward the water's edge. Its
roar diminished, and the airplane dipped downward: it must
be coming in for a landing on the smooth sands where the
lake had receded. In the distance, a man was waving at the
pilot. All else forgotten, Sonny joined a small crowd of excited men and boys running in that direction.

Off to the right, the descending airplane was now close
enough for him to watch the yellow disc wheels hanging
under the golden fuselage, not even turning as they glided
swiftly over the earth, waiting to touch the moving shadow
on the sand. Suddenly they were spinning and exploding
small clouds of dust as the plane rolled, slowing now, bits of
dried grass catching in the settled tail skid, idling propeller
quieter in its breezy flutter, the broad yellow wings poised as
if eager to keep flying. Engine cut, the flashing propeller
slowed its heavy clicks and was still. The front cockpit was
empty; from the rear, the pilot—all white teeth and moustache—smiled down at the assembling admirers, and with
black-gloved hands he lifted his goggles onto his close-fitting
leather Lindy cap. He called to the man who had been signaling him.

"Hey Charlie, wheels chocked?"

"All set, Bud."

"Okay!" Bud removed his helmet, used two gloved
fingers to wipe sweat from around his eyes, and climbed
down from the plane. On the ground and without his helmet,
he seemed to be a more normal man; his short, dark hair
reminded Sonny of Craig's older brother James, from school,
except that this fellow Bud was shorter, and under that light

leather jacket, he probably didn't have the muscles that James had. The field boots and flaring tan boot pants made him look pretty special, though. "So!" The pilot was looking around at the faces. "Who's gonna be the first to take a ride with me? Just two dollars, and away we go!" He pointed at Sonny: "How about it, young fella?"

Behind Sonny, plenty of takers crowded in and past, pushing him so close he could reach out and touch the smooth, yellow surface below the pilot's cockpit. He was surprised to discover that it gave under the pressure of his finger: it was just cloth, stretched tight over the hard frame. "Hey kid!" He looked up at the sharp command. The other man, Charlie, was scowling at him and motioning with his hand: "Don't touch the aircraft, kid! Let's everbody move back!" The fear that he'd done something wrong quickly subsided, and Sonny watched as Charlie herded people back, collected dollar bills from those ready for a flying adventure, and then helped the first one climb up into the front cockpit. Sonny felt the quarter and nickel that remained in his pocket: the glory that had been close enough to touch for a brief moment now seemed far, far away—could he even dream of doing such things? The lucky passenger was buckled in and had donned the extra helmet and goggles. Bud swung up into the pilot's seat, and Charlie gave the orders: "All right, everbody, get back now. Way back!"

As the throng receded, Charlie removed the wheel chocks. He stood in front of the propeller, and he and Bud began the very same ritual that Sonny had seen in the movie about airmail: "Contact." "Contact." Charlie placed both hands flat on the blade, lifted one leg high, and with an athletic, sweeping motion pulled swiftly downward. The propeller jumped, and sputtered pops came through the exhaust smoke up front. The engine again clattered with power. With the other onlookers, Sonny backed farther away, hands protecting his face from the sand and loose weeds flying through the air. Then the yellow fuselage and broad wings were moving away, the tail jerking back and forth and the wing edges up and down, as if the airplane were flexing muscles, impatient to be aloft. Beyond the spot where wheels had first touched sand, the airplane again faced into the summer breeze. Sonny could hear the authoritative surge of power as it moved the throbbing yellow machine ever faster until— just coming by them—open space appeared and widened between the still-turning wheels and the ground. It was flying.

Wide-eyed, breath suspended, Sonny stood apart from the others, watching the phenomenon of flight, almost feeling the sensation of becoming airborne alone in the wondrous yellow machine climbing toward the sky, free of everyday constraints, dependent upon no one else, moving with a thrust of power that led up and away, into the blue. He felt strangely detached from everything, as if in a dream, and as he watched the diminishing double line of wings, he struggled to figure out what was real and what was not. The airplane and the pilot, they were real, all right, and they were up there flying through the air right now. The thirty cents clenched in his pocketed fist was just as real. It would take eight quarters to make two dollars. For a moment, he let his soaring imagination carry him to unreality: Bud, the pilot, and Charlie are still smiling at him and they know how much he would like to ride in their airplane and they are saying, "Sure, for you old pal, why not? Thirty cents is plenty this time"— but he stopped himself. No. This is not a fairy tale. That Charlie guy is not smiling at anybody, and the pilot doesn't do any magic, either, not like some King Arthur or Merlin. He's just an ordinary man dressed up fancy who maybe when he was a kid found out about airplanes and now has learned how to fly one. The quarter and nickel clenched in his hand could be a start toward saving enough to take a ride someday. Someday.

For now, it was enough to stand on this spot and watch the airplane circle back, fly over the casino, turn for the landing, and roll up to take on another passenger. Eight, nine times, he lost count as he followed every move in the airplane's rounds of maneuvers. Gradually the little band of onlookers thinned. Wayne and his friend had been among the first to leave the lake-bottom group, and by the time the sun glowed red in the west, Sonny was standing alone. After the last passenger descended and headed back toward the casino, Charlie climbed into the front cockpit. The pilot craned to inspect both sides of his aircraft, and when he was looking in Sonny's direction, he paused for a long moment. His leather-jacketed arm appeared above the cockpit, and the tip of his elegant glove touched his goggles. Slanted rays of sunlight deepened the warm tan of his face and highlighted the white teeth and moustache. Suddenly Sonny knew that this was a special, personal salute meant for him alone, a salute meaning—what? "I see you there, you have proved your interest in flying, you are like me." His own sweaty hand released the quarter and nickel in his pocket and came up to imitate the airman's salute, and the white under the moustache flashed broader. He continued to watch as Bud pulled down his goggles, gunned his engine, and headed into the wind. Against the hazy blue, the yellow wings and fuselage gradually dwindled into a moving speck and disappeared into infinity, and the only sounds came from the midway and picnic grounds, where people were still celebrating the Fourth.

"Where you been?" His mother sounded a little angry when he appeared back at the scene. But there was no time for her to listen. Everyone else had eaten their share of the evening picnic; she handed him a bun and chicken leg and packed up the empty dishpan. Pa's brothers were no longer

around, and Ma's younger sisters and brothers had already
come and gone home again early in order to get chores done
and return to dance at the casino. Clarice asked why they
couldn't stay until after dark for the fireworks, but Pa said
better not; it had been a long time since early-morning milking, and "some of those cows shouldn't wait much longer."
But when they got to the car, the tire Pa had fixed that morning was flat again—"sun got too hot for the patch, I guess"—
and he had to jack up the back wheel to put on the worn
spare, bulging with a boot inside where the hole in the tire
showed through. When they finally got going, Pa had to drive
more slowly than ever to favor the worrisome boot, which
made the back of the car wobble with each turn of the lame
wheel. The worry was not baseless: halfway home, a plaintive
hiss came from down below, and the Ford rumbled to a stop
on the gravel. No choice now; Pa peeled off the flabby rubber and they proceeded on the rim, a ringing crunch of metal
against pebbles as the Ford crawled along, leaving its trail of
shame double-cut into the roadway. To avoid permanent
damage, Pa turned off onto dirt roads and watched carefully
for large rocks.

It was long after dark when they finally eased into the
driveway. The cows stood waiting at the barn door, and in the
lantern light their bags looked swollen and stiff. Sonny could
muster little energy as they went about the evening chores,
and the wayward Old Holstein managed to add both insult
and injury when she kicked him into the manure gutter just
as he touched her. She had a mean, bloody gash on her bag,
apparently from another attempt to jump the barbed-wire
fence. Pa had to take over milking her, tying a rope around
those menacing legs. "Dang fool cow," he muttered as he gingerly applied Bag Balm. "Never satisfied with what's on this
side of the fence; always got t'get in trouble."

An hour later, tired, sore, and morose, Sonny sat with his

mother in the dim yellow glare of the kerosene lamp between them on the kitchen table. Their shadows loomed high and dark on the walls behind them. He ate slowly from the cup of bread soaked in milk that she'd set before him. The girls were long since asleep, and Pa was finishing up the chores.

"You're not talking much," she observed. "Bet you're pretty tired. Long day."

He glanced up briefly but offered no reply. The lamplight shining on just one side of his mother's face made her look sort of glamorous, like a star in a movie magazine. This chance to talk with her, just the two of them, calm like this, came along every once in a while, since her moods seemed so much better now.

"That cow didn't really hurt you, did she?"

"Naw." Old Holstein's dumb ways were not what was bothering him the most. "But we sure have to work a long time around here just to take a few hours off."

"Well, chores is part of farmin'. You had fun today though, didn't you?"

"Mmm, yeah, guess so. Different."

"Who'd you see, besides Wayne?"

"Hardly anybody I know. Nobody from around here."

"Well, what were you doing all that time, then? You never did say."

He held his empty spoon upright to emphasize what he wanted to tell her. "Ma," he said, "I was down there by that airplane. I touched it. I, ah, sort of talked with the pilot, even."

"That so."

"Did you know that airplanes are just made out of cloth? Stretched over a frame of wire or maybe wood, and painted?"

"Hmm. Makes them light, I spose."

"Sure. And the way you say 'contact' and pull down on the prop to start it, like in the movie show, remember? And that big old motor just roars and kicks up a windstorm, and the plane rolls along, and in a little while there's nothing between it and the ground—but air!"

In the silence his spoon clanked again in his cup, and he swallowed the last of his soaked bread. He could feel her eyes still on him and returned the gaze. "Just imagine," he said, "what it must feel like, flying around in the air like a hawk."

She nodded, half-smiling. "You'd really like that, wouldn't you."

He felt the realization glow inside him. No one else in the whole world understood him like his mother. "You think I could ever really fly an airplane, myself?"

She looked at him matter-of-factly and spooned another portion of her bread and milk. "Don't see any reason why not," she said. "A person can do anything, if he wants to bad enough. First thing is, you got to want to do it."

He thought about this for a moment, then turned to get up from the table. He saw his shadow rising toward the ceiling, and he spread his arms, waggling shadow wings. "Look," he said, "I'm flying already!"

"Better fly upstairs to bed."

Shoes off, he turned from the upstairs door with another insight to impart. "The wheels on an airplane—they turn only because the plane is rolling on the ground. They don't move, even, when the plane is flying. Did you know that?"

She shook her head, and there was that relaxed smile between them that came only once in a while. "No," she said, "I never thought of that."

He raised his hand, touched an eyebrow with the tip of his fingers—bent just so, as if encased in the most elegant kid-leather glove—and with a farewell salute, he turned to climb the steep stairs.

NEIGHBORS' WORK

Clarence
1935

Clarence was late getting back to the house for breakfast. At the porch door, he paused only briefly on the new concrete steps to stamp encrusted snow and manure off his heavy, four-buckle overshoes. Inside the enclosed porch, Bernice already had her two round, galvanized washtubs up but still empty, the corrugated washboard tilting on dry legs.

She stood at the kitchen stove, lifting high a bucket—wet rope trailing from its handle—to pour soft water dipped from the cistern into the oval-bottom copper boiler. Warm humidity filled the room. The three older kids must have left for school already, he judged from their empty oatmeal bowls still on the table, and the two littlest ones were probably in bed yet. He hung his blue denim overall jacket on the nail at the kitchen door and turned back the earflaps of his dark woolen cap before hooking it over the jacket. Heat from the hissing wood fire flushed his craggy face as he crossed toward the pantry sink.

"Ice in the tank pretty thick already this morning," he

said, easing around his wife and stopping at the stove reservoir. She made no reply but bent to pull at a triangular length of split firewood from the battered tub on the floor. When she opened the front stove grate, her face and brown hair glowed rosy and the flame danced in her glasses. The rosiness darkened when the grate clanked shut again.

He lifted the reservoir top and saw that it was almost empty. "You got a dipper pan, for the warm water?"

She reached to the other side of the stove to pick up the gray-speckled dipper. It clattered and bounced against the lifted reservoir top and finally tumbled into the square opening. She's still sore from yesterday, he thought, and she don't even know about today yet.

When she spoke the mood seemed to show through. "You can take off them stinking overalls before you sit down at the table," she said. "Clean pair on the porch." He dipped out the soft water, splashed it into the chipped enamel basin in the pantry sink, and inspected his hands. Trying to fix the engine, he'd had to work without gloves, even in the cold. New smudges of dirty grease covered the blackened, never-clean cracks on his thick and hardened fingers and around the irregular, dark-tipped nails. In natural reflex, both hands wiped themselves against old stains on his overall legs before he grasped the square of P&G and worked up a little lather. Clean enough, he figured, dabbing them into the damp of dark turkish towel; they'll be greasy again in a few minutes anyhow. A quick glance in the mirror above the sink reminded him he hadn't shaved for a couple of days. He smoothed dark strands of hair down with moist fingers, then went back out to the porch to remove his top overalls—she was right, the cowbarn and the old engine oil did make them smell pretty bad—and returned to sit at the table.

She set the plate of fried eggs and potatoes before him, poured his coffee, and gave herself a half-cup. He could feel her looking at him for a while before she said anything. "What took so long? Engine trouble again?" For as long as they'd been on this place, the gas engine at the stock tank had been a daily concern; the well was too deep, the pump too heavy to work by hand. Now, with colder weather coming, it worried both of them.

He nodded and reached for a square of corn bread. "Dang thing won't start. Guess I'll try to heat it up, see if that helps."

"Ought to get a different engine."

"Ehh, costs money. This'n's good enough, can be fixed."

Her glare sharpened. "Good enough! Everything's good enough for you! But you spend all morning monkeying with that engine, and you never will get your other work done." She sipped her coffee and went on: "Wasted enough time yesterday helping the neighbors. You thought you'd have the corn picked before the snow flies, and now winter's almost here."

There it was, he thought, her old complaint, "helping the neighbors." Yesterday he'd been over at Schleuters' to help them cut silage, and she didn't like that. He could hear her last words before they went to sleep last night: "Seems to me a person should tend to his own fields before spendin' time at the neighbors'." Now he would have to find a way to mention that he had promised to lend a hand again this morning to butcher a hog.

He said, "Well, only a few rows left in that cornfield. I can finish it up in three, four days, some good weather comin' yet."

"Anyway, good idea to get at it this morning."

He paused briefly. "Got to get the engine going first." He took a spoon of sugar, let the coffee seep over the edge to turn it brown. "And Julius needs help to butcher a hog later."

Once more she was staring at him, grim-faced. "So today again, too! Can't they do anything without you? First it was haying this summer, then after threshing it was their corn to shock, and the silo-filling yesterday!"

"Oh, they do things for us, too, y'know." He thought about times when neighbors had helped him in exchange; he would need Julius around to butcher, too, pretty soon. It would be nice to have some pork and headcheese to go with the johnnycake. But he said no more and simply left the table. His wife, with a sigh of exasperated weariness, returned to the dining room and the task of sorting out piles of family clothing for the wash.

On the porch, he pulled on the clean, patched, striped overalls over the faded blue ones worn underneath and, hand at the outside doorknob, paused for a minute to regard silently the two washtubs standing there. They had agreed, years ago, that someday Bernice would have a washing machine. Such hard work for her it was, every few days washing on the board for the seven of them, the baby's diapers still and those smelly overalls—he knew it was true. No wonder she feels sore sometimes, he thought. I should have bought her a washing machine long before now. Maybe this year we could afford it; at least we got a crop—maybe we could find a way to get some money ahead.

But first he had to get that engine started. It squatted there in the open air, waiting to be coaxed and tinkered with, green and greasy except for recessed spots between the two flywheels, where he had not been able to brush away the fresh snow. He found a length of heavy wire, wound an old rag around one hooked end, and poured onto it gasoline from the gallon can. It ignited with a whush, black smoke wafting from the flame, and he placed it to heat the underside of the engine. With pliers drawn from his overall side pocket, he removed the spark plug, scraped off carbon with his knife blade, and tapped the plug's open end to narrow the gap. He made certain that the ignition cable was firm and followed the oil-covered line to the magneto. "Maybe better take a look at that consarned thing," he said aloud.

It took a while to get it apart, and then, moving its inside mechanism with his fingers, he thought it seemed to have more play than it used to. He found a piece of twine to wrap around the shaft as a temporary washer and rebolted the magneto box to the engine's warming side. A few minutes later he had everything ready and slid the heavy crank over the axle. With the crankcase warm, the engine turned over with less resistance than before. Eventually a first tentative exhaust explosion rewarded him, and before long it was running evenly, but too slow. He tried weighting the crank with a bent wire hooked onto the governor rod. There, the engine's popping came faster. He slipped the belt onto the pulley and watched in satisfaction as the pumpjack gears suddenly started their grind. There would be water for the stock. For today, anyway.

"Engine's about shot, at that," he told himself, standing back to watch the water finally flowing into the near-empty, iced-up tank. He recalled Bernice's mocking words: "Everything's good enough for you!" Well, maybe he could do better. Best way to keep this old engine running through the winter would be to build a shed to keep the weather out. A few posts, walls of double woven wire with straw and horse manure in between, some of those old boards on the roof— it would work. All he would need was a day or two.

"Get your own work done instead of spending time at the neighbors'." Again, her words echoed in his mind. Can't say she's wrong about that, there's work to be done here. He pondered the dilemma as he watered the stock and began walking the quarter-mile toward the Schleuter place. How can you say no when a neighbor asks for help? Neighbors have always exchanged work, not only at harvest time but all year long, too—butchering, or vaccinating and cutting the pigs in the spring. Always something. No farmer could do everything himself. Maybe, he had to admit, he did spend more time helping others than neighbors came to help here. But the other side of it was that often he had to borrow machinery from others—the trailer from Elmer Krause, the single-row cultivator from Adolph Knutson, the grain-fanning mill from Julius. He thought about the drinking water obtained every couple of days from the Schleuters' pump. He remembered, above all, this spring, when his own granary was empty from last year's drought and crop failure; it was Julius who offered him the loan of a hundred bushels of stored old oats for seeding. And he remembered the pride and good feeling when the hundred bushels were paid back to Julius with the first oats threshed on this place just weeks ago. Good neighbors help each other.

He stepped off the road, crossed the shallow ditch and low fence, and cut through the stubble field toward the Schleuter yard. Around the corner of the graying granary-garage, Julius was at the grindstone, sharpening the knives. He looked up, peering from under the cloth cap that was always pulled low.

"Mornin', Clarence," his high-pitched greeting came through the tobacco-stained teeth clenching his pipe stem.

"Harya. Hope you wasn't waitin'." Through the open garage door he could see the butchering platform of planks on sawhorses, the wood-staved barrel at the far end, the wire-stretcher ropes rigged above as block and tackle. A three-foot singletree from an abandoned buggy balanced under the dangling stretcher, ready to hoist.

"Naw," Julius pedaled slowly and spoke over the grating scratch of knife held against stone. "Vernon's over to the hoghouse now, gettin' a rope on that shoat to herd him over this way." The younger Schleuter, in his twenties, still lived at home but farmed on his own.

The two neighbors chatted about the weather and the corn crop, and after a while Vernon appeared, tan corduroy hunting cap askew, arms flailing. He and the dingy white hog, a front leg tied with a thin rope kept slack in the young man's fist, traced an irregular course across the light layer of snow. Julius, sliding off the grindstone seat, said, "Might as well get at it, I guess."

While Vernon and Clarence held the hog—its shrill squeal so loud it made uncomfortable vibrations in their eardrums—Julius did the sticking and worked the long blade several times deep into the soft throat. They let the hog loose, and the squeal subsided into a grunty moaning as it wandered erratically, the red draining pink into the snow around the yard. When it finally weakened and fell, they hauled a boiler of scalding water from the house. A cloud billowed up as they mixed the hot water with lye and ashes in the angled barrel. Then they hoisted the carcass high, using the singletree hooked into its spread back-leg tendons. Julius pulled the stretcher rope while Clarence and Vernon guided the dead weight into the steaming barrel. After a few seconds, at Julius's signal, they exerted strength together to pull the carcass out, roll it slightly, and haul it up and into the barrel again. At last it rested steamily on the platform. The wet hog odor helped get them ready for the stink of warm guts, soon to come.

"Yeah! That worked fine!" Julius was triumphant. "Boys, I think this customer is ready for a shave."

They all set to work scraping, and as the clean, smooth whiteness spread on the scalded hide, their conversation touched topics of neighborhood interest. They doused the hog twice more and were doing finishing touches around the ears when Julius brought up a new subject.

"Say, Clarence, you heard yet about this guvvamint deal, for workin' on the road?"

"No, what's that?"

"Well, we was over to George's last night—he's always our road boss, y'know. Says Roosevelt has a new program for us farmers, haulin' gravel and actually gettin' paid for it." Neighborhood farmers were accustomed to working together on local roads one day a year, but they never saw any money: it was a way of "working out the poll tax."

Clarence became very interested. "Oh? Paid how much, did he say?"

"Not sure," Julius said. "You hear, Vernon?"

"He said about five dollars a day for man and team," the younger man said. Vernon and Julius had both stopped to stoke their pipes.

"And when would this be?"

"Said maybe next week, as long as the ground ain't froze."

Julius nodded. "Guess he'll let us know when he has the whole story." He looked at Clarence through the blue of his new smoke. "Vernon will work a team for us. You'll want to be in on it, eh?"

"Bet your life. We could use some hard cash right now." The idea excited him. He'd worried about having to sell off the spring pigs too early for needed fall cash. Now maybe working on the road could get them some money ahead. Maybe, just maybe, that washing machine for Bernice.

The notion grew in his head, like a good seed in nourishing soil sending out shoot and roots. By the time he had walked halfway home, he had turned it into a plan: he would make it a surprise for her. It would be something to let her know he appreciated all the unending hard work she'd taken on since coming to work for him years ago. It could be, even, one of those romantic things. He thought, now, about matters that he usually tried to keep out of his mind: the awful time after Gunda died, leaving him with the two baby girls; young Bernice coming in as housekeeper and staying on as wife and stepmother; and the years since, with four babies of her own. There'd been no chance to go out courting or romancing, as normally a fellow and his girl might. He'd never driven his buggy team or Model T by her house or taken her to a neighborhood dance. There were no letters exchanged that she might, like other women he'd heard about, save and bind together with pink ribbon to look at sometimes and remember bygone days of sweetheart foolishness. With him and Bernice, it had all been right there in the house, natural and practical, first just working together, gradually coming to appreciate each other, then feeling the powerful man-woman urges before they decided to get married. So she'd never had her share of romantic things that women like when they're young.

"Oh," he told himself, walking along, "she wouldn't expect me to pick a handful of flowers and kneel in front of her like Charlie Chaplin or some sap in the funny papers. Real people don't talk about 'love' and things like that." But he was ready to admit that once in a while a man should show his wife that he cares about her. He had to admit, too, that in these last years especially he had not done enough of that; the move to this place and the bad drought last year, and all. Maybe a washing machine would make it up to her a little bit.

That very afternoon, while Bernice was washing dinner dishes, he sneaked a few minutes in the dining room to look in the Sears, Roebuck catalog. Lowest-cost washing machines were hand-powered models; the "High Speed Wizard" could be ordered for $15.95. But it wouldn't be much improvement for Bernice to trade her washboard for a handle she'd have to push and pull. Machines with motors were alarmingly expensive. Anything under a hundred dollars seemed to be made to work with electricity—for town people, or those few farms with their own generators. Machines equipped with gasoline motors would cost up to a hundred and twenty-five, more if you bought it on time, even if only five dollars down and eleven a month. What if some month a person couldn't scrape together that eleven dollars? Would the company send a man out to repossess the machine? The way so many people around here lost their farms because they couldn't make payments in the Depression and the dust storms? He decided to compare prices next time in town.

The weather warmed, and confirming word came from George Roecker about the road project. "We'll plan on four days' work now, more next month. Start a week from Monday, early mornin'." Much had to be accomplished before then. Clarence had to pick the last corn, build the engine shed, and prepare the wagon box for hauling gravel.

On a trip to town to buy a few two-by-six planks for the wagon bottom, he stopped by the Gamble store and then at Kittleson's Hardware to see about washing machines. It was discouraging. He just hadn't realized that gas-motor machines were going to be that expensive. Young Nort Kittleson, showing him what was on hand at the front of the store, presented another idea: "Tell you what, Clarence, you might want to consider a used machine. We happen to have a pretty good one out in back, fella just west of town traded it in on a new electric." It was a beauty all right, a gleaming white Maytag, the automatic wringer there on the top. Kittleson placed the muffled end of its exhaust hose out the door and kicked the motor's starting pedal twice. The little engine popped smooth and steady. "We could let you have it for, let's see . . ." the young man scratched his balding pate, "say, fifty dollars?"

Clarence nodded affirmation; if only he had the money. "Would you sell it on time?"

"I think we could let it go for twenty down and five dollars a month, if that sounds okay."

"Seems a fair price," Clarence said tentatively. By Friday he should have the cash in hand from working on the road. "I'll have to let you know, though. A week from Saturday too long?"

"I guess we can hold it for you till then."

He was jubilant at the prospect and threw himself into a frenzied work schedule. The weather held clear and mild, and he vowed openly he was going to get the corn out of the field before the roadwork began. Bernice was skeptical, for she assumed the road project was more of his spending time with his friends, and he kept secret the fact that they were all to be paid. But she pitched in and got the kids to help, too, doing more than their normal share of the chores. Every morning in early light, Clarence had old Jim and Birdie—his buggy horses, getting older now, but still his best team for cornhusking—hooked to the wagon with the towering bang-board riding on one side of the high box. He made good progress, stooped between the two rows hour after hour, his left hand seeking and holding each ear as his right palm with the hook flashed and returned for the grasp and wrist-snap and throw, all in a repeated rhythm. He let his hands and arms do the work, and he could keep his mind on other thoughts. He wondered how much faster and cleaner the champions could husk and toss at the big cornhusking contests; some year he would go to watch them. He speculated on his yield. Maybe thirty, thirty-five bushels—no bumper crop but a whole lot better than last year's drought and no corn to pick at all. And his thoughts turned often, during those long hours in the field, to his secret plan: the roadwork money soon to be earned, the Maytag waiting for them, the surprise and delight that would be on his wife's face when he told her about it, in less than a week now.

Even the old gas engine seemed in a cooperative mood, at first. Every noon, after unloading the morning's husked

ears, he needed to spend only a few minutes to get it started pumping the stock tank full. He felt he was sort of reward-
ing the worn contraption for its good behavior, or maybe brib-
ing it for the future, when he started to build the shed to keep
it from the weather. He gave an hour or so whenever he
could, late afternoons before the light faded completely, and
worked on it full time after triumphantly finishing the last
row of corn Saturday noon. But on Sunday—the day before
the roadwork was to begin—he was nailing the final boards
on the roof when the unpredictable engine decided to go hay-
wire altogether. One minute it was popping away just fine,
cozy and protected within its new walls, driving the pumpjack and making the water flow, and all of a sudden there was
a god-awful racket from down there and everything stopped.
This time it was more than the spark plug or magneto.
Cautiously turning the flywheels, Clarence could hear that
something had come apart inside.

"What you going to do now?" Bernice asked at the supper table. "Can't very well work on the road with the engine
broke down again."

"Well, the tank's about full—enough water for the stock
tomorrow and maybe next day. I'll haul gravel with the rest
of them tomorrow, better do that much. Then Tuesday morning I'll take the engine to town, get it fixed." He hated to lose
even one of those precious earning days; and he still wanted to keep his secret from her.

He trotted his horses along most of the two miles through
the chill air the next morning and found George's car already
at the gravel pit. Harry Koppman was with him, and soon the
three other wagon drivers pulled up. George had them meet
together and gave instructions, left hand at his sheepskin-cov-
ered bay window while his right—part of the glove turned
inside out for the finger lost in a threshing machine accident
years ago—gestured and pointed toward the recently grad-

ed road now to be graveled. "Let's get the wagons loaded from this gravel"—he jerked his jowly head toward the pit— "in this order: first Vernon, then Clarence, then Elmer, and then Shorty, and by that time Vernon should be back for his second load. Me and Harry will help shift the planks to unload, and we'll spread it even on the road." The six of them worked steadily according to plan until noon. As they huddled next to George's car, out of the wind for their sandwiches and thermos coffee, Clarence told them that he would not be able to work with them tomorrow.

"Dang, that's too bad," George grimaced, his gold front tooth catching the sunlight. "Goin' to be hard to finish this part of the job if we're short-handed." He took a swig from his cup. "Wonder if they hain't some way we could use your team and wagon anyway?"

After a little silence, Vernon spoke up. "I could ask Dad tonight. Maybe he can fill in."

It worked out that way. Julius used Clarence's team and wagon the next day, while Clarence borrowed Elmer's two-wheeled trailer to take the broken-down engine to a mechanic of good reputation on the edge of town. Bernice came along to do the trading, so the cream can and square egg case rode in the back seat. The mechanic had bad news for them. "You got a busted connecting rod there," he said. "See, scored the cylinder wall pretty bad."

"Can be fixed, though, can't it?"

"Well, hell, cost you fifteen, twenny dollars to repair the damage, and then what you got is still a piece-a junk. Magneto and governor both about gone, loose bearings, leakin' oil. If I was you I wouldn't put more money into this thing; better t'buy another one."

Clarence felt confused and uncertain, but he knew he did not want to have to buy a different engine now. Getting this one to run ought to be good enough to get by for a while.

What he earned on the roadwork might have to take care of this repair, and maybe he could sell the hogs early to find the money for the down payment on the washing machine.

Bernice was watching him. "What now?"

"Well, a new engine would be nice, but no use thinking about that—maybe a coupla hundred dollars."

"What about a second-hand one?"

Clarence told the mechanic he'd have to let him know later what they decided. They stopped at several implement dealers. At International Harvester, past the new, shining red Farmall tractors lined up outside, they were shown what might have been an ideal gas engine. "Just look at that," Clarence said when they stood next to it in a corner of the shop. It seemed almost new. The gold "IHC" against the green cooling tank was not even chipped or smudged with oil. But the asking price—ninety-five dollars, or thirty dollars down and five dollars a month—would be too much, they agreed. Clarence nodded at the familiar feeling of disappointment. Most things that looked good were out of reach.

"I wonder if you couldn't find something cheaper in Estelline or Watertown," Bernice said when they were in the car again.

"Maybe so. We could drive around there, I guess. At least we got one engine that still works pretty good!" He tapped his hand on the Model T's dashboard.

"Too bad you can't use it to pump water," Bernice said.

"We used to, in the old days—bolt a pulley to the back axle, jack up the wheel, and line it up with the pumpjack." An idea was coming into his head. "You know, Julius has one of those old pulleys hangin' in his garage; I saw it last week butcherin'. If we got that, we could use the Ford here to pump water tomorrow and until the engine is fixed—or we find another one somewhere else."

"Why don't you try that," she said. "I just don't think you

should put more money into that old wreck unless you have to."

Such a temporary solution appealed to Clarence: it would let him get back to the roadwork to earn cash both for fixing the engine and, he hoped, for the down payment on the secret washing machine.

Doing the chores late that afternoon, he kept an eye out for Julius returning from the roadwork. Instead, George Roecker's blue Chevy appeared at the driveway. Julius was with him. "We left your horses over to Harry's, closer by," Julius explained. "You want to work tomorrow?"

Clarence explained his problem with the gas engine and said he'd like to borrow that axle pulley from Julius to put the car on the pumpjack. "Don't know if it's still any good," Julius started to say, but he was interrupted by George, who leaned his girth from behind the wheel to talk through the opposite car window. "Hell, Clarence, we can do better'n that. I got that John Deere gas engine—you know, Julius, we used it with your fanning mill last spring—why don't we get that over here and put it on your well for a few days?"

That's what they agreed to do and Clarence felt relieved. A lot better to keep that borrowed engine in place, he knew, than to fool around lining up the Ford wheel every morning. But he had to ask Julius to take one more day of the road-work—another five dollars lost, he silently lamented—to give himself time the next morning to get George's engine belted to the well. By noon Wednesday, the machine was lined up and doing the job. Clarence was tempted to get Bernice to drive him at noon over to the roadwork, but he decided it wouldn't be fair to Julius to take a half-day of work away from him after he had been so neighborly. Bernice, still assuming there was no money involved, liked the idea of having Clarence around their own place instead of joining the other men, though now that the corn was picked she did not begrudge him one more day of "being with others."

On Thursday he took over his team and shovel from Julius, and George's round face showed satisfaction to hear the engine was working fine. "Keep it as long as you need it," he said. But for Clarence, the decision time would be two days from now: Saturday was when he planned to take Bernice into Kittleson's to give her a look at her new washing machine. And at the same time they could go over to see what's-his-name, the mechanic on the edge of town, and tell him to fix up the old engine the best he could.

He was not prepared for a surprise development that started Friday toward noon, as he was finishing up the barn cleaning, driving the team on the empty spreader back from the stubble field. He'd been feeling good to get caught up on work to be done around the place. The little borrowed engine within the new shed, barely audible, worked away in its irregular John Deere rhythm—pop, sniff-sniff; pop-pop, sniff-sniff-sniff. He could see some of the cattle standing leisurely around the filling tank, and the rest of the herd at the straw pile where he would now pick up clean bedding for the whole barn. Then a movement over at the distant driveway caught his eye: it looked like George's car, stopping briefly at the house, then looping around and back to the road. Later, in the kitchen just before sitting at the table, he asked Bernice, "Wasn't that George drove in?"

She was looking at him in a peculiar way, with a kind of half-smile. "It was him, all right." She knew something he didn't know, and she was enjoying it.

"Didn't say he needs his engine right back, did he?"

"No, he brought this." She reached into the cupboard and placed a yellow rectangle on the table. "Your check for the roadwork." She chided him with a gentle nudge: "Why didn't you tell me you was earning money there!"

They exchanged sly grins for a moment, and then

Clarence began reading aloud: "Twenty and no one-hundreds dollars, man and team, four days—" He looked up, incredulous. "Hol' on here, *four* days? I only did two, Julius did the other two."

"That's what I said, too. George says Julius won't do it any other way, just paying you back in exchange work. I told George, you guys shouldn't have done that, it's too much, and George just said—you know how he looks like a teddy bear sometimes—he said, 'well, that's what neighbors are for.'"

Warm elation filled him as he listened; Bernice couldn't seem to stop talking. "First they borrow us that gas engine, and now Julius even lets us get paid for his work. I guess we do have good neighbors, all right." He nodded, and she went on. "But we shouldn't take advantage of them, either. We better get Roecker's engine back to him pretty soon, don't you think?"

"Well, let's see. Maybe now I can tell you about . . . something. Nort Kittleson has a Maytag washer he's holdin' for us, just about new. With this check now, we can make the first payment and bring it home tomorrow. Eh?" He awaited her reaction.

Another kind of smile was there now, and her face glowed with pleasure as comprehension came. "Well, for crying out loud," she almost whispered, as if to herself. "You mean, you been into Kittleson's and found a *washing machine?*"

He nodded briefly, half-embarrassed at her pleasure. "Thought it was high time you got some help with all this work for a change."

She reached over and patted his thick forearm. "Well, just your doing that, it's awful nice," she said, and in silence, for a long moment, they looked at each other in a way that made him think of how it used to be.

Then, in tone more brisk, she continued: "But I been

doing some thinking, too." She pushed her chair back, stepped across to the cupboard again, and returned with the old orange-iridescent sugar bowl that had been her mother's and where she now stowed savings from egg and cream money.

"Look," she said, dumping its contents on the oilcloth alongside his plate after she'd moved over the dish of corn bread. "There's nearly ten dollars here. Put that with the check, and we can buy that good engine at International Harvester!"

He regarded her quizzically now. "But the washer . . . we can just get the old engine fixed good enough to get by."

"Good enough again!" It was only teasing this time, but there was some exasperation there. "No, what I mean is, we should get that good engine now and let the rest go—forget looking all over for a cheaper one, and forget that old piece of junk. Like the guy said, it's so worn out it could break down again anytime. You need an engine out there that will be dependable, winter and summer, for a long time to come. The landlord won't put a windmill up for another few years yet, I betcha."

"That straw shed keeps the snow and ice off now, though."

"It's a big help, sure. But the shed ain't gonna keep that old magneto or the bearings from flyin' apart. How would you water the stock if that old engine would break down again in the middle of a blizzard?"

The picture of thirsty cattle and blocked roads convinced him. "I know you're right about that," he said, "but darn it all, we should be able to get that washer, too."

Her hand was on his arm again. "I sure do appreciate you thinking about it, anyway," she said, nodding slowly. "But we can't do everything all at once. What's most important now is to make sure there'll be water in the tank this winter. Other things can come later."

"I don't know how long Kittleson's can hold that washer for us."

"Well, if it's not still there when we get some money ahead, that's all right too. I been washing on the board all my life now; guess I can do it a little longer."

"All right then. Tomorrow we'll pull Elmer's trailer to town and we'll haul that new International engine home. But before long we'll find a washing machine, too." He stood to reach up for his jacket on the nail above the door. "You know, I seen in the catalog, they have those hand-powered washers, only about fifteen dollars, new. Better'n nothing, I spose. But I thought one with a gas motor would be a lot better."

"Well, we'll see. One of those hand machines might be good enough."

He was pulling on his cap, and at the familiar words his callused fingers paused on the dark wool visor. He looked sidewise at her. It must have been ten years since they'd felt such a playful mood between them. "How's that again?"

She cocked her head at him, then realized the words she'd used, and she had to laugh. "Well," she said, "good enough for a while, maybe."

WHERE CHURCHES GROW

Bernice
1936

By the time Bernice began to feel settled in as part of the Hidewood neighborhood, the Overhome household had broken up, the brothers and sisters scattered to wherever they could find jobs. Like his two older brothers, Harry had headed for the West Coast. Margie had moved to Sioux Falls, where a girl could earn two or three dollars a week, plus board and room, doing housework in the fancy homes of the well-to-do. Bert was now in Iowa, where Leona and Zena— the two girls closest in age to Bernice—had gone years earlier to seek their futures. "Zee" had arranged for him to live with a local farmer and to work for board and room. Maybe she thought having her youngest brother close by would help her get over her husband's tragic death; she still treasured the flashy car that she and her wonderful "Steffy" used to drive into the Amerson farmyard, melodic horns blaring, when they traveled the 150 miles to visit. Bernice hoped she would continue to come now and then. Maybe young Bert could ride along, stay awhile. An oldest sister had a responsibility to offer a temporary home to footloose brothers and sisters.

Thankful that at least two sisters remained nearby, Bernice focused her attention on Irene and Ruby. She felt proud that they had taken the initiative to get more schooling, had trained themselves as secretaries, and held good-paying jobs only thirty miles away in Watertown. She had helped them get started there; Sonny and the girls always seemed eager for the big-town experience of carting boxes of eggs and garden vegetables up to the second-floor apartment on Kemp Street. Within a few months Irene and Ruby had established themselves, and now sometimes when Bernice and Clarence had to make the trip to Watertown, the two sisters rode back to spend the weekend with the family on the farm.

Her kids loved having Irene and Ruby visit. An exciting glamour surrounded these two high-heeled, single women who worked in offices and lived in a town big enough to have names on the streets and numbers on doorways. They might bring little dime-store gifts—paper dolls or Big Little Books for the girls, maybe a toy car or black sticks of twisted licorice for Sonny. Best of all, just *doing* things with them guaranteed fun—laughing at jokes and reading books and telling stories and singing together. One time, inventive Ruby had put on a show for them, cutting up a chicken and having them remember the names of all the parts. At Christmas, when little money could be found to buy gifts, she had led the way in creating lovely presents out of ordinary things found around the house. Both aunts always seemed to enjoy being at home with family again. Carefree times of their own childhood having been cut short, they could relax in play with their only nieces and nephew.

As for Bernice, she relished the moments of family closeness, when the girls called her Big Sister and shared small confidences. The thought often came to her that if Maw were looking down from somewhere, she must approve. Thus, it came as a complete surprise to Bernice that one weekend she actually got into a spat with one of her sisters—about church, of all things.

On a Friday afternoon in May, rain having made field-work impossible, Clarence had agreed to stay in Watertown until after five, when Irene and Ruby got off work. Then they had to hurry back for evening chores. Sonny could get the cows into the barn but, small for his age at eleven, he still couldn't milk several of the kickers or stand up to rambunctious hogs at the feeding troughs. Clarice, just out of grade school, and the three little girls had also stayed home to leave room in the Model A, the "new" used car bought to replace the old Model T; by dusk they'd already gathered eggs from the chicken coop and set the supper table with two extra places, anticipating the evening. But it was nearly dark when the car drove into the yard. By the time chores and supper were finished and the davenport opened in the east room for the visitors, everyone seemed too tired for real fun. Irene and Ruby volunteered to do the dishes—usually the best time for singing together—but energy lagged, and besides, Clarence needed to hear the ten o'clock news on the radio. Ruby reassured the disappointed kids. "Wait until tomorrow," the frail girl promised, small face shining, blue eyes appearing larger through her new, gold-framed glasses. "I've got something special to show you!"

Next day they all made up for whatever they may have missed the night before. The younger children conducted the honored guests on a tour of the farmyard to see puffball chicks and their clucking mother near a hidden nest, new calves in the barn, and cute piglets sunning themselves at the soft, nurturing belly of mother sow. Bernice enjoyed a midmorning cup of tea with her sisters, listening to them exclaim about the fresh air, even the musty barn—"all those homey smells of the farm," as Ruby put it. Irene, more sassy, had to add her own twist: "Yeah, but I just came in from the backhouse—some of those homey smells can *stay* on the farm!" Bernice laughed with the rest of them at that, promised them "an indoor toilet around here, too, someday," and urged them to take a long hike into the open spaces of pasture and wet ravines. They went off, then, with the children to dangle bare feet in new, brown rainwater and look for minnows. When they returned, all smiles, they told of scaring up two beautiful rooster pheasants and spotting a jackrabbit loping along a hillside.

Their good mood continued into the evening. Singing started right after supper, when Clarice and Sonny rendered for the aunts their song, to the tune of "Wanderer's Warning," about a winter bout with the measles. Usually shy Baby Jeanie, only three, was coaxed into offering her version of "In the Valley of the Moon," learned from the radio and older sisters. Elaine and Snooky teamed up on a nonsense tune from school called "Intry Mintry Cutrey Corn." Sonny suggested one of the hymns they all knew, and that's when Ruby, making a show of it, produced her promised "something special": a hymnal borrowed from the church she and Irene attended in Watertown.

Now music filled the house. Clarence grew interested, too, and Sonny ran up to the attic to fetch the fiddle. Irene led with melody lines; Ruby blended in the alto and organized others to follow; Clarence filled in, completely absorbed, a faraway look on his face. They did all the old favorites—"Softly and Tenderly," "In the Garden," "Bringing in the Sheaves." Clarence had a personal request: "Do you know 'Shall We Gather at the River'?" Neither Irene nor Ruby did, so they found it in the hymnal. Clarence led the way, and Ruby got Sonny and Snooky to follow her on the harmony. Bernice, at the edge of the group, had never heard her husband play a church song before—probably one that had stayed with him from the old days in the Norwegian Lutheran church, she thought.

A little later, leaving the others practicing a new hymn, Bernice found herself alone with Irene, side by side at dishpans on the kitchen stove to work at the supper dishes.

"It's amazing!" Irene said, applying the floursack dish towel to another plate. "Listen to those kids hold the harmonies out there. Beautiful!"

Bernice glanced at her middle sister, always such a good-looking girl with a bright personality, and now working in the big town as a receptionist and secretary for a respected doctor. "Yes," she agreed. "They take after their father, I guess."

"But from our side of the family, too. The way Ruby can teach the alto parts . . ."

"Where did she learn that, anyway?"

"Some of it's natural, I guess," Irene said. "And she's been singing alto in the choir of our church."

Bernice remembered their speaking, weeks earlier, of some church with a long name, not Lutheran, anyway. "What church do you go to, did you say?"

"Christian and Missionary Alliance. Reverend Thompson—wonderful man, wonderful family—wonderful place!"

Church talk gave merry Irene's pretty face a serious look. "You never went to church much before, did you?" Bernice asked her.

"No, Overhome none of us did. You know how it was."

Bernice's parents had never taken their children to regular church services, except for funerals. "Going to church was not so important for Maw and Paw, I guess," she said.

"I'm not so sure about that. It might have been, for Maw."

"What makes you think so?"

"Well, remember that magazine we had around home, *Evangel?* And when we were in school in Hayti, Maw always wanted us to take that hour each week for Bible training over at the Lutheran church."

"She did?" This was news to Bernice.

"Yes, and she told me something, too. Her father, our grandpa DeGroot, he was one of the founders of the Presbyterian church in Ashton, Iowa."

Bernice said nothing. She had never heard of Maw's family being church people. Now here was her younger sister telling her things about her own mother that should have been told to her first, by rights. She concentrated on scraping the bottom of a kettle. Neither of them spoke for what seemed a long time. Then Irene laid the damp dish towel on the stove reservoir and moved around it to look more directly into her sister's face.

"You know, Bernice," she began, "going to church, it *is* important. I have found out something. God is *all*-important—in my life, in *all* our lives!"

Bernice regarded her sister in silence. She seemed so earnest, so holier-than-anybody. And the next remark just escaped on its own: "Where'd you find *that* out, from the Lutherans in Hayti?"

But Irene's pretty face only softened again into a smile. "No, no. I realize you had a bad experience over at the East Norden church. But churches are not all like that. Reverend Thompson just took us in, so friendly—he's almost like a father to Ruby and me."

Ah, that's probably it, Bernice thought; a couple of young girls, without parents or kids, new in a big town, they would find comfort in a friendly church. "Well, I'm glad you have good friends there," she said.

Irene looked impatient now. "But just having friends is

not the point, Bernice! A church is the House of the Lord, where you hear the Holy Word, where you feel the presence of God."

"Well, I—"

"Think of your kids, their everlasting souls!"

"Think of my—"

"I mean, those girls have not even been baptized yet, have they?" It sounded like an accusation.

"I don't baptize my kids anymore," Bernice said, failing to keep the bitterness out of her voice. "Tried it once."

"Don't talk that way! Bernice, you may not like what I say, but I am going to speak God's truth, to do what I can to add to His Kingdom. I think you owe it to your kids to take them to church and Sunday school."

This was too much. The nerve of a kid sister who only yesterday was just a snot-nosed baby needing a diaper change, who don't know the first thing about raising kids—trying to tell me how it should be done. Now she's a city girl with funny notions about having to save the souls of other people's kids. Bernice could feel her anger rising, her mouth line tighten as she glared at Irene. "You just mind your own business," she blurted out, "and *I'll* take care of *mine!*"

She reached over to yank the twisted, moist dish towel away from her sister's hands at the reservoir top and occupied herself with drying the kettle she'd just washed. Irene, silenced by the outburst and by the lingering tension, turned away slowly and shuffled, shoulders dropping, toward the east room. They did not speak further with each other that night.

Sleep would not come easily. As always, Bernice used the quiet dark to think things through. Why had she let herself get out of control? The last thing in the world she wanted was argument with any of her sisters or brothers. And yet, with her cutting remark, she had hurt the feelings of one of her favorites, who surely meant well and whose interest in this family was genuine, after all. If only Irene had not used that preacher talk, taken the holier-than-thou Norwegian attitude. Bernice recognized that all those bitter memories should be pushed aside now, should not be allowed to stand in the way of good sisterly relations. And maybe the very future of her own children *was* at risk here. Their "everlasting souls," as Irene had put it. How should a mother give her kids opportunities to make their own choices in religious faith?

She was not even sure of what she herself believed, had never really thought much about it. She did not doubt the existence of God, the "Almighty Creator of Heaven and Earth," in church people's words. She recalled again the spiritual mystery surrounding her mother's death, when Maw, in a kind of ecstatic agony, had moaned about a bright light just before passing away. Weeks after the funeral, when a traveling salesman had come to the house hawking religious material, Bernice had found the coins to buy two placards to hang on the front-room walls. One reminded everyone that "The Fear of the Lord is the Beginning of Wisdom"; the other, blue-bordered with a portrait of Jesus, proclaimed more boldly: "CHRIST is the HEAD of this HOME." She had been willing, then, to identify herself and her family as believing Christians. (And, thinking about it, she remembered with a smile how Sonny—about eight at the time and proud of his reading and reciting skills—had paraded around the house endlessly repeating the latter quote, with all the emphases, until she told him it was not right to talk that way.)

But beyond going along with what nearly everybody seemed to believe in, Bernice had little personal experience in the religious side of life. In contrast, all of her sisters, especially Irene and Ruby, openly declared themselves Christian believers and sometimes used such expressions as "born again" and "our Saviour." The subject had always made Bernice feel uncomfortable, embarrassed at her own inability—or maybe her stubborn, deep-down resistance—to forget doubts and simply agree, in blind faith, to what churchly religion seemed to demand. Irene and Ruby had become accepted members of that Watertown church filled with friendly people, where apparently everyone could "feel the presence of God." How to explain why God had made His presence known to her sisters, and never to her? Would this happen only within a church? How should one listen for such messages? How can you make children aware of such things?

Clear answers did not come. But she knew she could not leave things as they were. Before her eyes closed, she had determined what she must do.

Around the breakfast table next morning, talk was subdued, confined mainly to Ruby's appreciation of the fresh fried eggs and salt pork and the pancakes swimming in Karo syrup. But afterward, Bernice found a way to have a moment alone with Irene, and she placed her hand on her kid sister's arm.

"Listen," she said, and couldn't think of what should come next. Bernice could not make herself utter such emotion-laden words as "I'm sorry," or "Please forgive me" any more than she could say a prayer out loud at the dinner table. But Irene seemed to need no spoken message; Bernice could feel the necessary communication pass through her fingertips.

"I know," the sweet, relaxed face told her. "Sometimes we say things we don't mean. I shouldn't have come at you so strong."

"Well, I understand what you were saying," Bernice said. "And I been thinking. Maybe you're right. These kids ought to have experience in a church."

"Really? Oh, Bernice!"

"As part of their education, if nothing else."

"Oh, there'll be lots else! They'll go to Sunday school?"

"Well, I imagine so."

"Where will you take them? Want to come to our church, in Watertown?"

"No, that would be too far to drive, Sundays. Maybe the closest one, over by Gaugers' corner, four miles."

"What denomination is that, do you know?"

"I can't remember the name of it," Bernice said, "but it's not Lutheran."

Not many of the Hidewood neighborhood families attended church, her inquiries showed. Bessie and Elmer Krause went nearly every Sunday with his German-Lutheran folks some distance away. Vera Schleuter sometimes got her children to Sunday school, but in town, where they had family connections. Vera thought that Annie and George Roecker went now and then to the Evangelical, over by Gaugers' corner. (Ah, Bernice remembered, *that* was the name.) None of the other neighborhood women she'd become acquainted with seemed likely insiders in that church, waiting to welcome newcomers. She would have to handle this problem on her own, to go hat in hand to yet another strange church and ask for acceptance. She hated the idea, but she had made the promise to Irene. To the kids. To herself.

As she had expected, Clarence offered little help. When she mentioned the idea of church and Sunday school for the kids, he nodded with some sign of interest; but later, he made it clear that he would assume only the role of caretaker at home while others attended. "Youse can go," still his stock phrase for such occasions. Bernice had never figured out why he used that old-fashioned, immigrant word only when he wanted to be left alone. She saw this as yet another way he sealed off his deeply private past, including church-associated memories, away from others. She admitted to herself that she might be partly to blame for his passive attitude, and she knew that she had to learn to live with it.

During the week she made sure the kids got ready. They reviewed printed religious material at hand: Maw's old Bible, which Bernice had inherited, and a new book from Irene and Ruby called *Stories of the Bible.* She urged Clarice and Sonny to memorize the Ten Commandments (when Sonny asked her to explain what "adultery" meant, she mentioned something about "what grown-ups do, sometimes" and told him to ask his father if he needed to know more). She found three pennies each for Elaine and Snooky to drop into the collection plate that she figured would come around. Clarice and Sonny—who together had washed and swept out the Ford Saturday afternoon—each got a nickel. She also dipped into her egg money and allocated one dime, then another, to herself. Sunday morning the kids would be freshly scrubbed, wearing their best clothes. Her own hat and good dress would make her look respectable, and not too stylish or modern.

At the highway intersection, the lone structure glistened white on its grassy lot. Only four or five cars—nice cars—showed around the space next to the cemetery, so she knew they'd arrived in plenty of time. Inside the door, a slight, red-headed, balding man in a blue suit peered at her face expectantly, his hand extended. Little Jeanie hid behind Bernice's skirt.

"Oh, yes!" he smiled when she identified herself. "Come right in! Welcome! And these are the children?" He bent, with hands on his blue serge knees, to the eye level of Elaine and Snooky, who were rescued from having to reply by the appearance of a round-faced woman beaming a pleasant smile. The wiry redhead sprang erect again: "Oh, I forget my manners! I'm John Gauger, and this is my wife."

It was as friendly a reception as Bernice could have hoped for. Irene had been right, not all churches were like that. She shook hands with a half-dozen people standing near the entryway—another Mrs. Gauger, two Schiefelbeins, she couldn't remember other names. Someone took the children in tow to sit with their age-divided Sunday school classes down in the front pews. Bernice sat herself and Jeanie near the back to wait and watch.

The wooden interior seemed plainer than that of other churches she had seen. More people filed in gradually. They all seemed to know one another. She looked in vain for George and Annie Roecker but recognized no familiar face. The preacher—a youngish man with straight black hair, rimless glasses, and a very serious expression—finally arrived and took his place near the pulpit up front. The kids below him stayed in their Sunday school pews when the regular service began, the preacher going through a prayer and various announcements. Bernice tried to pay special attention to the prayer. Everyone stood to sing a hymn, the number posted on a little wall rack with black-and-white numerals, its title unfamiliar to her. She listened hard to the words of the singing, then remembered that she was supposed to be joining in; she felt uncomfortable at letting others hear the sound of her voice and decided that the kids really made better music at home. When the collection plate came by, she covered her two dimes with her hand as she released them, noting with relief that others, too, had dropped pennies, nickels, and dimes among the quarters and few half-dollars. The preacher read from the Bible out loud; she wondered why they had to confuse people with those *-eth* endings. His sermon seemed sensible in places, but she found her mind wandering. She tried to concentrate on listening again and kept listening through the final prayer, wondering just how Irene and Ruby felt when they believed they were in the presence of God. Here, in this church, nothing seemed to be happening to her. Maybe she had to concentrate still better. Maybe it would take more time, more practice.

On the way home she tried to judge from the talk among the kids what they thought about their first Sunday school. Elaine and Snooky, with Jeanie listening in, spoke of others in their class; at least they liked the notion of acquiring new friends. On the other hand, Clarice, at fourteen, was more interested in sharing secrets with old pals than in breaking new ground; she complained that "there was nobody there I knew." Sonny, in the front seat with Bernice, said little until she asked, then merely shrugged, wagging his head to imply mixed feelings. Bernice decided that it had been a day of mixed feelings for all of them: better than expected, if not really satisfying. People friendly enough, but no miracles. Yes, it would take time.

The next Sunday they—except for Clarice, who said she'd rather not go this time—got dressed up again and drove the four miles. Courteous people at the door greeted them once more, and Bernice at least recognized a few faces this time. The prayers and the readings and the sermon and the hymns all seemed about the same as before, and she had heard Ruby teach one of the hymns to the kids: "Softly and tenderly, Jesus is calling." This put her into a listening frame of mind, which lasted during the rest of the service. She waited for a soft and tender voice to signal to her, somehow, deep inside, but nothing became audible to her mind. She began to think about what she had heard or read about Jesus, how His presence might be different from that of God Himself, and how that other part of what they called the Holy Trinity—the Holy Spirit, that was it—how the Holy Spirit was supposed to fit into all this. By the time the service ended she felt more confused than ever about what her relationship should be, or could be, to church beliefs.

The preacher's announcements included plans for the annual picnic in two weeks, so on her way to the door, Bernice looked for the Mrs. Gauger, who had been so nice the first time. She found her talking with a group of three other women. Bernice stood behind them, unnoticed, hesitant to break in. They were having such a good time together; likely they had known each other for years, and maybe got together only Sundays, like this. Churches can do that for a person, too, she reflected—give you a place to meet and make friends. She remembered Clarence's telling her, in the early days before their marriage, about his homesteader father's work helping to build the Lutheran church, and how the family used to go with horse and buggy every Sunday, the highlight of the week. She had missed all that somehow and had never learned to join groups easily. Now she wondered if it was too late.

One of the women noticed her, nodded a smile, and Mrs. Gauger beckoned her to join them; she mentioned names. Bernice asked whether they might like to have some rolls or potato salad brought to the picnic. The ladies received her offer with genuine appreciation, she thought, and she felt proud of herself for making some progress, anyhow.

Heavy rains prevented church attendance the next two Sunday mornings—Bernice didn't like to drive through mud—but they all made ready to take in the annual picnic, which was being held just a mile away at George Roecker's sheep pasture. It had plenty of space not only for good food under the trees but also for horseshoes and a kittenball diamond, too. Many of the Hidewood neighbors came as well, which made it seem to Bernice more like a picnic for folks of the community than for the Evangelical church. Clarice and Sonny had some of their friends from school to help keep them from feeling the outsiders. The strong Koppman brothers made a good showing in the ball game, and Sonny seemed to benefit from that: at one point she noticed one of the older Schiefelbein boys casually leaning against Sonny's small shoulder, as if they were the best of friends. She thought this must have made her son feel good about church and the people who ran it. Clarence also seemed to have had a good time talking and playing with both neighbors and strangers. As he drove the car home from the picnic, Bernice tried to figure out why she felt vaguely disappointed. It had been nice to see the men and the kids having a good time. But it could have been *any* kind of picnic—for neighborhood, or school, anything. If the family was going to take in a picnic, wouldn't it be better to meet with people you already knew, rather than to pretend friendship with those from another township just because they belonged to church?

The family got to church twice more before the fall season. With the threshing, and then getting ready for school, and then bad weather coming on, some complication always seemed to make Sunday morning outings difficult. During the winter months, they didn't go at all. Bernice knew that bad roads and busy schedules weren't the only things that kept them away. She simply had a hard time maintaining any enthusiasm for carrying out her promise of last summer. Nothing much seemed to happen when she and the kids did sit through church services. She supposed it might be her own shortcomings: too little schooling, too little knowledge about the Bible, too little faith in accepting what other people might preach at you. She still worried that her limitations might be keeping her *children* from feeling the presence of God, from hearing the voice of Jesus, so soft and tender. But how long must she go on trying?

Two conversations finally helped her find answers to the question. The first came during another visit from Irene and Ruby, who over the months had expressed pleasure that Bernice and the kids were attending church. At one point,

during a quiet moment in the dining room following an especially harmonic version of "Old Rugged Cross," Irene asked
Bernice whether she had talked with the minister about baptism for the three smallest girls. Bernice, taken aback—she
had completely forgotten that her sister placed so much
importance on the ceremony—shook her head.

"No-o-o. Well, not yet. I haven't asked."

"They must do baptisms there, don't they?" Irene said.

"I don't know." She did not relish the thought of standing with her girls up at the front, all eyes on them.

"You could always bring them to Watertown," Ruby put
in. "Irene and I have done it there—twice."

"Twice?"

"You remember, we were sort of baptised when we were
younger, before we had truly accepted the Lord. Last week
we went through baptism as adults. Total immersion, in Lake
Kampeska."

"Under the water? I don't think the kids should—"

"No, no," Ruby assured her with a calm smile. "For children, only a symbolic sprinkle on the forehead. More of a
dedication, for the parents."

"We could help arrange it for you," Irene urged.

Bernice nodded slowly. Among friendly strangers, it
might be easier. "All right, we'll do it sometime soon," she
said, and she knew that when they did, she would be keeping promises. It would be a good thing for *all* the family. If
her children were all baptized, nobody could say they had
been completely neglected in their spiritual life. Eventually,
they would make their own decisions anyway, about church
and about religion in general.

The second conversation that helped Bernice to clarify
her thoughts occurred a few weeks later—in the cow barn,
of all places. She and Sonny, getting started on the milking
one evening while Clarence worked late in the field, got onto

the subject by accident. They had each finished a cow, and while Bernice waited for the boy to pour his half-filled milk pail into the five-gallon can, she dropped her T-stool on the straw-covered earthen floor, regarded the gutters, and sniffed the air.

"We should have cleaned the barn today, I guess," she observed.

"Yeah." Sonny held the can cover while she poured. "This way, we have to sit in the pew, like in church." The kid was always making word games.

"Well, church pews may be hard, but they're easier than this to take. Don't you think?" Now that he'd introduced the subject, she wanted to hear more.

"I dunno. I guess."

"You and the girls liked it those Sundays in church, didn't you? And the picnic, too?"

"Picnic was all right. None of us like Sunday school and church, much."

"I never hear Elaine and Snooky complain."

"That's because they're good little girls, and they do what they have to."

"I thought maybe you liked having new friends there, and learning about all those things. Praying and everything."

"Don't have to be in church for that. I say my prayers every night anyway."

"You do?"

"Sure. 'Now I lay me down to sleep,' that one that Ruby taught us."

"But prayers said in church are better, aren't they?"

"Nah. Don't think so. Besides, us kids never feel like we *belong* there."

"Yeah, well. You should have gone long before, even before we moved here."

Sonny replaced the milk can cover. "'O Lord, we've never

lived where churches grow,'" he intoned, as if at the county speaking contest.

"Where churches *grow?* Farmer talk from a magazine, or what?"

"No, that's *cowboy* talk. From a poem I learned at school. Called 'The Cowboy's Prayer,' by Badger Clark."

"I've heard the name."

"He's South Dakota's best poet. I know the first four lines. Wanta hear?"

"Sure."

One small hand rested on the can cover, while the empty milk pail dangled from the other. The boy apparently remembered the speaking-contest training from his first-grade teacher:

> O Lord, I've never lived where churches grow,
> I've loved Creation better as it stood
> The day You finished it, so long ago,
> And looked upon Your work, and called it good.

Looking pleased with himself, he awaited her response. She regarded him for a moment, thinking. It's true for me, too. I've never lived where churches grow, either. "That's pretty good," she said to him, and she picked up her stool. "Now, you take Old Blackie down at the end. I'll try Jersey here."

Flies were already getting bad; next time in town, better buy some spray, she made a mental note. She had to clasp Jersey's tail between her knee and the milk pail. Soon her milking had covered the bottom, and the only sound was her regular squish into the foam, keeping time to the echoes in her mind of Sonny's rhythmic speaking voice: "NEver LIVED where CHURCHes GROW." Maybe if she had lived around churches as a youngster, maybe if the Lutherans had not been so strict, she might have turned out more like her sisters, she thought. More able, like them, to feel the presence of God; more attuned to spiritual voices that might call out softly and tenderly.

But then the realization came: I am not like them. Somehow, the Creator made each of us different, and we all have to be honest with ourselves, true to ourselves. My family and I don't have to stop going to church altogether, and getting the girls baptised is good, what everybody expects. We can live decent lives, and we need to keep listening, keep our minds open. But, right or wrong, we don't have to worry just because religion does not affect us the same way it does some others. Even others close to us.

The steady, swishing rhythm of her own work gave her familiar comfort. For the first time in months, she felt at peace with herself, deep within what she thought church people might consider her soul.

VERA'S PARTY

Vera
1936

"I don't think I'll ride into town with you this afternoon," Vera told her husband as she poured his customary second cup of breakfast coffee.

"Oh?" Julius looked up through billowing blue clouds of smoke, still holding the match at his pipe. He took two more long draws, pulling the flame deep into a fresh stoke of Half & Half. "I thought you wanted to see your dad, if he's sick."

"We-e-ell." Her resonant purr told him she had everything in control, as usual. She seated herself across the oilcloth from him and sipped at her own cup. "I called Olive this morning already. Dad's all right—just a cold, is all." Her aging father some years earlier had moved from the homestead into town, where he lived with her sister. Now Vera reached to pick up a grocery list she had penciled while Julius was doing the morning milking, and she dangled the paper at him, flirting, eyebrow arched. "You wouldn't mind doing the trading for me, would you?"

Her husband grinned and waved away smoke wisps that

hung suspended between them; George Weisel's dazzling daughter had always been able to charm him into anything. "All right," he said, rising from the table, "as long as you don't expect me to go hold your old man's hand."

Her expected guffaw was his reward. "Oh, you! Get on out of here now! I have important things to do."

"Yeh. Ee-yeh," Julius kidded her through clenched pipestem as he lifted his cap and denim jacket from the nail on the wall. "I can see you're gettin' itchy about something." She feigned haughtiness, arms akimbo as she followed him to the door.

"Never you mind, mister man. You just finish your chores, and let us women be mysterious, that's the way of it." Her easy patter accompanied an affectionate farewell squeeze on his shoulder.

At the kitchen window she watched his familiar figure move across the frozen yard—the faded blue overalls and jacket, the old brown cloth cap worn low over his eyes. The suggestion of a limp made her worry about his recurring bunion problem. Traces of smoke swirled after him and dissipated into the shifting late-autumn breezes. When he disappeared behind the weathered barn door, she kept staring absently at the spot, becoming aware for the hundredth time how badly the barn—all the outbuildings—needed paint. That's the way it is when you rent instead of owning your own place, she knew. But she had never imposed, would never impose, her father's standards on Julius. Sweet, witty Julius, who understood her: "You're gettin' itchy about something."

Of course he's right, she smiled wryly now at her own reflection in the window, the pale October sun glinting on her silver-rimmed glasses, her short, wavy hair seeming too gray in this light. She moved back a step but continued to gaze beyond the colorless farmyard to the amber stubble field, where snow flurries had dusted the black strips of fall plow-ing. Some white was staying now on the north sides of the irregular clods. Beyond the field, tall cottonwoods marked the Amerson place—a reminder of the special challenge fac-ing her now. Still farther beyond, to the hazy horizon, her eyes caressed the smooth, tan-shaded folds of the Hidewood Hills that she had loved for as long as she could remember. "Yes, my dear, you are right; I am feeling itchy again."

She had to laugh at herself. It happened every year about this time. Through that window, she recognized all the signs. The harvest mainly in, the granaries adequately filled. Behind the barn the straw pile, a fluffy, bright yellow, new two months ago, now settled and faded from the September rains; soon the cattle, browsing in colder weather, would begin rub-bing at the edges of the entire straw pile, and by midwinter the cow-high convex wall would be eaten away all around the base, making the pile look like a huge, pale chocolate drop behind the barn. Out there, to the left of the stubble field, corn shocks stood like tall sentinels to guard the remaining checked rows of browned leaves and proud ears jutting from the stalks, the husks pulling away from the golden kernels, ready for picking. This was the time for bright orange pump-kins and Hallowe'en; for blackbirds flocking by the hundreds one day, gone the next; for high V-formations of ducks and geese winging southward, some of them descending toward evening to circle a picked cornfield, offering excitement to hunters. A time when kids were back in school again, pleased with their new pencil boxes and tablets and double-row Crayolas; when everyone could enjoy new clothes for a new season, the rubbery scent of fresh, clean overshoes from the open box. It all meant the fall season had come again to her Hidewood Hills. "Oh, pshaw, I know I make too much of all this," Vera told her reflection, and she turned away to pick up the breakfast dishes.

Her seasonal restlessness was real. The paradox was that just when others could start thinking about leisure, now that the dawn-to-dark fieldwork season was mostly over, her own social responsibilities really began. Relaxation would mean evenings free for neighboring, opportunities to give fun and meaning to the folks of the Hidewood. Today would be the first "working day" of this fall season, and it somehow fell to her to get things organized.

Not that she had ever been elected or appointed social leader of the neighborhood; indeed, it would have bothered her to hear herself described by such a title. For Vera it had always been a natural thing: "Why, somebody has to start things, get people together—that's what neighbors do!" She was her father's daughter, she knew. George Weisel had been famous for his leadership: it was he who had organized a company to bring telephone service to the Hidewood, and he who had first mapped out the rural route for mail delivery from town. He had also been the first in the neighborhood to pipe hot and cold running water into the house, the first to use gas from a tank for kitchen and living room lighting, the first to buy a gasoline-powered tractor to replace the steam engine. It all had seemed so easy, so natural for him: "We are who we are," he would repeat to his family, "and someone has to lead the way." Little wonder, then, that his first-born daughter found it natural to assume leadership in the special world of women's affairs.

She had the personality for it. "Isn't that just the way of it, though? I should say!" Her repertoire of stock phrases, delivered with an air of genuine cordiality amid smiles and hearty laughter, carried an infectious quality that made it easy for people to admire her self-assured grace and to follow her initiatives. She was the main organizer of the Extension Club, a loose organization that provided opportunities for Hidewood families to gather for occasional evenings during cold-weather months. The wives would show and tell about homemaking projects while the men played cards and the children horsed around upstairs until toward ten o'clock, when the food was piled onto plates. She also served as a kind of neighborhood social conscience, welcoming newcomers here, lending a hand there. Vera was the one to count on, just about everyone agreed on that.

Just about everyone, but not quite. A few of the local families were simply not sociable or didn't fit, for various reasons. One old neighbor ("gruff as a bear and independent as a hog on ice," as Vera put it) seldom took his wife and kids anywhere; there were hints that he held long-standing grudges against the Hidewood's more established families. Some other households on the edge of the community seemed substandard, either in their general responsiveness or in their personal hygiene. Vera had about given up on those. But this year she saw a particular challenge in the new family—well, not so new anymore, she corrected her thoughts; it was two years ago already that the Amersons had moved in just down the road. For some reason, she still hadn't been able to convince Bernice to become a regular member of the club. Now she had a plan, and today was the time for action.

Julius wouldn't need the car until the afternoon, so she could take a couple of hours to get things going. First she needed to talk privately with Annie Roecker. She lifted the black receiver from the side of the varnished-oak box of the wall telephone. No one on the line; she reached over to crank out Roecker's call—a long, a short, a long—and smiled at the three stealthy rubberneck clicks before she heard Mrs. Roecker's husky "halloo."

"Annie, you home this morning?"

"Sure." The two women had known each other all their lives, and little protocol was required.

"Well, get your coffeepot on. I'll be there in about ten minutes."

Past rows of box elder that lined the long Roecker driveway, Vera rumbled the heavy Dodge over George's cattle guard—tubular metal crossbars laid into the roadway over a shallow pit between the gateposts, a device that served instead of a swinging gate to keep within the yard dozens of blackface sheep that kept grass trimmed neatly under the trees. Another of George's innovations, she thought. It was always such a pleasure coming onto this place—to see the big, red, hip-roofed barn neatly trimmed in white, with the windmill towering above it on one side and on the other the gray, cement-block silo with "F Roecker & Son" proudly lettered up there. Old Fred himself, she thought, would be pleased to see how his son, having had to take over the homestead when still a boy, had kept improving it. And now George's boy, Clarence, was farming with his dad, too, and was soon to be married. Eventually there might be a fourth-generation son to take over this good land that his great-grandfather had worked to break from prairie sod. Maybe there will be Roeckers in the Hidewood forever. The thoughts made her feel good.

Annie's stout, aproned form appeared at the kitchen door. "Okay," she called out, "coffee's poured and I'm ready to listen." Annie enjoyed serving as the outspoken foil for Vera's schemes. At the table, Vera got right to the point.

"What we need to start off this fall is something special—not just another meeting of the club, that can come later. But some special reason for a neighborhood get-together. Don't you agree?"

"Wouldn't do me any good if I didn't." Annie furrowed her dark brows but did not succeed in hiding a smile of enjoyment.

"Well, I've been thinking," Vera went on, "this is the year, you know, that Henry and Bertha celebrate their fortieth wedding anniversary." She inclined her head toward the east, where the aging Goldbecks, a mile across the hills, still worked day and night building their farm.

Annie nodded. "Good, good. Be nice to do something for Henry and Bertha. But maybe they won't want a party. Eh?"

Vera merely smiled, perhaps too smugly, she suddenly realized, and blurted out, "Oh, I can handle Bertha—I mean, she'll want to do this, I'm sure." Old Bertha had never failed to follow Vera's lead in all these years.

The women agreed that Vera should drive over to have Bertha pick a date, and then Annie wondered aloud who should be invited. "The whole club, I suppose?"

"Well," Vera began laying out her plan, "maybe we should go beyond our regular club members." She counted off on her fingers several names of old Goldbeck friends from homesteading days. "And some new folks, too," she added. "I want to try Bernice Amerson again."

Annie grunted. "You got her to club once last spring. She didn't seem too interested, never came back." Vera recalled only too well: she had made it clear that invited guests need- n't join the club until a second meeting, and her new neigh- bor had resisted attending any second meeting.

"Oh well, you know, she does have those five youngsters there. And I think she's kind of shy, you know what I mean?"

Annie's scowl darkened again. "E-eh. Whatever you want to call it. Looks like she thinks she's either too good for us— or not good enough. One or the other."

"Now, Annie." Vera's alto tones were loaded with sooth- ing persuasion, and she laid a freckled hand upon her friend's sturdy forearm. "She's a good neighbor and a good person, too, I just know it. But she still feels she's an outsider here. We probably scare her off."

"We? Speak for yourself, Miss Vera Weisel——Emily Post!

I ain't even seen the woman but once or twice." Her husky
chortle bothered Vera: sometimes Annie overdoes it, trying
to be witty and cynical, she thought. Still, she could be right;
maybe I do put newcomers off just because I've always
belonged here. But Vera only laughed out loud and gave her
friend's arm a playful poke. "Anyway," she smiled, "we'll invite
her again."

There would still be time today, if she hurried. At the
Goldbeck place, she spotted Bertha, bending over her chick-
en-feed troughs, the dark rubber men's overshoes like heavy
weights anchoring the hunched figure to the farmyard; a faded
kerchief framed the familiar weathered face as the old woman
peered out above reflections in round glasses. She's so perma-
nently bent, Vera thought, that we only see her now looking at
us over slipped-down specs. But as Vera had expected, the
leathery skin crinkled around those old bleary and squinted
eyes when she heard the plan, and the kerchief nodded vigor-
ously. "You betcha," the gravel voice affirmed, "we'd like to
have folks—over here—to help us celebrate. You betcha."
They picked a date; it would be fine to have Vera take care of
the inviting and other arrangements. It was working out, Vera
nodded to herself with satisfaction, hurrying on toward her
third stop, where a more difficult job of convincing might await
her: how best to approach her shy young neighbor?

Their foolish, car-crazy dog alternately nipped front tires
and barked her arrival, and before she got around the car,
Bernice was there at the open porch door, toweling flour and
dough off her hands. The baby peeked her small blond head
and blue eyes silently around her mother's print dress. Vera's
greeting elicited a tentative smile from the younger woman.
Vera liked her open face and the intelligent eyes that had
seemed so often averted during the few conversations
between the two of them since the family had moved onto
the place.

"Can't you come in?" came the expected—required—invitation.

"Oh, can only stop a minute." Vera wanted to reassure her neighbor that opening her house to unannounced inspection would not be necessary.

The invitation was insistent, and Vera smiled her way through the doorway, bending to pat the little girl's beribboned blondness and to whisper an animated "And how are *you*?" The child, pleased but embarrassed at being fussed over, averted her gaze, rolled a pink tongue under her lower lip, and retreated farther behind the protective maternal skirt; it made Vera wonder whether shyness might run in the family. The mother remained equally wordless for the moment, and Vera filled the space with her patter: "Yes, the wind does have a little chill on it today, doesn't it? I said, winter'll be here before we know it, isn't that just the way of it, though? Guess we're all used to that, all right, hah-hah, I should say! But it's nice to have the harvest in, and a pretty good year it was, too, wasn't it? Especially compared with the drought and dust storms we had two years ago, that was awful, I should say. . . ."

An aroma of fresh bread filled the kitchen; four new loaves and a square of sweet rolls cooled on the table, and a second rising batch awaited the oven. "Isn't that a beautiful sight!" Vera exclaimed in genuine admiration. "I've always just loved the smell of bread coming out of the oven."

"Maybe you'd like to try a cinnamon roll? I'll make some tea."

"Oh, I don't want to put you to all that trouble—"

"No, the water's already hot, you just sit a minute."

Though Vera preferred coffee to tea, she knew she must accept the tendered hospitality; and the rolls were perfection. Chatting away, her private thoughts were reaching a conclusion: this woman may be shy with words and among people, but she certainly expresses herself in baking skills. Vera paused to savor a final morsel, but her hostess still did not volunteer to fill in the silence. Still too soon to bring up the party, Vera reasoned, and decided to open a new subject. "You know, I said when I was driving in here just now, doesn't this place look nice these days! Before you came, I always felt so bad about these buildings left empty. It's so much better to see them all painted up and people and livestock on the place."

Bernice nodded. "Whole lot better'n it was, all right." And after a moment, "We got a long ways to go yet, though. Can't expect the landlord to do too much right away, I guess, these hard times." Much of this declaration, lengthy for her, was directed at her teacup.

Vera saw an opening. "Well, believe me, over at our place we know about landlords who never do enough. We've been trying to get ours to paint our old barn—nothing doing! These insurance-company landlords." Focusing upon what they had in common as neighbors might help dispel the younger woman's misgivings, Vera's instinct told her, and she was encouraged by the steady hazel eyes regarding her thoughtfully. Their exchanged gaze did not hold long, but it was long enough for Vera to try to transmit without words the thoughts she wanted to implant into Bernice's mind: Yes, that's right, shy Bernice: your closest neighbor in the Hidewood, this daughter of Big Shot Pioneer George Weisel, she lives on a rented farm too, like you do; you need not be afraid of her. The silent moment was broken when Bernice picked up her teacup again, murmuring abstractedly, "Yeah, guess lots of us have problems like that."

"Bernice—" it was the first time Vera had used her given name—"could I ask a favor of you?"

The hazel eyes reflected puzzlement. "Favor? I guess, if—"

Quickly seizing the moment of new confidence, Vera out-
lined the plan for the Goldbecks' anniversary celebration. She
carefully laid emphasis on the merits of the old couple, how
they would be counting on everyone in the neighborhood to
come and to share this occasion, how each family might contribute to making it a celebration worthy of these Hidewood
pioneers, whose hard work and generosity had meant so
much to so many. "I know you and Clarence will want to be
there—"

"Well, I don't know." The interrupting demurral surprised Vera; and then she understood when Bernice continued: "I'm just not very good at joining things, your club—"

"Oh, of course!" Vera instantly projected relaxed assurance, while thinking behind her words: How worried this shy
woman seems to be about getting involved with the rest of
us. Will she always feel herself the outsider here? "No," she
purred aloud, "what we're planning is just this special evening
for Henry and Bertha. I was hoping you would be there and
that we could count on you to bring some sandwiches,
maybe." Vera gestured toward the handsome loaves at the
other end of the kitchen table.

The younger woman visibly relaxed. "Oh, well, sure.
Guess we'd be glad to do that."

Driving home, Vera allowed herself only partial satisfaction. She had made a good first step at drawing this young
woman out, but what would it take to get her to lose that newcomer's sense of inferiority? To give her self-confidence
enough to join the other neighborhood women and accept
regular membership in the club? Vera knew she'd have to
bide her time until the Goldbeck party.

An early snowstorm worried them for a while, but by the
afternoon of the big day, she and Annie and Bertha had

agreed on the telephone that there was no need to cancel: most of the local roads had been shoveled out, and the weather had turned cold but clear. She got Julius to finish chores early, and the whole family crowded into the Dodge so they could arrive in plenty of time to help in Bertha's last-minute arrangements in the house. She wanted to try out their old upright piano to make sure it was still in tune. As a surprise, she had composed a special narration to honor the celebrating couple, and she was planning to play while leading general singing. Privately, almost subconsciously, she felt the aching lack of her own piano, but emphasizing the positive as always, she told herself how lucky she was that her parents had provided those childhood music lessons. Besides, having to go into town to practice the program had given her extra opportunities to see her father, still confined to his sickbed.

She hardly recognized Bertha, who was decked out in brown velvet with a white lace collar. "Went into town last week, got me a new dress," the old lady grinned, squinting over her glasses. Vera told her she would be the prettiest girl at the party, and she obviously relished the joshing. "Oh sure you betcha," she scoffed, flicking a hand, but the self-conscious grin glowed long after the two of them began bustling about their preparations. I'll bet this is the first real party dress this woman has ever owned, Vera thought. She pictured Bertha as a homesteader child, shouldering her share of farmwork even then. All the following years had been filled with hard work and little play here with Henry—who at that moment shuffled down the stairs in his dress-up celebration suit and tie, which could never cover his own disfiguring hunch. Testimony to sixty years of too-heavy labor.

Others began to arrive. Before long, undrifted patches in the white yard were sandwiched with a dozen cars, newer models proudly reflecting the bright moon. Old quilts hung over several radiator caps to preserve warmth. Children, encumbered by layers of coats and scarves, waddled in and were consigned to the upstairs to play their games, while the women carried dishpans or baskets of food into the pantry and the men began to gather near the card tables, filling the air with a haze of pipe smoke as they talked farming.

Vera, helping to greet and direct guests, kept an eye out for her young neighbor and was beginning to despair that her plan might not have worked after all. Then, with relief, she heard Henry's gruff, welcoming voice calling out from the porch door. Into the gas-lantern glare Bernice appeared, the five children behind her, the oldest girl bearing a covered dishpan in both arms, as if it were crown jewels offered to the queen. Bernice responded to Vera's greeting as she urged the girl forward to present the pan. "The sandwiches," Bernice said tentatively, "two dozen, just minced ham, hope that's all right."

Vera's musical assurance was overpowered by Bertha's husky "You betcha," as the old woman smilingly took the proffered dishpan and headed toward the pantry. Then Bertha's attention was diverted to her husband. "Henry! What the Sam Hill you puttin' on your sheepskin for?"

"Ahh," came the familiar growl, "I'll help Clarence get them horses in the barn." He lifted one of the gas lanterns from its ceiling hook.

"Horses?" Vera was delighted at the very idea. She had always felt romantic about sleigh rides, even before Julius had courted her with team and cutter. She turned to the new arrival. "Did you come with horses and sleigh?"

Bernice seemed embarrassed. She concentrated attention on removing heavy coat and overshoes as she replied. "Well, the old Ford radiator . . . froze up yesterday . . . sprung a leak." She straightened, then set her overshoes alongside others in the corner. "But *he* thought we should go anyway, fixed up the bobsled."

"Now isn't that wonderful! A sleigh ride in the moon-light!" Vera couldn't contain her enthusiasm at the idea, but the younger woman regarded her silently, uncertainly. Vera suddenly was aware that she must sound silly, gushing that way. Her neighbor might even suspect ridicule. But then the moment was past and it was time to mingle, to get on with the evening.

The evening, indeed, went along as she had planned—no, even better: as she had *hoped*. The arrival of the Konolds—her aging uncle, Alois, his wife and son—gave Vera personal pleasure for two reasons. First, she loved family his-tory and continuity, and it lent the party a special meaning to have one of the original settlers present, especially this one. Alois and his brothers had brought the wood from Wisconsin to build on the Hidewood plain the very house that Vera and her family lived in today. Second, her concern eased about having overpraised sleigh rides, for the Konolds also arrived by team and bobsled from their distant place below the Hidewood Hills.

"Ve had to cut a few pass-ter fences," the diminutive homesteader chuckled, "but better den comin' around by d' roads." And his wife—jolly Myrtle, who had been a teacher right there at Hidewood's Plainview when widowed Alois courted her forty years earlier—added to the merriment, while removing layers of wraps, "Oh, we had a good time! Walter played his mouth organ, and we sang in the moon-light—kept the wolves away!" Unmarried Walter, big mouth agape, acknowledged the introduction like a vaudeville per-former, waving his instrument to the cheers of onlookers hud-dled around the entryway, who knew that the Konolds and music went together. Vera noted with satisfaction that her young neighbor, taking all this in, now smiled in her shy way. Then the women took an hour or so for just sitting around and talking, while the men played cards. Vera observed that there was nothing shy about Bernice's husband: Clarence joined right in the card game, obviously enjoying every minute.

When it was time for the program, she got Walter to pull his mouth organ out of his pocket and play a few numbers to set the mood for entertainment, while she and Bertha hustled the rest of the men to crowd into the parlor. The kids dropped to the floor to claim front-row seats. She sat at the piano, got their attention, and began working from the five-page script she had prepared. "Memories," she intoned in theatrical style, "let us turn back to days gone by and see what they held." In words and music, she touched on the stories of Bertha and Henry, how as youngsters they had come to Dakota Territory from Wisconsin (at the piano: "School days, school days, dear old golden rule days"); how they had met, courted ("Bertha, Bertha, I been thinking"), and married ("I love you truly"); and how this house has always been their home ("Home Sweet Home"). Vera concluded her program: "As time has passed, this happy couple have enjoyed everything that life can offer. It is the heartiest wish of all their friends that they keep well, and that for their golden anniversary we can all be here again!" She turned once more to the old piano, banged out the first bars of "Put on Your Old Gray Bonnet," and lifted directorial arm to lead her audience. "All together now!" Everyone knew the words: "Through the fields of clover, we will drive to Dover, on our Golden Wedding Day." Their voices became more lustily enthusiastic with each note, and if the piano was a little out of tune, no matter.

It was a splendid moment, filled with warm sentiment for the honored couple and with genuine community camaraderie; a tear crowded Vera's eye. Bertha led a round of applause for the artist. A buoyant mood of good feeling remained in the room, as gradually they began dividing up again. Old Henry, in his good-natured growl, had let it be known that since this was a special occasion, there might be a little schnapps out in the back room for some of the boys to nip. A few of the women who would never tolerate "booze in the house" tittered at the very idea of such proximity to sin, but Vera was confident it would not get out of hand back there. Laughing to reassure one another, they turned to their work at the kitchen woodstove and to the serving tables to arrange hot-dish casseroles, heaping platters of sandwiches, and seven different pastries.

Vera looked for her young neighbor, who had at least joined in mouthing some of the words during the group singing. Good sign, Vera thought; now maybe I can convince her to join us regularly. She found her in the kitchen, volunteering to lend a hand to Bertha, who, still fairly bubbling from the emotion of the evening, was beckoning over her spectacles at the newcomer. "Sure, Bernice—that's your name, ain't it—I need you t'help me out here in the back pantry." The two of them disappeared through the pantry door, and Bertha's voice drifted back: "Froze a gallon a'ice cream today, we'll get that ready."

They still had not returned several minutes later. Vera began to feel uneasy. Shy Bernice would be doing the listening as old Bertha—always gruff and forthright, and now all worked up—filled her ear. Bertha is a good woman and she means well, Vera thought, but too much gruff, plain talk right now might ruin the plan, might scare Bernice off for sure. Maybe I should go on out there to see if I can help with that ice cream, she rationalized, and moved toward the pantry doorknob. She didn't really mean to eavesdrop, but the old woman's husky voice coming through the door made her hesitate.

"Ee-yeh, I'd handle things a little different, if I could do it over again."

Bernice's softer words were harder to make out: ". . . own your own place here . . . proud of that."

"Oh, sure, sure. It's what we all want, ain't it, own our own land." Vera had never heard the old lady charged up like this. Surely she had not been at Henry's schnapps? "But it ain't ever'thing, neither. Sit down here, let me tell you somethin'."

The husky tone became quieter, more confidential. Vera could not stop listening. She removed her hand from the doorknob but edged closer to the door, pretending to be occupied with a detail of the dish towel she held. She hoped no one was watching. Bertha must have been sitting close to the door now, because she could hear her every word.

"When I first come here to the Hidewood, more'n forty years ago, stayed over to Fred Roecker's. That's where me and Henry met. Him and his dad and brother, they was staying there, too. Old Fred was in the middle of everything those days, him and George Weisel, Vera's father, you know. And I was the outsider, young and green. Alone, not much schoolin'. I thought, these Roeckers and Weisels, they're all so special, I can never be like them."

A pause, and something mumbled. Bertha went on: "But I figured, maybe I don't belong here like they do, maybe I ain't as rich or as smart. But I can work. That's what I could do best. So I'll outwork 'em, and someday—we'll see, I said. Well, here it is, forty years later, and now I wish I could do some of it over.

"I got to thinkin', listenin' to Vera's program. She talked about 'this happy couple that has everything life can offer,' was the way she put it. Oh, we have a lot, and I thank the Lord for that. And I don't mind havin' worked hard all my life, it's still the only thing I know how to do." Another brief pause, and the husky voice became louder. "But I wish now there'd been more time to be with other folks more. To enjoy life more. Wear pretty clothes. Learn to play that dad-burned piano in there, been standin' around for years. Take some trips, learn about other places."

More murmurs from the milder voice, and Bertha resumed, speaking now as she might to a daughter. "Take some advice from an old woman who was a lot like you, once—new to the neighborhood, and maybe a little too impressed by some of the other folks who been here longer. Don't be put off by who their fathers was or how much land they own. They're just folks, like you and me."

". . . spose that's true."

"You betcha. Take Vera and Annie. They don't come any better. You come to club regular, you and your family, and you'll see. Get to know these folks, have some fun. You'll be glad you did." There was a shuffling of chairs. "Well, we better get this ice cream in there 'fore it melts." The gruff voice was nearing the doorway now, and Vera snapped the dish towel over one shoulder and moved quickly away, joining the women getting coffee ready to pour.

Conflicting emotions to sort out. She felt a little guilty for having listened: this had been more than rubbernecking on the telephone, when those talking knew others would be on the line. Sure, it *was* nice to hear Bertha's words of praise for her and Annie. But . . . something about it—ah, Vera suddenly thought, I guess this is what bothers me: Bertha, understanding things so clearly. All these years I have underestimated her, thought of her as only a simple soul who means well but can't be expected to handle delicate situations. Now she shows that she is just as intelligent and sensitive as any of us, maybe more. It took *her* to see what assurance Bernice needed most. Where George Weisel's social butterfly daughter failed, old gruff, hard-working Bertha showed the way to success.

But was the young woman really convinced? Vera had to

find out during the confusion of departures, as sleepy children got wrapped in woolen snowsuits and guests shouted farewells through the steam wafting in from the night. Chatting all the while, she helped Bernice wind long scarves around the little girls, preparing for their sleigh-ride home. When the bundled family headed toward the door, she caught Bernice's eye.

"I'm awful glad you could be here tonight."

The younger woman smiled shyly back. "Me, too," she said in that quiet voice. "It was nice, all the neighbors and everything."

"Don't we have wonderful neighbors!" This was the time: "We'll be meeting again next month, at club over to Annie's. Sure would like to have you folks join us."

Bernice's eyes seemed more intense, and she nodded in her heavy kerchief. "If I could bring something," she said. "Maybe some lemon pies?"

"Lemon pie is my favorite! That would be fine!"

Bertha burst back into the steamy light of the room, having helped the elderly Konolds into their bobsled. Vera regarded her old friend, who somehow looked different, and it was not merely because of Henry's sheepskin, which she had thrown over her brown velvet dress. "Oh, Bertha," Vera called out. "Bernice will bring lemon pies to the next club meeting, isn't that nice?"

The old woman peered, owl-like, over steamy glasses, first at Vera, then at their young neighbor. "You betcha," she nodded, "Bernice here, she's a good baker."

Vera could almost hear her father's distant words wringing fresh insight from an old truth: "We are who we are." We all do what we can in our own ways, and one way is not necessarily better than another. Each of us has something special to contribute. That is the way of good neighbors.

She watched through the steam as Bernice and Clarence

got their family under quilts in the waiting bobsled. Snow crunched in the cold under the horses' hooves, and the bright moonlight glistened blue on gentle drifts. Later, on the way home in the car, she sat too close to Julius, her mittened hand resting lightly on his shoulder. He would kid her afterward about being so sentimental. But he would understand.

DOCTORING

Clarence
1937

The wind seemed to be coming in stronger and colder out of the northwest. Over there, beyond the miles of treeless hills still streaked with old snow, a cloud bank loomed dark in the gray sky. Already, hard little pellets, nearly invisible in the dim light of late afternoon, stung the face and began to pile in miniature drifts around the bleak and frozen yard. No mistaking the signs. A good January blizzard was on the way.

Clarence latched the granary door. He steadied the filled feed sack with one knee and used both ungloved hands to button his denim jacket more tightly at the collar. While he was at it, he swiped off his dark wool cap to let down the earflaps: still a lot of outside chores to take care of. A glance toward the house revealed no light yet in the kitchen window. "She's most likely looking after those sick kids," he said. Years of mainly solitary work had nurtured his habit of sometimes speaking aloud the notions that came to him.

Snowstorm now, on top of the sickness. Well, he told

himself, feeling the cap warming the tingle on his ears, we each do our job, and there shouldn't be much to worry about. Bernice, she's always been good at taking care of kids, even when they come down with colds and the dang flu that seems to hit every winter as regular as the snowstorms. She even knew what to do when Clarice and Sonny broke out with the measles two years ago.

"Pretty good at women's work, all right," he nodded, taking another look at the darkening sky to the northwest. "And now I better get my own done." With a quick grunt, he hoisted to his shoulder the heavy bag of ground corn and oats and headed for the barn. The load afforded some protection from the wind's stinging fury. "Don't you know each cloud contains, pennies from Heaven," he intoned the words of a popular song, something he vaguely remembered having heard on Major Bowes's radio program. Music just came to Clarence; sometimes he made it a game to figure out why this or that tune would be running through his head. Once in a while, he let the tune follow imaginary fingering on the fiddle, in A or D or maybe both, to keep in practice.

In the barn he carefully mixed minerals, bought in town, with the ground feed and apportioned a ration to each milk cow. Next, the six horses got their whole oats; just hearing the resonant crunch from their feed boxes as they plunged deep into that first bite always made him feel good. And then there was hay to throw down from the mow, corn fodder to carry from the stack for the cows and young stock, clean straw from the still-high pile out there to tote in for bedding. He did the milking and took time to teach the newest brown calf to drink from a pail, letting the little critter suck on his fingers while holding its slippery nose into the fresh milk. He noted with satisfaction, by the lantern's shadowy light, that the seven calves in the pen were growing healthy and strong. "Soon time to get you fellas vaccinated for cholera,

too," he told them; he had, in fact, already mentioned it to
Julius Schleuter, who could be counted on to help.

Finally, milk cans and lantern in hand, he paused inside
the barn door to review his storm-preparation chores, to make
sure no task had been overlooked. The warm, moist aroma of
the cows and horses, quietly bedded down for the night, blended with the smells of the clean straw and cured bromegrass
stored in the haymow above, plenty to last over the long weeks
of winter still to come. He inhaled the sweet perfume.
Everything taken care of for now in his tranquil barn.

As he reached to open the barn door, the old dog stood
up where he'd been curled in the feed alley. "Naw, you better stay inside, Pup," Clarence told him. "No table scraps off
the porch steps tonight. I'll bring you and the cats out something later." The aging collie seemed to understand; he
stretched, yawned, and lay down again.

Outside, the wind howled around the barn roof, and
Clarence's kerosene lantern blew out after two steps. Larger
flakes filled the air now, nearly obscuring the pale orange
glow from the kitchen window, which reminded him of his
other set of worries. People worries. This time his voice
formed no words, but thoughts came at him, thoughts about
the differences between livestock and people. At least you
know what to expect when you're taking care of animals; with
people, even ordinary life was always so complicated, hard to
understand. And sickness just made things harder.

The first to come down with the flu was Clarice, home
for Christmas vacation after starting high school over at
Hayti, where her older sister, Marie, attended and worked at
a job, too. When Clarice said she was sick and didn't want
to go back to school, they'd thought at first it might be just an
excuse. She was lonesome and unhappy over there and really would rather be out working on her own than stuck in a
classroom.

Clarence had been glad—more glad than he could let on—to see the girl again. As she grew older and prettier, she reminded him more and more of her mother. "Long time ago," he heard himself saying to the wind now; that was another life, another life that left some things to be remembered and some things best to forget. For fifteen years he had been trying to keep his private memories of that past separate from his new life with Bernice and the four babies that had come since. Sometimes, he could feel it, there was a resentment and an anger in the house when his memories seemed too close. "It ain't been so easy for her either, I know it," he confided to the cold wind that numbed his face in the black of this night.

And he knew, too, that some of the tension was his own fault. There were times when the feeling in the house would build up and he just took the easy way out, escaping to his barnyard and fields instead of trying to settle anything. And all this had been hard on the two oldest girls—his and Gunda's daughters. He could never allow himself to fuss over them as any father naturally might, for fear it might look like favoritism, bringing back into the house those unwanted memories. Maybe he went too far in not giving them attention. Sometimes he felt confused and exasperated, but he knew a man had to be patient, too. "I don't know," he said, fumbling in the darkness for the tar-paper-covered porch door. "It's too complicated to figure out."

He left his overshoes and top overalls on the porch and carried the two filled milk cans into the kitchen lamplight toward the pantry, where they kept the cream separator during winter months. The kitchen was empty, but after a moment Bernice shuffled in from the shadows of the other room. She wore two old cardigan sweaters under a faded blue housecoat, which she clutched together at her throat; her short brown curls hung uncombed, stringlike, over her pale brow. She supported herself against the pantry doorway and watched him stretch a clean floursack cloth over the pail to strain milk into the separator's high tank.

"Sounds, ah . . ." She had to clear the congestion from her voice and start again. "Sounds like the wind's come up."

"Ye-ep. Snowin' hard now, too. Be some good drifts by mornin'." He leaned into the separator crank, and the mechanism's growl rose to a whine.

After another moment she called in, "I'm getting kinda worried about the kids." The working machine made it hard for him to hear. "I said," she repeated, louder, "the kids, they feel so hot. Fevers must be awful high."

He nodded, leaning back and forth with the turning crank. "Well, bound to have some fever with the flu, I spose." Clarence could always make that baritone voice heard when he wanted to.

"Yes, but . . ." She turned slowly away toward the cookstove. "I'll fix some supper," she said, as if talking to herself.

A few minutes later she set his plate of fried eggs and bread before him on the table. She grasped the back of a chair and eased onto it. "Wasn't much in the cupboard," she said.

"Ah, this is plenty." Clarence seldom let himself complain about anything, and certainly not the meals she served.

"I was going to open up a couple jars, the tomatoes and that beef I put up last fall. But I just don't have the gumption today, those cellar stairs."

"This is plenty for me," he repeated. Then, aware that she was not eating, he asked, "You had supper? What about the kids?"

"Well, like I said, they been down all day, high fevers, no appetite. And I guess I'm coming down with something, too."

"I wondered." He wiped eggs from his plate with the bread crust.

"Must be the same thing, headache, fever, sore throat." Her hand touched her neck, around which she had wrapped an old flu remedy learned from her mother: a work sock that Clarence had taken off yesterday, the slightly gummy sole next to her skin and the top end fastened with a safety pin. "I rubbed in Vaporub, took some aspirin, like the rest."

"Well, you go on now, if you're gettin' the flu, too. See if you ain't better in the mornin'."

Her eyes went to the bedroom doorway, and she shook her head. "I don't know," she said. "Seems worse this time. We might need to call the doctor." She pulled herself up from the chair and disappeared into the dimness.

He sat there alone for a minute. "Call the doctor." Something about her words disturbed him, deep inside. But no need to face any of that just yet. "We'll see how things are in the morning," he told himself softly. First, get at the work that had to be taken care of—and some of Bernice's work too, looks like. He would put off until morning light getting the eggs from the chicken house, he decided, as he poured soft water from the reservoir into the dishpan for cleaning up stacked dishes later. Then he readied the milk to feed his calves and found something for old Pup and the cats, too. While he was outside, he thought he'd better take on one of Sonny's usual chores and carry plenty of split wood into the porch to keep dry in the storm.

The night turned out to be a long one, a bad one. Bernice, there in the bed beside him, seemed to be getting warmer with fever. The five kids were spread in makeshift beds around the dining room and living room so the two wood heaters would keep them from chill. They needed attention every few minutes, it seemed—a drink of water or a cool washcloth on a face, or else they had to throw up in the pail or to use the "white owl" chamber pot. None of them got much sleep. And through it all, the wind outside reminded him that snow was drifting high.

Just before dawn, when he was up to stoke the wood fires yet once again, he decided he might as well get started on this day that would require extra effort. He returned to the bedroom to dress for the cold and paused to look more closely at his wife. In the dim lamp-glow, she blinked up at him, pale and weak.

"How you feeling?" he asked.

Her eyes closed. "I don't know," came the murmur, "not so good."

That meant she was really sick. He stood there a minute before speaking. "Well, I'll get at the chores," he said. "You all right here for a while?" She managed a nod.

The drifts had piled up. He had to strain against the packed snow just to squeeze through the porch door with the shovel. It was still coming down, whipped by the unabated wind; the nearly total darkness made it tricky to find his way over irregular new drifts between house and barn. He remembered his father's stories of blizzards on the pioneer prairie, of having to string a rope between sod shanty and cowshed to avoid wandering blindly across the fenceless plains. There were stories of farmers' frozen bodies found after the snowdrifts thawed in the spring. "At least we ain't that bad off; we got the yard fenced in." His instinct took him to the barn door, humming the tune to "Little Old Sod Shanty on My Claim." He shoveled a passage in the blocking drift so he could open the door. He didn't mind the extra work. He knew that the only hard decisions he would have to face would come when he returned to the house.

It took him a couple of hours to get all the stock fed and the milking done. Gray morning light made it easier to find his way back to the house. The kitchen was empty, as he had left it. He set his milk cans down and stopped at the doorway to peer into the shadows of the adjoining rooms. Only sounds of sore-throat breathing greeted him. Everyone seemed asleep—Bernice in their bedroom to the left, the three little girls beyond in the front room, and here, nearest him on the open davenport, Sonny, his form under the quilt seeming small for his eleven years, and Clarice. Almost grown up, she was now. Fifteenth birthday in just a few days. Fifteen years ago. He moved a quiet step closer. The girl slept silently on her back, the pillow folds in the dim window light seeming to radiate from her dark shingled hair, the gray light giving her face in repose a strange, haunting quality. He was aware of staring as if transfixed by a curiously numbing sensation. Then he made himself blink rapidly to clear the blur, and what had seemed for a moment funereal silk returned to the normal pillow and blanket of this life. Shaken, he quickly turned away; he needed to find out how Bernice was feeling.

"Don't seem any better," she told him in hoarse whisper as he leaned over the bed. "And the kids, neither. A while ago I felt their foreheads, still hot."

"I'll put some water on, make you some tea. Maybe open a jar of soup later, see if the kids can eat something."

She made no response as he left. He shoved more wood into the cookstove and found the green teapot. The tea was ready to serve before the whine of the cream separator had died down, but though she tried a sip, she had to give up and leaned back in the bed. "Just can't," she said in that weak whisper, gazing at him intently with red, watery eyes. "I think we better find out about the doctor now. Before it's too late."

He did not respond immediately but shifted his gaze to the bedroom windowpane, white with thick frost on the inside, through which the pale daylight filtered though snow was still heavy in the wind. "Roads must be blocked good by now. Maybe I should boil up some onions, that's a good cough syrup."

Her head moved feebly to one side, and a frown creased her damp brow. "It's the fever that's bad! Those kids are really sick—aspirin or cough syrup just ain't enough!" She fell back upon her pillow again.

"Well, I spose . . ." He didn't know what else there was to say.

"See if you can get the doctor?" she almost implored. "You could phone from Schleuters'."

There seemed to be little choice but to try. "All right, I'll go over there this morning."

First he needed to water the stock, which took longer than usual in the storm. He had to let the cows out two at a time, practically herding each of them to the tank where the popping engine pumped, then getting them inside again before the cold wind could freeze the tender teats of the milkers. As soon as he could, he put on his long sheepskin for the quarter-mile walk to Schleuters'.

His thoughts swirled with the blinding snow. "Get the doctor." Damn, how those words brought back bad memories. It would be next to impossible for the doctor to get through in this storm, but he knew that his holding back on even trying had more to do with fear than with the ten miles of blocked roads or with the doctor bills that would come later. The last time serious sickness had made him run for the doctor, it had ended up in a funeral; and the image of the face in the coffin passed before his consciousness once again before he shook free.

Why was it that about every time you went for the doctor somebody was going to die? He thought of his parents and of Bernice's Paw and Maw; they shouldn't have died that young, either. Doctors called, then the funerals. When babies come you hardly ever need a doctor, just another woman who knows what to do. And you sure don't have to run for the vet every time a cow comes in with a new calf. He wondered if it might not be better sometimes to stick with the natural ways, the old remedies.

Julius and Vera, in the kitchen having coffee when he pounded on the door, immediately got him in out of the storm. He explained the situation. Vera was quick to respond. Yes, Doc Bates was in Clear Lake, been there twenty-five years; of course, let's see if the lines are still up in this wind. She wound the little crank of the telephone on the wall, then shot an affirmative glance at the men when Central answered. After introductory words with the doctor, she turned the receiver over to Clarence.

He had never really used a telephone before, and it took him a minute to get adjusted to the idea of talking into the mouthpiece in reply to the little metallic voice in his ear. As best he could, he again described the illness of the family and answered several new questions. "Sounds like I better come if I can," the voice said. "I'll have to call back after I check to see if the snowplows are clearing roads yet."

Julius was doubtful about the roads—"they might not run the snowplows before this storm clears up"—but the men agreed that when the doctor called back Julius would walk over to let Clarence know. Outside, the wind was as strong as ever, though the gray sky seemed to have brightened a little. On the way home, Clarence breathed the notes from "Tell me why the stars do shine." It was an old number he and his brothers used to harmonize, at home; they had always laughed at "the ivy twines," picturing poison ivy used in the grain binder to tie bundles of oats.

The quiet house remained as he'd left it. Bernice seemed relieved to know that the doctor would at least try to come: "Those kids're gettin' worse, we need help . . . I can't do much anymore." She seemed pretty sick herself, the way her words slurred together.

And she might be right, he could see it now. This sickness must be something more than ordinary flu. He would have to do more himself to help out—no, to take over—in the house. Now a new worry presented itself: What if he, too, should get so sick he couldn't work? If the rest of the family could come down with something, why shouldn't he?

He'd almost finished his morning barn chores when a scraping of the opening door and sudden daylight announced his neighbor's arrival, along with a snowblown draft of cold air. Julius doffed his snow-encrusted cap to slap it against a manger. "Well, he's comin'," he said through his clamped pipe. "Doc Bates says they're plowin' out 22 now and expect to be over at Schiefelbeins' corner by about three." Clarence fished in his overall bib for his Waltham to confirm the hour at half past twelve. They figured he should be able to make the three miles over there by then with horses and bobsled.

He welcomed the need for fast, decisive action to clear his mind. The sled had last been used for barn cleaning, but he shoveled out the snow and frozen manure leavings and then forked clean straw into the low box for the doctor to sit in. He'd take the old buffalo robe along. Now: which team of horses to harness up? Jim and Birdie? High-steppers in their time but getting too old and poor now. The big mares, Roxy and May? No, they never did work right as a team. He would take Tim and Diamond, Roxy's foals, pretty well broke in at three and four, young and strong—and steady. Don't need skitterish horses today.

Hard-packed drifts in the driveway supported the young bays and sled runners without breaking through. As he turned onto the north road, the bitter cold wind in his eyes made it hard to keep looking ahead to guide the team among the irregular drifts angling infinite patterns of barriers along the way. Over open, windswept stretches, gravel showed through the white, and the metal edge of the sled runners scraped and screeched until he eased closer to the ditch grass that held more snow. When they came to higher drifts, he let Tim and Diamond pick their way over the top slowly, cautiously. On the Kluckman hill, trees close to the roadway had captured a six-foot bank, and here the horses' hooves started breaking into the drifts. "Whoa, whoa, easy now," he spoke to them, lines held taut, and their incipient panic eased as, still nervous and trembling, they stopped thrashing and waited for their master to solve their problem. "Ho-boy, tha-a-t's it," he calmed them, moving to pat their necks. He felt proud of his colts; a team with less horse sense might have struggled wildly, breaking legs in the crusty drift.

It took some twenty minutes of digging with the spade before he opened a pathway past the trees. Then it was clear going to the corner. They had covered three miles that no car could have made, even with chains. "Heh," he snorted in satisfaction, "nothing like a good, old-fashioned team of horses." It made him think of the early days: "Get a horse!" they used to yell. He found himself whistling a tune under his breath— "My merry Oldsmobile"—about a fancy town car. He got to wondering what kind of man this Dr. Bates would be. "Soon find out, I guess," he answered himself. His pocket watch told him he'd made it on time.

He waited at the windswept corner for what seemed a half-hour—stamping numbing feet and swinging arms violently in a self-embrace of his sheepskin, worrying that the team was getting chilled. Finally he discerned the spray of moving snowplow, and the machine, drawing closer, exploded two or three more smaller drifts before he could confirm that a car followed close behind. The yellow plow mounted on a gravel truck rattled by, the driver taking his eyes off his work only briefly to wave, and the black Chevy pulled to the edge of the clear road.

From it emerged a tall man in a long gray overcoat and black fur hat; a wide, red-plaid wool scarf circled his neck several times. Wear a long scarf like that on the farm, Clarence thought, and a fella might hang himself when it gets caught. The man pulled a satchel from the front seat and approached the bobsled. "Mr. Amerson," the husky voice in the wind sounded different away from the tinny telephone. "I'm Doctor Bates. How're those sick folks this afternoon?" Without slowing his brisk pace, he clambered onto the rear of the sled.

"About the same, I guess." Clarence started climbing up over the front runner. "Pretty bad."

"Well, let's go have a look."

A shake of the lines got the team moving. The doctor kicked straw into a mound, nestled onto it, and reached to pull the tattered, hairy brown buffalo robe over his lap. Horses at a trot, lines loose, Clarence gestured a mittened hand at the sled's snow-speckled box, which still showed stains of recent manure-hauling. "Not a very fancy rig, here," he shouted out.

The doctor wagged his fur hat, and over the wrappings of plaid scarf came a reassuring scoff: "Ohh—don't worry about that. I spent time on a farm myself, know all about chores in the winter." His exposed face and glasses disappeared again, turtlelike, behind his upturned collar and all that red scarf. The horses followed their earlier trail, only partly drifted over; they were making good time. Now and then Clarence turned to check on his passenger. No further words came from the figure huddled under the robe. "So he is a farm boy, too." Funny, Clarence thought silently, I never thought a doctor would turn out to be a farm boy. I guess if any doctor can bring together some of the old remedies with new medicines, it might be a man like this. He wondered whether the doctor had ever vaccinated calves or mixed minerals with ground feed, as a boy.

The doctor, all business, entered the kitchen ahead of him and without ceremony draped his outer garments over a chair and dug into his satchel for his instruments. He asked Bernice many questions about the early stages of their illness. Efficiently, methodically, with a frequent tender word of sympathy, he examined each patient—all were fully awake for the occasion—inserting his thermometer into obedient mouths, listening through the tubes of his earphone contraption, tapping, feeling. Clarence kept waiting for him to say something about . . . something. But the doctor kept his analysis to himself until, with all the chidren again covered and reclining in bed, he motioned Clarence to accompany him to Bernice's bedside. Owlish behind his horn-rimmed glasses, the tall, gray doctor frowned toward each of them as he wound his rubber-tube equipment and returned it to the satchel.

"I think I found what I was afraid of." His voice was quiet, without any suggestion of alarm, but what he said next hit Clarence like a kick from a horse: "Looks like we have scarlet fever here."

He could not breathe. Those words *scarlet fever,* uttered aloud for the first time in fifteen years, set off a sudden, private tightness that gripped his entire insides. Dizziness made him lean against the wall; he was vaguely aware of Bernice's weak voice.

"Is it . . . real bad?" she asked.

The doctor considered for a moment, and in the silence Clarence thought he did not want to hear anything more about the killer disease that had again found its way into his house. He wondered just how what the doctor said affected Bernice. They had never talked about Gunda or her sickness, but Bernice must have heard about the scarlet fever.

"Well, it can be serious, of course," the doctor replied. "And there can be complications, like something called erysipelas, we have to be aware of that. But it can be treated, too. I can give you some medicines I've got with me. Send out some more, stronger ones, tomorrow morning. We *may* have caught it in time." He inclined over his case again to select several bottles and vials, and then he added, scolding over his round glasses: "Would've been better, of course, if you'd called me a day or two earlier."

Clarence could feel Bernice's quick glance toward him. No one spoke as the doctor finished setting out the medicines, made a quick round to treat each patient, and began giving instructions for treatment through the night. "When I get back to the office," he concluded, "I'll put together a package of special medicines for you. Now"—looking intently at Clarence—"how can we get that package out here quickly?"

The need for practical action, directly stated, brought Clarence around. "Well, the road—this stretch between here and the highway—it'll be a couple days before we can get that shoveled out for cars."

"Hm. So no mailman this far." The doctor had put on his overshoes and reached for his heavy overcoat. "But we could get Roy Konold to take it with his mail run tomorrow as far as the corner, where we met today. Couldn't make it 'fore about noon, though."

"No. No, I'll go." Clarence felt the need to do something. "I can take the team all the way to town first thing in the morning. That way we can be sure." He pulled his cap down hard above his eyes. "We need some other things from town anyway," he said to Bernice, who lay against the pillow. She barely nodded, lids half-closed. He wondered again if she knew what those words *scarlet fever* meant to him. He wished they had talked about the dreaded disease and what it had done before.

On the porch with the doctor, out of earshot of the bedroom, he could ask: "How bad is it?"

"Hard to tell. Always danger with scarlet fever, I don't want to mislead you. But we'll start treating it now, and if we're lucky they might all come through it. With no aftereffects."

"Why . . . How could we catch it out here?"

"Best I can figure out from what your wife told us, must've been the oldest girl. She apparently picked it up at the Hayti school. I heard they had some cases there." The doctor adjusted his fur cap over his ears and paused with both hands lifted to add an afterthought, as if to himself: "Strange, though, that girl's not as sick as the others."

They walked to where Clarence had left the horses waiting out of the wind and remounted the bobsled for the cold ride back to the doctor's car. The doctor adjusted his scarf and pointed his mitten at Clarence, "It's a lucky thing, you know, that so far you haven't caught this bug. And you have got to stay healthy now to take care of the rest." The doctor gave him a gruff, man-to-man pat on the arm. Then the encouraging smile became hidden again behind the red plaid as they were accosted by the continuing northwest wind, still bitterly cold.

Standing there, holding the lines of a team that needed little guidance, Clarence found that the absence of action made the cold wind easier to deal with than the piled-up questions. What will happen now? Call the doctor and there's a funeral. Who might die? Why did it happen that the girl brought her mother's fatal disease into the house again, to work its awful . . . what? Revenge? Why haven't I caught it— either time? Who would provide for this family if I was gone? There were, he knew, no answers to such questions, which seemed to come from outside his own head; for now, all he could do was see to the everyday things that he could handle.

For the rest, it would have to be a matter of faith—faith in the knowledge of this educated man under the buffalo robe behind me, he thought, this farm boy turned doctor. And faith, too, in the Almighty, the All-powerful. "A Mighty Fortress Is Our God." Then, strangely, the Norwegian words to that old Lutheran hymn he had learned as a boy came coursing back through his memory: *"Vor Gud han er saa fast en Borg, Han er vort Skjold og Vaer-ge."*

Such a long time, nearly fifteen years now, since even being inside a church, after all those Sundays growing up with his brothers and sister around the East Norden Norwegian Lutheran, and then with Gunda. And even afterward, with Bernice—until they made her feel like such an outsider that she wouldn't go back even to get married, and so he never went back either. He had come to believe that a man can live a Christian life, a decent and right life, without having to sit in a church; but no strict Norwegian minister would agree with that. Maybe the Almighty expected you to line up in a pew and pray with the preacher. Was the sickness now some kind of punishment? "Too much to figure out," he whispered into the biting wind, and images appeared and receded—memories of the steepled white structure in the trees back home, of spaded clay covering the coffin as it was lowered into the cemetery ground, of old neighbors chorusing the hymn: *"Vor Gud han er saa fast en Borg . . ."* The powerful harmonies ran through his mind and would not leave him.

"The next forty-eight hours should tell the story," Dr. Bates reminded Clarence in the morning when he picked up the package of medicines. "You call me if you see any change for the worse. And I'll drive out next week, for sure, to look at 'em again. Meanwhile"—the doctor handed him two printed signs reading QUARANTINE—"you have to put these up on your doors. Very contagious."

Back home, Clarence concentrated on the multiple tasks that fell to him. He tried to spend most of his time in the house; the stock would have to get along on fodder only once a day and sleep in stalls not cleaned regularly. The sick children needed attention often, and he watched them—and himself—carefully for any signs. He took time to cuddle the three littlest girls, rocking them to sleep. But both the next two nights, whimpering or vomiting or some need for assistance interrupted sleep. Once in the gray light of dawn, while handing Sonny a glass of water, he felt Clarice's big eyes on him, but when he turned she quickly closed them, pretending to sleep. He kept himself going, all the while fearing that lack of rest might make him more likely to catch the disease. So he determined at least to feed himself properly, even though he felt guilty enjoying Bernice's canned treasures when the others could not even keep tea and crackers down.

For two days he kept at it, alert for any signs of change, uncertain about even what an uneducated farmer should look for. A sense of despair grew within him. What if, in his ignorance of doctoring, he had missed important medical signals? Might the sickness have worsened for someone in this family? Would this awful menace from the past use him to claim victims again?

On the third morning, after chores, he stood over the cookstove to heat up stew in his mother's cast-iron black spider; he'd inherited the old frying pan and always used it whenever he had to cook anything. A little sound from the other room caused him to turn. From the shadows beyond the doorway slowly appeared the figure of Clarice, her yellow nightgown a mass of wrinkles, her dark hair disheveled and matted. She blinked in the brighter light of the kitchen.

She looked different now, fully awake, but shy, taking him in with those big and haunting eyes.

"You feeling better?" How seldom, these last years, he had taken occasion to speak to his two older girls directly, alone. She seemed so tall, so grown up, so distinct a person in her own right, now that he had this good look at her.

The girl nodded, uncertain. "I ain't been as sick as the others, I guess."

"But you been sick in bed."

"Well, the flu or somethin'."

He nodded his understanding. "Guess you didn't feel quite good enough to go back to school over there?"

Her eyes turned downward in acknowledgment. "But I'm hungry now."

"Hungry." The first time anyone had mentioned food in what seemed a very long time. A good sign. He lifted the steaming spider off the stove. "You want some of this stew meat? Or no, better, some soup. Here, I'll warm up some of your ma's good soup for you."

As he looked for another pan, his own words came back to him: "your ma," he had said. Well sure, he now told himself, that's the way it should be. Bernice *is* their ma. Maybe I haven't really seen it myself until now. Maybe her getting better is meant to be the good sign I been waiting for. If she brought the sickness, maybe she'll be the one to lead the way for the others, make them feel better, too. The thought cheered him. "A Mighty Fortress, A Trusty Shield . . ." He could hear the choral harmonies in his head.

By the time Dr. Bates came by a few days later, Clarice had taken charge of the housework. Sonny was up and around, too, eating better and absorbed in catching up on the *Argus Leader* funny papers. Bernice felt well enough to help with the small kids, and that morning she had even sat up at the table.

"Very good. Oh, this looks very good!" The doctor kept nodding his bespectacled gray head as he depressed tongues and took pulses. "Yessir," he told them, lifting his closed bag from the kitchen table. "I think any danger has passed. We have been lucky."

"Well, I should say," Bernice said. "Lucky you could come when you did." She seemed still weak but determined to give credit where it was due. "We might have—it might have been a lot worse."

The doctor only nodded silently, and Bernice poured coffee for him, herself, and Clarence. For a few moments, the three of them chatted over the kitchen oilcloth of the weather, of the roads mainly open now, and of the doctor's next call, some twenty miles away, to a farm family that had lost a child because of diphtheria. "The thing is, they just didn't know, and I got there too late." He stared into his cup, shaking his head slowly.

"Well, I guess none of us do much doctoring until we have to," Bernice said.

The doctor spread his hands in a gesture of helplessness. "Ah, sure, it's hard—when you live out in the country, I understand that. Hard to practice what I call preventive medicine, even keep everyone clean."

"The kids bring home ideas from school sometimes," Bernice said. "Last year we were all going to start brushing our teeth, but we never kept it up regular."

"Good example!" The doctor pointed an animated finger at her. "This is why so many of the older folks have to get false teeth by the time they're forty or fifty. Think of it"—his husky voice kept rising—"someday, maybe, everybody will understand better how to take care of themselves. Someday maybe there'll be more than just one country doctor for a whole area like this, too, and we'll have a hospital right in Clear Lake so we won't have to run thirty miles to Watertown for a simple appendectomy—" He caught himself, and began to laugh, embarrassed. "Didn't mean to go preaching at you," he apologized. "Sometimes I do get a little frustrated, I guess." He tipped his cup and scraped back his chair. "I'd better get going. Thanks for the coffee."

Listening to the doctor, Clarence had held back, recognizing the truth, knowing he'd been wrong. He should have paid more attention himself to the sickness, should have called for the doctor earlier. Maybe I should have found a doctor earlier that other time, too, fifteen years ago, he thought. These connections between that past life and today—what could they mean? Why have we been spared death in this second attack? How should he listen to that spirit from the past, alive in the pretty face of his daughter?

The departing doctor, halfway into his car, extended a bare hand and regarded Clarence, watery eyes blinking against the cold breeze. "I'm not a religious man," he said. "But something more than medicine has been working here. Looks like you've been watched over from up above." He smiled and, suddenly all business again, found his mitten and settled into his car.

Clarence, standing alone, watched the dark Chevy back through the white glare of shoveled driveway. "Maybe that's it," he told himself. Maybe those words from the former farm boy contained more wisdom than even the doctor himself knew. "Someone to Watch over Me." Once more he saw the sweet face, the dark eyes closing to release him, and the connection between past and present became clearer in his mind. Maybe there could be no sure understanding of spiritual presence from the world beyond, or the influence of the Almighty in ordinary lives. But he knew that somehow powers had combined to grant him a second chance—a chance to learn from experience, to grow with the times, to appreciate and preserve what exists here and now. In the face of unknowable mysteries, this seemed an idea good enough to put a man's faith in.

He turned toward the barn, cold snow crunching underfoot, old Pup frolicking on the drifts ahead of him. He felt better and began stepping in rhythm, fingering imaginary strings, in the key of D, for "Turkey in the Straw."

TO HAVE IT NICE

Bernice
1937

Bernice knew she had to keep her mind on the bread loaves browning in the oven, but thoughts of Nathalie's letter kept distracting her. When she lifted a length of cottonwood to add to the cookstove fire, a swirled knot in the split surface made her think of the dark spit curl that Nathalie used to wear low over her left eye; flickering flame in the grate somehow took her back fifteen years to the farewell wienie roast the night before Nathalie left for California. She could hear her best friend's last girlish words that night: "Oh, Bernice, I wish we was going to be together!" Now, after half a lifetime, the two of them *would* come together briefly once again. "How much have we changed and grown apart, I wonder?" Bernice asked aloud, gently closing the heavy stovelid over the flame.

The question was hardly new to her. Indeed, over the years at Christmas-card time and whenever either might take a sudden notion to write, the contrasting images of their chosen lives would parade past Bernice's imagination. City versus country, palm trees versus blizzards—sometimes, it seemed, glamorous paradise versus "stuck out there raisin' kids on a lonesome farm," as Nathalie had warned, dark eyes flashing so long ago. She's a city girl now, I guess, Bernice thought; my old pal, a big city girl, used to the easy life.

Once more she reached into her apron pocket for the torn envelope and reread the penciled lines: ". . . been wanting to get back there for a long time, and this is the year! In August I and Clyde can catch a ride with my cousin to Estelline. We could drive over and spend a day or so with you." Nearly all the rest of the letter was devoted to Clyde this and Clyde that—her only child, about the same age as twelve-year-old Sonny, and obviously the main person in her life now. Nathalie didn't seem to write much about her husband, whom she'd married about the time she went to Los Angeles. Bernice read again the page describing how Clyde's school chorus had visited Hollywood to perform with Deanna Durbin. "Who knows," went Nathalie's scrawl, "maybe some day he'll be a movie star."

A smell of burning abruptly demanded attention. "Damn! You dumb ox!" Bernice castigated herself and dashed toward the stove, waving her dish towel at the fumes beginning to emanate from the chrome-trimmed oven door. But only two or three of the eight loaves were too dark; almost everything could be salvaged. She glanced at the green clock on the wall. The three older kids would be home from school in a few minutes, and they always enjoyed the twice-weekly batch of fresh bread, maybe with butter and chokecherry jelly today. She decided to wait until they came before fixing a slice also for four-year-old Jeanie, playing in the dining room. A little more time to think.

Nathalie, coming to stay "for a day or so." Bernice crumpled a torn piece of newspaper to daub butter over the dark crusts of her loaves. What will Nathalie think of what she will see here? Thank the Lord we got wallpapering and painting done last month. The worst part now is the bedroom, that old mattress sagging between those paint-chipped, wrought-iron bedsteads, just not good enough. Maybe now is the time to get new furniture there. A person should be able to have *something* that's new and nice.

She stepped briskly to the shelf where she kept mail-order materials and consulted the thick Montgomery Ward catalog. There it was, under the bold headline BEDROOM SUITE—that odd word, *suite,* like a suit of clothes, only spelled with an *e* to make it fancy, like that hat shoppe in Watertown. "Five-piece set," the small print read, "mattress, box spring, walnut bedstead, dresser, chest of drawers, $54.50." She pictured Nathalie entering such elegant sur-roundings, nice as anything in California. There must be a way to do it, maybe somehow with chicken money. Always, any funds she could call her own came from the chickens.

She had a plan formulated by the time the three schoolkids and the baby had finished their bread and jelly. While Sonny was changing out of his school clothes, she told him about the coming visit. "There's something I want to do before they come," she concluded. "I could use some help."

"What kinda help?"

"Well, there's a bedroom set we need to buy, more'n fifty dollars. So we'll raise more chickens this summer."

"You want me to help sort out more cluck hens, to hatch their eggs?"

"That, too, but we're running out of space for brood hens. We'll hatch our own chicks in the incubator, and we'll raise them in their own brooder house."

"Incubator?"

"Maw's old kerosene incubator from Overhome. Darn thing's just been collectin' dust up in the granary for two years, we might as well put it to use."

"Oh, yeah!" He was getting intrigued. "I've seen that thing up there, wondered how it works."

"You'll see, kind of interesting. But chicks take a lot of care. I can't do it all alone, and your father's so busy this year. So I need to count on you."

"Sure, okay." The boy was willing enough.

"You help me with the work, you can have part of the chickens."

He was grinning now. "Chicken parts? I'd rather have a whole pony, or even a cow."

"Not a bad idea, at that. We don't have a pony to give, but I'll talk with him about you getting one of the calves for your own."

"Let's shake on it, podner," the boy drawled in a mock-solemn western twang.

The pact started a season of concentrated activity for the partners. Late that night, Bernice worked out a schedule, and the next day they lifted down from the granary rafters the four-foot-square incubator box, cleaned away dust that was encrusted over its chipped varnish, and made sure the burner functioned. They began setting aside, in the cool cellar, eggs selected for incubation. "How many we going to need, anyway?" Sonny wondered.

"Two incubator trays, about a hundred eggs each."

"Two hundred baby chicks! Wow, with—"

"Wait a minute," she interrupted, laughing. "We'll be lucky to get three-fourths of that. Didn't you learn in school about counting chickens before they're hatched?"

"Oh, that's right." Then, after a minute: "But how can you tell if the eggs will hatch or not?"

"You can't, really. Just have to hope they're all fertilized."

"Fertilized?"

"Well, you know. When the roosters chase the hens. I don't have to explain *that* to you, do I?" She regarded him sidewise, suppressing her grin; too seldom, these times just to be alone with one of your kids.

"Nope. I heard about the birds and the bees a long time ago from your brother Bert, and I watch the bulls and the boars once in a while, too."

"Uh, the brown eggs, here," she pointed out quickly, looking for ways to change the subject, "they're the Buff Orphingtons. White ones are the White Rock. Might be a Leghorn or two in there."

"Well, all of 'em future spring fries." Sonny closely inspected an egg held between thumb and forefinger. "Baby, some day you're gonna make us a delicious dinner."

"Better not think about chicken dinners," Bernice said wryly, raising an eyebrow. "Concentrate on money instead."

According to plan, one Saturday morning in April they set the readied incubator box upon its spindly legs in a corner of the dining room, prewarmed it with the burner turned high, and placed, one by one, the two hundred eggs upon the rectangular trays. Before inserting the loaded trays into the warmth, Bernice wrapped a small wad of cotton batting around a matchstick, brought in from the porch her bottle of laundry bluing, and began marking a large X on each egg.

"What you doing that for, Mama?" asked nine-year-old Elaine, who had helped place the eggs.

"'Cause they have to be turned, just like the hens do it," she told them. "The X up in the morning, under at night."

"How do the hens know which side is up," Sonny wondered, "with no X on the eggs out there?"

"Mothers just know things," his mother said.

Three weeks later, Clarence had fashioned from scrap lumber a small brooder shed next to the henhouse, complete with a kerosene brooder stove with its six-foot, metal-cone hover—"hoover," Bernice called it—under which small chicks could huddle for warmth. Miniature feeding troughs, bags of special mash and ground millet as scratch feed, and tiny watering stations awaited customers due from the marked eggs. The other children became involved each time the eggs were turned, watching for evidence of new life. Precisely on the twenty-first morning, while Bernice was sliding the first tray from its warm chamber, little Snooky squealed with a seven-year-old's delight at discovery: "I see it! A l'il beak pokin' through!"

The hatching process had indeed begun. Over the next several hours, the children checked the trays frequently to marvel at the transformation from quiet, smooth eggs to strange, pop-eyed, wet, and ugly creatures. They lay briefly in apparent helplessness amid jagged shards of their former confines, and then in the welcoming warmth of their new world, turned into individual fluffball baby chicks peeping their own announcements of arrival. Bernice herself never tired of witnessing the wonder of it all. She held one of the bright-eyed powder puffs in her hand for all to admire. "Just look at this little fella—ain't he just about the cutest thing you ever saw?"

"Hey, remember, Ma," her partner in the enterprise reminded her, "this 'little fella' is gonna look cuter by July in somebody's frying pan."

She pushed him away in playful disdain. But Sonny is right, she thought, I do tend to get sentimental about babies. And men always think they have to be the practical ones, while it's all right for women to admire pretty things, from flowers and babies—to bedroom sets.

During the next hours they gently lifted a total of 162 yellow and buff chicks from the hatching trays and onto sheets of newspaper in a washtub set near the cookstove. Toward evening they carried the tub, its peeping chorus under protective blankets, out to the brooder house and set the chicks one by one near the feeders. By yellow lantern light they watched the first tentative pecks at mash and dips of small beaks into water fountains. "How do they know how to do that!" Sonny whispered in obvious awe. "Just natural," Bernice said. "All we have to do is help Mother Nature out a little bit."

Some of their helpful attempts failed. One gusty night, cold for May, the brooder stove blew out, and in the morning they had to pick out twenty-three dead chicks, smothered in the mass huddled under the hover. In spite of the special "boughten" mash from the hatchery in town that was supposed to have the right nutrients, a dozen or more of the chicks began to look droopy and finally died; "the croup, I guess," Bernice figured. But gradually the flock began to show promise. Incipient feathers became discernible on enlarging, fuzzy tails and wings; the chorus of tiny peeps grew lustier. "Oh-oh, I was afraid this might happen," Sonny said one day when they opened the brooder house door. "Those cute little things we hatched in the living room are turning into big, dumb chickens."

"Bet your boots," she told him. "What we have to do next is turn big chickens into big profits." Now who's being sentimental and who's practical, she smiled to herself.

"Is the money going to be enough?"

"We'll have to see."

By early July she had reconciled herself to compromise. Some of the flock would soon be ready for market, but they would not bring enough to cover the cost of the complete bedroom set. She consulted the catalog once again and sent in her mail order—with five one-dollar bills as down payment, scrounged from cream-check money—for the bed and dresser only. "What about that chest of drawers, supposed to come with it?" Sonny asked.

"Have to wait, for now. Before long, the chicks those brood hens have been raising on their own will be ready to sell. We'll send for it then."

"Too bad." The boy sounded dejected. "Maybe I didn't help you enough."

"No, we did our work just fine. We're going to get our bedroom set. And you deserve your pay, too."

"You mean the calf?"

"I talked with your father yesterday. The Hereford cow that's comin' in, that's going to be your calf." She wanted to share the optimism she felt in her bones that the plan was going to work—good enough, anyway, as Clarence might say.

Notice came that the bed and dresser awaited them at the warehouse in Watertown. On the same day, a penny card from Nathalie in Estelline—at times like this Bernice longed for a telephone—confirmed that "Clyde and I will drive over Tuesday and can stay overnight if OK." One week away. It was not until the next Monday, though, that a fortuitous rain gave Clarence enough excuse to keep him from haying, and they loaded their own chicken crate alongside another borrowed from Elmer Krause on Elmer's two-wheel trailer and hauled the largest of the spring fries the thirty miles to Swift & Co. in Watertown.

Bernice felt the triumph of bringing home her prize packages—various cartons and long objects shrouded in protective wrapping paper, all of which they stowed in the dining room corner where the incubator had stood. They seemed like giant, angular eggs, waiting to hatch. After a hurried supper, while Pa and Sonny did the milking and finished the chores, she worked with butcher knife and pliers, keeping the intrigued little girls well back from the danger, to get at the contents. Each revealed carton offered a distinct piece of the wondrous puzzle: the big mattress and box spring; the beautiful walnut grain of the dresser and bedstead; the strong metal support bars; the smooth clarity of the wide mirror, which would be attached by the dresser's curved, graceful embrace. A rare perfume of newness permeated the house.

After they had finished the assembly—the kids in bed long since—Bernice could not wait until morning to see the overall effect. Over the sheets she spread first her own patchwork quilt and then the pink chenille bedspread. She surveyed her new bedroom from the doorway, and the combination of the beautiful wood with the soft, rosy luxury was really something. "Nicest bedroom I ever saw," she said through the lump she felt in her throat, and Clarence, leaning with her at the doorway, put an arm on her shoulder. "Want to try it out tonight?" He seemed to understand when she suggested they open the davenport in the living room instead, now that the new bed was all made up for company tomorrow.

Nathalie had not specified what hour she might arrive, so Bernice decided she would be ready any time. She had Sonny put on a clean pair of bibless overalls and got him excused from helping Clarence pick up hay, so that he might be on hand when the guests showed up. It was afternoon by the time a new-looking green car tentatively probed into the driveway. Yes, out-of-state license plates below that shiny radiator grill. "Boy, a '36 Plymouth!" from Sonny as they waved from the porch steps. Behind the windshield's reflection a waving hand responded; then the car was still, and Nathalie's expressive smile beamed above the opened door. "Bernice!"

The spit curl was gone, and streaks of gray showed now in the fluffed black hair, but that face and voice were unmistakable. "Hello, stranger," Bernice said, her own smile breaking into a self-conscious laugh at the emotion of the moment. The visitor's yellow-flowered blouse and brown skirt bounced into the sunlight, and there was a squeal of delight (how like Nathalie!) as the tan high-heeled pumps scuffed excitedly through the stony dust of the yard. Bernice extended her hand, but Nathalie had both arms open and came right on for a tight embrace that surprised Bernice—they had never hugged each other in the old days; after the briefest hesitation she hugged back, accommodating to her friend's new city ways and luxuriating in the spontaneous, mutual affection. A perfumed fragrance enveloped them. "Let me look atcha!" Nathalie was exclaiming, standing back, her hands still grasping Bernice's shoulders; her enthusiastic smile now made those rouged cheeks into ripe apples, and familiar merriment sparkled in the dark eyes. She seemed more dazzling than ever. "So good to see you!" the Betty Boop lips said. "This must be your Robert—ah, Bobby?"

"Sonny, we call him," Bernice said. "Nickname's always stuck." They both laughed, and Nathalie devoted attention to the three girls, who by now had joined the excitement. "This is Elaine. And Snooky. And over here, Jeanie. Marie and Clarice, they're away." Bernice hoped that each of her small daughters would get to offer a responsive greeting, but before she finished talking, Nathalie pointed back at the car.

"Come on, Clyde," she called out. "Come say hello."

After a moment the Plymouth door unlatched, and from it emerged a somewhat heavyset boy dominated by a shock of shaggy auburn hair and the brilliance of his garb—all white, shimmering in the summer light. Polo shirt, long pants, even shoes—all white. Bernice was sure she had never before seen a boy wearing white shoes. "Say hello to Bernice and the girls," his mother instructed, her metal bracelets jangling lightly at his shoulder. "And this here's Robert—Sonny, I mean. You two can be friends!"

The boys regarded each other, both mute with undisguised curiosity. Clyde's fleshy face seemed to give him a built-in pout; Bernice felt relief to hear Sonny finally make some kind of shy effort: "Ah . . . nice car. Aerial for a radio, even!" He fingered the antenna.

"Oh, yeah," Nathalie responded. "This is a real boat out

on the road." She giggled an aside to Bernice: "You know my cousin Harry, he had to do all the driving himself on the highways; wouldn't trust me behind the wheel until we got out here on these country roads."

Clyde stirred. "Harry says the dust out here is worse than the exhaust fumes around LA." His pout disappeared; he was trying to be sociable.

"Oh, now," Nathalie half-scolded. "The dust ain't so bad. Nothing like those dust storms out here two, three years ago. Guess that was kinda tough, eh Bernice?"

"Coulda been worse, I guess. Say, Sonny," she gently nudged him, "you take Clyde out and show him your calf, hm? And watch for your father comin' in with the hay to unload." The boys moved toward the barn, Clyde in pressed white seeming to Bernice so much more grown-up and cared-for than the smaller, familiar figure with the flapping shirttail. Nathalie called out. "Clyde, you be careful, don't get your clothes dirty, now." Bernice wished she had made Sonny change his shirt, too; it might have let Nathalie relax a little if Clyde had not looked so distinctly fresh and clean.

"Nice-looking kid, that boy of yours," Bernice said.

"Yeah, inherited his charm from somewhere," Nathalie said, her wistful gaze still following the boys. "Ever since he was a baby. Y'know," she giggled again, confidentially. "Like I tell all my friends out there, maybe I should of named him Rudy. He looks a little like Rudy Vallee."

"That's the guy who sings through the, watchacallit, megaphone?"

"Right. I told you about my Clyde in Hollywood, singing with Deanna Durbin, didn't I?"

"Yes, your letter, pretty nice. Say, let's get your suitcase in the house and sit down for that cuppa tea."

It was a wonderful afternoon. At the kitchen table, they reviewed times they had shared years ago in the Norwegian community by the lake, before Bernice had married. Nathalie's eyes glistened as she touched upon their old dreams of "getting away," and she related details of her first real travel adventure, the long midwinter drive in a rickety Model T to a new life in California. "I'll never forget that first morning," she said. "After those cold days through Nebraska and Wyoming, then fighting snow in the Rockies, we had driven across the desert all night, and when the sun come up that morning, there was oranges growing under those tall palm trees along the road. I was in heaven!" For more than two hours, they chatted and dawdled with spoons in cold tea leaves, and gradually in Bernice's mind a more complete picture of life in paradise came into focus. She felt the fascination of the colorful contrasts: Pacific Ocean beaches and burglars in the house next door; Nathalie's clerking job at the dime store, her concern about rough kids who could get Clyde into trouble. Another world, all right, Bernice thought.

Sounds of activity out in the yard drew them to the kitchen window, and they watched as Clarence, standing atop a teetering load of hay and holding reins taut to his horses, guided the hayrack close to the barn, stopping exactly under the high yawning space of the opened loft door. From the top of the big opening, at the extended peak of the barn roof, dangled a heavy rope. On the ground the two boys stood near the horses; Sonny, one hand on a bay's flank, bent behind the horses to unhitch, while Clyde held back, the incongruity of his white costume suggesting an errant baker asking directions. Nathalie looked concerned. "You think it's, ah, safe out there?"

"Oh, sure, don't worry." They continued to watch. Clarence reached up to connect the dangling rope to slingrings pulled from his load, and Sonny drove the unhitched horses around, with Clyde now helping to carry the wooden evener still attached behind the team. Sonny faced the horses

away from the barn, and the boys knelt to hitch up the tow-
ing end of the same thick rope that dangled from the high
peak and ran through pulleys two lengths of the barn, emerg-
ing at ground level near the hayrack. Nathalie seemed more
relaxed now. "Hmm," she intoned, "this is kinda fun. Been
a long time since I seen a loaded sling pulled up into a haymow!" Clarence now descended and urged the team ahead,
pulling away from the barn; the big rope tightened and rose
parallel to the ground behind the horses. Up on the hayload,
moving tension pulled the two ends of rope sling together
and began to lift the loaded sling like a huge green knapsack
toward the peak of the gaping door.

Watching, the women could hear the clank of sling metal
hit the rail mechanism and the melodic whir as the carrier
suddenly jerked along the high rail into the dark of the barn,
giving a quick tilt in midair to the slingload and making it follow along, like a funny-papers cartoon policeman might yank
a thief by the ear. Clarence's "whoa" suspended the slingload
where he wanted it, still visible among the shadows, and he
nodded to the two boys to tug on the long cord attached
directly to the mechanism holding the sling. A distant ping
as the sling suddenly released, tumbling the loosened hay out
of sight. Bernice picked up Nathalie's words, uttered some
moments before: "Yes, me too," she said. "You're right. There
is something satisfying about hay going into the barn like that.
It's knowing you're getting ready for what's coming, I guess."

When the boys burst in a few minutes later, enthusiasm
rounded Clyde's flushed cheeks. "Did you see me, Mom?" he
asked, just through the door, his green eyes shining as his
mother ran fingers through his tousled hair. "The second
sling, I pulled the trip-rope by myself!" "Yes," she said quietly, "you got a smudge on your pants, there, but that's all
right." Bernice was pleased to see the boy having a good time
but disturbed by the distinct odor she detected; when she got

Sonny alone she put it to him bluntly: "You two been smokin' out there?"

Sonny looked offended by the suggested accusation. "No-o-o," he growled. "Not me. He had a package of Old Golds, though. Dumb cluck was gonna light it right there in the barn."

"He didn't, did he?"

"Naw, I had to tell him about fire danger, made him go outside behind the barn. He inhales, too." A pause. "This was after I showed him Slicko in the calf pen, while we was waitin' for Pa. You know," he suddenly became earnest and confidential, "Clyde, he thinks he's pretty smart, but there's a lot he don't know, too."

"Oh?"

"I mean everyday things. He didn't know that oatmeal comes from oats. He said he never read about King Arthur and Sir Galahad. He was afraid of animals, wouldn't even touch the calves, at first." Sonny burst into a little laugh. "You shoulda seen the look on his face when I got him to let Slicko suck his fingers!"

Bernice smiled softly. "Well, don't be too hard on him. He hasn't had the chance you have to learn about some of these things. Just treat him nice."

These first few hours of the visit had Bernice feeling buoyed, and she could sense that Nathalie was fully appreciating the experience as well, in her own way. For each of them, probably, it seemed to Bernice, the process of digging out old memories illuminated both the past and the present. She was aware that these new insights somehow revised the dimensions of her life, and she tried to think more clearly about all this during the busy hours of the afternoon and evening. She chatted off and on with Nathalie while fixing supper and attending to the needs of the children. They took longer than usual at the supper table to let Clarence and Nathalie have a turn at catching up on news of mutual acquaintances. She hovered in the background, at the dishpan or getting the girls ready for bed upstairs. She planned to share a bed up there with little Jeanie while Clarence and Sonny slept in the north room. Nathalie protested weakly when she guessed that Clarence and Bernice would be giving up their bedroom, but Bernice made light of it and felt the awaited surge of pride when she showed her visitor the elegance of the new bedroom set. It was a feast for the eyes, Nathalie's well-dressed good looks complimented by the beautiful walnut finish and pink in the background, her presence seemingly doubled by the big mirror. The satisfaction was there, even though Nathalie did not say anything special about the bedroom, except to insist that Clyde could share the double bed; "no sense making up your davenport with another pair of sheets for you to wash."

Bernice showed them how to dip warm soft water from the stove reservoir for washing up in the pantry, how to drain the basin "right into the slop pail here, underneath the sink." She poured glasses of drinking water from the can for brushing their teeth. She provided a flashlight for when they would need to go to the toilet behind the house. She showed Nathalie where extra pillows and blankets could be found. She dropped off to sleep believing she had thought of everything to make their night a comfortable one, though during the predawn stillness she became aware of movement and surreptitious flashlight glare down below and then outside; she wondered whether she might have served her guests too much tea.

Clarence and the kids were halfway through a quiet breakfast before the visitors peeked through the door. Nathalie, her dark hair still disheveled, finished tying her bathrobe belt and groaned apologies. "Such sleepyheads we are!" No, no, Bernice assured her, explaining that Clarence had to get going early this morning to pick up the rest of the hay and then do cultivating some distance away. Clyde was disappointed that he had missed the morning milking, having become fascinated by the cow-barn scene last night, but his complaints were calmed when Nathalie agreed that they could stay long enough for Clyde to go along to load hay. "Maybe you'd like to drive the horses," Clarence suggested, and Sonny talked about how much fun they could have jumping off the barn rafters into the new mounds of soft hay. Clyde got into ordinary clothes, and a few minutes later Bernice had shoved "the menfolks" out the kitchen door, the three girls had disappeared toward their playhouse, and the women, once again alone, regarded each other in expectation across the oilcloth. Nathalie's lips shaped a crooked smile, and in a gesture that implied both impatience and uncertainty, she ran her fingers through her hair. A dark looping strand detached itself from the waves and fell over one eye, like the spit curl of youth.

Bernice felt a tug of sentimental nostalgia. "So," she began, "you slept all right?" Maybe I'm fishing for compliments on the bedroom here, she warned herself.

"Oh, sure. Took me a while to get to sleep—"

"Mattress too hard?"

"No, no. I kept laying there, thinking about our good talk. Then I had trouble waking up, as you can tell." She flicked a self-deprecating hand at her ungroomed appearance and played her fork against the bits of pancake and pork rind left on her plate. When she looked up, her eyes seemed unable to open all the way, and it gave her a strange expression of melancholy.

"Are you feeling okay?" Bernice asked.

"Yeah, sure. Not sick, anyway."

"Something bothering you, then?"

Nathalie once again scrutinized her plate. "Well, not exactly bothering. A little mixed-up, maybe."

Bernice felt her sense of well-being start to slip. "What about?"

"Oh, I don't know. I thought I knew which end was up. But after yesterday, with all those old memories and feelings stirred up and everything . . ."

"Yes, me too! I sure enjoyed that—but was it somethin' I said, or . . .?"

"No, no." Nathalie's gaze was more direct now. "Bernice, we were always honest with each other, you and me, in those days when we used to look at movie magazines and dream about the future. Let me see if I can explain what I mean." She straightened in the high-backed chair and shifted her focus to a distant wall. The crooked smile again became prominent. "Before we came, I thought a lot about those old days, when I wanted to get away from here and you decidin' to stay and marry Clarence. I spose I've always wanted to prove that I was right and you was wrong. I wanted to impress you coming here. I guess that's why I got us dressed up in our fancy duds."

"Well, I—"

But Nathalie would not be interrupted. "I wanted to hear you say, yeah, I wish I'da gone with you to California. I wanted to hear you admit you'd like to be dressed up too an' living on Easy Street, instead of slavin' away out here washin' diapers with no runnin' water—" The dark eyes flashed. "Bernice, you should have an indoor toilet by now, for cryin' out loud!"

Ah, the toilet. "I guess it's not easy when you're not used to it," she began, blaming herself: I should have been able to figure out that people get to depend on modern conveniences.

"Oh, I talk too much." Nathalie's embarrassment had a

calming effect. "I know I am spoiled after all these years. I spose I couldn't get along without the comforts of my bathroom and electric lights and my winter garden." She reached over to lay a hand on her friend's arm. "But is it wrong to want those things for you, too?"

For a long moment they looked deeply into each other's eyes, and Bernice patted Nathalie's caressing fingers. "No, that's sure not wrong. It's real nice, you thinking that."

Nathalie's hand returned abruptly to her hair. "But having it easy is not everything, either. So much of what you have is . . . is so right! Me sittin' out there in my little plot of Pasadena paradise, I'd almost forgot what's nice about farm livin'."

"Well, like you say, the work out here does seem like a lot, sometimes. And it has been tough, the drought and Depression and all. But we're going to have it nice before we're done. Little by little." Bernice was warming to her subject now. "We want to own our own farm; we're thinking about the place Overhome where my folks used to live. Or if that don't work and we get some decent weather and prices, we'll try to buy this farm here one of these years. We'll put a fence around the house and plant more grass and flowers. We'll get a telephone line run in, and in a few years the REA will come through, I read in the paper—"

"What's REA?"

"You know, electricity, the government Rural Electric something or other. People put electric lights in the barn, even. And after that, we'll see about getting running water in the house. I'll write and tell you when it's safe to come and use the new bathroom!"

Each of them welcomed a chance to laugh, and they continued giggling and poking one another playfully, building on the joke. "Will I have to bring my own Monkey Ward catalog, or will this bathroom be completely furnished?"

"Oh, furnished—we'll even keep a basket of corncobs on hand for the old-timers!"

Bernice pulled off her glasses and wiped at her tears of laughter, reluctant to break the mood of shared silliness. "Ohhh, gol," she sighed. "Anyway, we're going to have all those good things—someday."

Nathalie also resumed a more serious mien. "You know, what's really wonderful is to hear you talkin' about all your plans and your hopes—kind of like the way we used to dream in the old days."

"Yes, but for you, lots of those dreams have already come true."

Nathalie was silent for a moment. "This is what kept me awake last night, I guess. Sure, I got electric lights and a bathroom and sun in the winter. But I don't want to kid myself. The rest of the dream is about over, for me. This is prob'ly as good as it's gonna get."

Some kind of protest seemed necessary. "Oh, come on now."

"Bernice, it's true." Nathalie's directness and candor seemed total. "I just go from day to day, workin' at the store, hopin' I won't get laid off. Any dreams I have left are for Clyde, but I worry about the bad influences of the neighborhood, the city. It's an easy enough life, all right. But I don't seem to be workin' *toward* anything anymore, like you are here."

"Yeah, well." Bernice searched for words. "It's about all we got, hopes and dreams."

"Oh-ho!" Nathalie looked at her askance to exaggerate incredulousness, and began enumerating on her fingers. "First, you and Clarence have each other. You've got neighbors you can trust. You've got all these great kids, and you're teaching them early about accepting responsibility. The way Sonny took over driving those horses yesterday, twelve years old, like a little man!"

"Well, kids do learn to work, on the farm." Bernice decided not to mention their summer project of raising chickens. "And he started learning how to drive the car when he was about eight. Guess you couldn't do that in California, eh?"

Nathalie snorted. "There's lots of things you can't do in California. But California's where I am. Too spoiled for anything else, so I spose that's where I'll stay."

"Enjoying your winter flowers and modern bathroom."

"Funny, ain't it, how the grass always looks greener on the other side, like they say. Guess you can't have everything."

She's right, Bernice thought silently. We envy others, and at the same time we try to make ourselves look good to them. It's only natural.

Later, in a new mood and ready for departure, Nathalie brought out her suitcase. "Say, Bernice, I meant to mention, what a nice bedroom suite!" She made it sound like bedroom "sweet" rather than bedroom "suit."

"Oh, it's not anything fancy, just a start. We'll get a chest of drawers goes with it next."

"Part of your someday."

"Guess so." The two friends walked toward the Plymouth, where the boys finger-scrawled in the thin layer of dust that dimmed the car's shiny green. Bernice cupped a hand over her friend's shoulder. "Thanks for coming," she said. "It was a really nice visit."

"Oh, Bernice, the best ever!" They embraced tightly for a long moment. From the car window Nathalie called a final farewell: "You've got to come to visit *us*, now."

"Maybe we'll do that someday, too," Bernice laughed. They all waved and the visitors were gone.

She started to return to the house, but an idea seized her.

"Sonny," she said, "before you go to the barn, run and catch two of the biggest spring fries you can find, for supper."

The boy showed his surprise. "I thought we had to sell all those chickens so we could buy the rest of that bedroom suit."

"Suite," she corrected him. "They call it bedroom *suite*. We'll do that later on. Today, we eat."

Bedroom sweet, she repeated to herself, feeling that inward smile again. The words did have a nice sound.

A HOBO RETURNS

Harry
1937

A haystack loomed above him against the brightening blue of early-morning sky. The familiar sweet smell of freshly cured bromegrass enveloped the softness where he lay. He remembered, clearly now, where he was and what this day would bring, and he sat up, pushing the gray cloth cap to the back of his head, squinting at the light.

For a long time he sat there, his face turned toward the scene that darkness had kept from him, walking the last miles before making his lonely nest. Slanting yellow rays glistened in nearby dewdrops and on the distant, rolling hills, illuminating an infinite green and amber patchwork of growing crops, as far as vision could take him toward the Hidewood. Here and there shadowed groves and tops of windmills and silos indicated farm places, where families would be at morning chores. He was conscious of comparing images that flashed from his memory—images of grimy railroad cars, of blurred crossties rushing by the glinting ribbon of track inches below, of mile-long freights puffing across desolate plains, straining through cold, forbidding mountains. And today, those beautiful fields of corn and oats. The moment made him smile through his three-day growth of beard.

"Damn near home," he said aloud.

He reached into his small knapsack of shapeless canvas and found the apple and slice of bread saved from yesterday. He inspected his troublesome left shoe—city oxfords not made for country walking, no wonder they're about shot. He munched the apple—core, seeds, and all—and on his knees he shoved back into the stack handfuls of fresh hay used for his bed. He relieved himself into the hayfield stubble, then fished into his faded blue shirt pocket for papers and his red can of Velvet, and rolled himself a cigarette. The inhaled smoke felt good but made him think of coffee. Shirttail stuffed into the belt of his soot-smeared denims, scuffed leather jacket over one arm and the knapsack on the other, he resumed his way. Another eight, nine miles—nothing next to the thousands traveled—and he could feel at home again.

Not really home, of course. At twenty-five, Harry had been on his own long enough to know the facts of life. There wasn't any home anymore, not since he and the rest of the kids finally broke up farming a year ago last fall and lit out in different directions, looking for work. By now, the ten brothers and sisters were scattered around South Dakota and Iowa and the West Coast. So about the closest thing to "back home" that any of them had these days was over at Bernice's, here in the Hidewood. She was the oldest sister, after all, married now more than ten years, and she and Clarence and the kids always seemed glad when someone in the family came by to visit. They'll sure's hell be surprised this time when I come walkin' in that driveway, he grinned to himself in silent anticipation as he strode along the section line, only barely favoring his bad-shoe foot. But a new thought clouded his visage and slowed his pace.

He had not really stopped to think much about it before, but now that homecoming was at hand, the sharper realization was there: they were going to want to know why. Why come back? He would be expected to explain. And sooner or later, around the neighborhood, somebody was going to taunt him: "Couldn't make it out there neither, huh?"

Well, t'hell with 'em, no skin off my nose what they think, it's a free country and a fella can do what he wants. That's the way to answer those guys. Still, he had to admit that the idea of failure bothered him some. Back on the farm, he would have been able to make it with a little more good luck and a lot less bad. Funny how he had ended up the oldest boy at home, stuck with picking up the responsibilities and signing for the loans and helping the girls get through high school. The drought, dust storms, and bad harvests and the bills and taxes to pay had taken their toll.

After the pitiful farm sale, Harry had headed his Model A toward Oregon, where older brother Chris, according to a letter, had found a fabulous sawmill job that paid $7.50 a day. But Chris had not encouraged others to come. For good reason, Harry thought now; ol' Chris and me never did get along too good at home. But he refused to think too much about all that. After a couple of hours in the growing July heat, it was enough just to keep going, putting one sore foot ahead of the other. He shuffled along the dirt road toward the Hidewood Hills, occasionally cutting diagonally across a pasture, feeling the sun on his head and hunger in his belly and weariness in his every bone, until finally he came over the rise and saw, there in the distance, Bernice and Clarence's place. Close to home.

As it turned out, Harry rode in style into the driveway, having encountered Clarence and Sonny a half-mile out along the road with team and rack, picking up section-line hay. Clarence seemed surprised but welcoming, in his good-natured way. The kid, as might be expected from a twelve-year-old, got pretty excited, and even before the load stopped he was scrambling down and running toward the house to announce the news.

"Ma! Bub's here! Rode the train from out west! Bub's back!"

His old childhood nickname, nice to hear it used again. When he opened the screen door, his sister was over at the black cookstove, a dish towel in both hands as she set down a heavy kettle. Mason jars, half of them filled with steaming green, reflected from the broad kitchen table: of course, bean-canning time on the farm. Bernice was peering over the mist on her glasses toward the doorway.

"Well, for crying out loud!" She half-whispered it.

"Hello, Bernice." Her welcome made him feel good.

"For crying out loud," she said again, finding her voice. "I thought you was in Ore-gon—my gosh, I don't hardly *know* ya, those whiskers an' . . . everything!" She moved toward him, and it seemed she might grab him for a hug, but it would have been their first ever, and she only held out her hand.

"Yeah, I been on the bum."

"Well, come in! You must be hungry, I'll fix you something and we'll have some tea—"

"Well, I sure could use a drink-a water, first, and some grub. And maybe a shave and even a bath wouldn't hurt, even if it ain't Saturday night."

"Same old Bub." She had always laughed at his jokes. Still grinning, she turned to the boy: "Sonny, you go put some soft water in the tub, and set it out in the sun so your uncle here can get cleaned up afterwhile." The boy left, eager to serve the enthralling traveler, and Bernice walked over to hand a kitchen cup to her brother. "Here now, take this, sit right down." When he accepted the cup, she paused, then reached her hand out a bit more to grasp his browned forearm tightly. Her suppressed, embarrassed smile as she looked him in the eye said everything. He was home again. For a while, anyway.

Thus reentered into the family circle, he savored each phase. They conversed, exchanging news of brothers and sisters. He luxuriated in the water from a clean cup and the baloney sandwich and tea she made for him. He fussed over each of the girls as they heard the news and came into the kitchen to get in on the excitement. Elaine and Snooky, nine and eight, and little Jeanie, now four—he had a special wisecrack for each of them, but they stood back, shyly self-conscious, leaving Sonny to join his mother in asking the questions. Between sandwich bites, Harry offered fragmentary replies:

"Got off the freight train in Aberdeen . . . caught a truck ride to Watertown . . . hitchhiked along the highway a ways . . . guess I walked the last twenty miles."

More questions poured from the boy. "What's it like out west? Are the mountains really high? On the freight train, where did you ride? Didja talk with other hoboes?"

"Now, wait a minute," Bernice said, laughingly raising her palms. "We all want to hear about being out west. So we'll let Bub get cleaned up, and when your father comes in for dinner we can sit around the table and maybe you'll tell us the whole story. Okay?" She looked at Harry.

"Sure," he said, "I'll tell you the whole story. Well, maybe I better leave a few things out." He looked sidewise at her, and they both laughed.

"Guess you better, at that." With the kids around, she wouldn't want him to start on his off-color wisecracks.

Harry actually welcomed the idea of a family audience to talk to again. A lot of thoughts went through his mind as he bathed and shaved. It would be good to share some of what he had seen.

At the dinner table later, feeling clean in fresh underwear and pants borrowed from Clarence, he was onstage. Bernice suggested that he might as well start at the beginning, and Clarence had a specific question: "How were the roads going west?"

"Well," he began, "you 'member me and Alvin Hansen, our old neighbor over by Hayti, we drove out together in my '31 Ford—damn good car, no problems a-tall. Had to get through some gumbo out in Colorado, no gravel or pavement for a long stretch. But the mountains, the Rockies, they was really somethin'—steep, narrow, sometimes ice on the road. One mornin' a brand-new Nash passed us going like a bat outa hell, a young kid drivin' and an old, gray-haired man with him. About twenty miles further—this little, iced-up road around them mountain curves—and there they are, back wheels of that Nash hangin' over the edge of the cliff, just teeterin' back and forth over the drop, about a mile straight down. They're sittin' in there scared shitless, afraid to move, even, and the old man a-prayin' and then yellin' over to us at the same time, when we come up, to *please* help get 'em off that damn cliff."

Harry paused to let the picture soak in. His audience kept silent, wide-eyed and serious; he pushed his empty plate away a few inches and began to roll another cigarette. The boy could not wait; hoarsely: "Whatja do? What happened?"

"Well, we couldn't just let 'em sit there. I got out my tire chains, hooked 'em together with one end over the front bumper of that teeterin' Nash and the other on the back of the Model A. Ol' Alvin, he was pretty nervous standin' there, and he says, 'Better not try it—that Nash goes over the side and it'll pull the Ford down, too, with you in it.' But I did it anyhow. Got the Ford on some dry footing and pulled that sumbitch right back on the road. The old man was so happy he was cryin'. And I guess the kid drove slower after that."

He flicked ashes from his humped cigarette into the saucer in front of him on the oilcloth. "Yeah," he concluded, "we all slept better that night, once we got past those mountain roads."

"Sure was somethin', all right," Bernice nodded. "Where did you sleep, those nights on the way out? Hotels, or what?"

"Hotels! Hell, I only had about fifteen dollars in my pocket when we left here, and Alvin not much more—and he was buyin' the gas. Nah, we changed off drivin' all the way, and when we was both too tired we just pulled off the road and slept in the car awhile."

"I bet Chris was surprised t'see you guys when you walked in!"

"Surprised, that ain't the word for it. Damn near had conniptions. But he put us up in his little shack there, while we tried for a week or more to find work. He's a planer at the sawmill, y'know, earns seven, eight bucks a day, but nothing for us there. No decent jobs anywhere around there, seemed like. Sold Chris the Ford t'help pay for food and rent—I still owed on it, anyhow.

"Finally heard about a farmer who was hirin', about thirty miles away. So I got out there, me and another guy, Shorty Webster, a farm boy from Kentucky. There was work there, all right—real work. Pitchin' wheat bundles out of a stack into the thresher and carryin' hunderd-pound sacks into the granary, then fourteen cows for three of us t'milk morning and night. The pay was fifty cents a day and board an' room— some board an' room!

"What they fed us was pancakes three times a day, maybe a little slab of pork, and for sleepin' they put us in a little bunkhouse with just a kerosene lantern and bedbugs as big as that goddam sugar bowl there."

Audience eyes darted to the middle of the kitchen table, sized up the glass sugar bowl, and returned to the narrator, hunched behind a cupped hand pinching his brown cigarette stub.

"So the second mornin' I says to Shorty, let's get the hell outa here. Shorty says no, I can't quit, my folks is dead, I need a job, ain't got no choice. Me neither maybe, I says, but I ain't workin' for this slave driver no more. So I waited for one more meal, them damn pancakes again, and right after noon I told the boss I was quittin'. You can't, he says, you got t'stay a week or I don't hafta pay you. He owed me seventy-five cents for that day and a half. If that's the way it is, I told him, you keep it. And I walked away over to the highway, 'bout seven, eight miles, and hitchhiked back to town." Harry reached out to trace patterns with his cold cigarette butt in the ashes on the saucer.

Clarence stirred and shook his head. "Funny a farmer'd treat a fella that way."

"Takes all kinds, I guess."

Bernice, eager for the tale to continue: "But then you worked in that rest'rant?"

"Yeah, can you imagine a Dakota farm boy slingin' hash in Bend, Oregon? There was this guy lived in the apartments next to Chris's shack, and we passed the time playin' cards. He was a waiter at the Excelsior Café, and one day he says his boss had fired the dishwasher, so might be a job there. He asks me, you got any money a-tall? I says no. Here's a nickel, he says, you go down to the café and order a cuppa coffee; ask for Wally and talk with him.

"So I went right down there and started shootin' the breeze with this Wally and asked him if he didn't need a dishwasher out there. How'd you know so fast, he says, and I mentioned Joe the waiter. He's lookin' at me hard and asks, you ever washed dishes before? Sure, I says, back in

Sibley, Ioway. Figured I didn't have t'tell him I never even washed a teacup hardly back home, all those sisters around! Okay, we'll find out, he says, come on back here and put this apron on.

"First time I ever tried to wear an apron, but I slipped the loop over my head and tied the long string, and he was laughin'. You ain't ever worked in a rest'rant in yer life, he says—you hafta tie that bow *underneath* the apron front so it don't show! But I like your guts, he says—when can you start? So I went right to work—three and a half a day and two meals, not bad. Had t'borrow a white shirt and bow tie from my waiter friend, and first had t'join the union, twenty-five dollar fee and me with no cash. But the boss paid it and later took it out of my wages. So I was finally earnin' a livin', wearing a black bow tie and a little white hat."

Sonny's enthusiasm got out of control, and he hit the table three times with his hand. "Boy! Working in a rest'rant!"

Harry nodded, amused, at his young admirer. "Bet you'd like that, huh? White hat and bow tie and everthing?"

"Yeah, like the guy at the White Castle in Watertown. Didja fry the hamburgers and wait on the customers?"

"Sure. After a while I got promoted, did some fry-cookin' and waited counter. Never forget my very first customer, a guy half-drunk, and he says, I'll have thish sheventy-five-shensh steak, and make it RARE. Never could understand why people want t'eat bloody meat, but that's how I ordered it. I guess the cook took the rare part too serious. When I brought it out for the guy, he looks at the plate and all that red juice and he says, hell boy I seen steers hurt worse'n thish an' still livin'! So my first order had t'go back to the kitchen."

Tickled faces all around.

"But yeah, I learned a lot about the rest'rant business and about people, too, workin' there a year and a half. Some of those ol' boys'd come in and sit talkin' half the night. Lots of 'em real educated, too, been around. Two, three of these older fellas, they was always readin' newspapers, and one of 'em told us about when he was in Germany after the World War. Said this crazy guy Hitler over there now, we're gonna hafta fight that Kaiser again; always called him that Kaiser. I wouldn't be surprised if we did, neither."

A silent moment, then: "If there was a war, would you go?" Concern was evident in Bernice's voice.

"Damn right," was his quick reply. "We can't let those tin-horn bastards push us around, if it comes to that."

"I spose there'd be a draft, anyway," Clarence put in. His brothers had been in the army in 1918.

"Yeah, and it might be a good thing, too—put some of these men t'work who can't find jobs. I seen dozens, hunderds of these folks on the bum. Good people, too, just outa work, is all. Some of 'em had women and kids with 'em, sittin' in a corner of the cold boxcar, wrapped in old newspapers tryin' to keep warm. Movin' from place to place, tryin' to find somethin'."

"Tell us about ridin' the rails, Bub!" The boy's eyes were glistening.

He nodded. "Lotsa parts t'all that. Ol' Chris"—looking directly at his sister now—"was surprised when I told him I was gonna bum the freights back home. What you wanna do that for, he says; you got a steady job at the café, don't make sense. Well, I'm goin' anyway, I says. He wanted to buy me a bus ticket, but I wouldn't take it."

"Pretty good of him to offer that," Bernice said.

Harry threw her a cynical glance. "Ahhh, he was plenty glad t'get rid of me, and all it cost him was a coupla cheese sandwiches he made for me to take along. Anyway, I hopped a lumber freight outa Bend headin' for Spokane and made two or three changes—that's where I first found out about the hobo jungles, they call 'em—camps run by the goverment, I guess, for people on the bum, some women and kids there, too. Cheap food, some of it free. You learn how t'get by without spendin' much money. I had thirty bucks in my pocket when I hopped that first freight outa Bend. Know how much I spent on grub the next five days, all the way to South Dakota?" Pride of achievement beamed from his face. "A dollar thirty-five cents is all, and that includes the makings and two cans of Velvet. 'Course, you hafta hustle for it, take some chances."

Bernice was frowning. "Dangerous, ain't it, ridin' on the outside of those trains?" And Sonny had to add, "Yeah, I read stories about police chasin' hoboes away from the boxcars—there's even a song about that on the radio."

"Well, it happens, all right. In Spokane I was tryin' to get on a big fruit train—the hotshot, they call it, with three locomotives. There was a railroad dick there, says you better git outa here boy. I snuck around the other side, but he caught me. Threw me in the cooler overnight, so—"

"You was in jail?" Bernice interrupted in alarm. "Wow!" chimed in Sonny.

"Nah, just sort of jail. Bed in a free hotel, y'might say. Anyway, next mornin' I was out and back around the yards—this time I made it. Climbed on that movin' train and moved around that baby the next three days, headin' east."

"Whatja do, sit on top all the time?"

"Well, you look for open, empty boxcars. The guys with families would always hafta be inside, of course—can't have kids and women go climbin' around movin' trains. But sometimes there wasn't no empty cars and the fruit cars was sealed up. Reefers, they call 'em, refrigerator cars loaded with fruit and sealed up tight.

"Around Missoula, the high mountains there, it got cold; some snow, July or not, and then it was rainin' like hell. So I had to get shelter somehow. I tried the rods—you know, those steel braces underneath the boxcars? But boy that was tough goin'—still the cold wind, and cinders in my eyes, and flyin' dirt and gravel to boot. So after about fifty miles, when the train was stopped and nobody around in the rain—I broke the seal on one of them reefers and crawled inside. I knew if they caught me it'd be real jail for sure, but I had to get outa the weather. So I rode with the fruit. Didn't eat none, though! All through that night, and next mornin'. Before they inspected the cars I peeked out as the train was slowin' down, and I jumped. Nobody saw me. Then I got on another box-car—by this time we was in Dakota and the weather had cleared—and I rode on into Aberdeen, got a lift from that cattle trucker to Watertown."

He reached for tobacco and papers once again. "So that's enough about bummin' around! Now I better find me a job. Think there'd be somethin' around this neck of the woods?"

"Yah sure," Clarence replied. "I know George Roecker's lookin' for a man for shockin' oats and wheat. Should be others, too, with the harvest beginnin'." He pushed back his chair from the table. "Guess I better get back to work. Finish that hayload, and then I got some binder canvas to fix. We'll start cuttin' the oats in a day or so."

Harry was standing, too. "Give you a hand. I think I still know how to use a pitchfork, anyway!" He would earn his keep, even at his sister's place. The two men ambled outside, and Bernice began clearing the dishes. The girls disappeared from the kitchen, but Sonny remained slouched over the table, elbow and palm supporting a head that was apparently still lost in distant worlds.

That evening after supper, Harry went out to sit by himself awhile on the porch steps. He needed a full measure of Dakota dusk to make his homecoming complete, and his cigarette would help keep away the mosquitoes. They were a good sign, actually—enough moisture this year for the crops and a few bugs, too. The sweet air had begun to cool, and a gentle breeze created waves of shaded gold in the tall, ripening oats across the fence. He looked up and around: clear sky, those low bright stars coming out from the glow still on the distant western horizon.

He became aware of someone behind him and swung about. "Hey, Sonny, howya doin'? Come on, sit down."

The boy shyly settled onto a corner of the porch step and looked up at his uncle, relishing this quiet moment of nearness. Then he said, "Gee, you sure did see a lot out west."

"Lots to see, all right."

"The mountains must be really somethin', those high mountain peaks, huh?"

"Yeah, all rocks and ice up on top, and below that evergreen trees, huge *forests* of evergreens, far as the eye can see sometimes. And quiet lakes, too. I went fishin' one time in what they call Crater Lake, made by a volcano, they said. Then there's those big, fast mountain streams and rivers. They just roar, there's so much water rushin' down toward the ocean."

"Wow. Didja ever get to the ocean, see the Pacific?"

Harry exhaled slowly, stubbed out his cigarette on the concrete, and flicked the crushed butt away. "No, no, never did. Wanted to, but never made it."

A pause, and another question: "Bub—why did you *do* it? Why'dja come back?"

He looked sharply over at the kid—but there was no criticism in the innocent question, no suggestion of any failure of purpose.

"... I mean," Sonny was continuing, "boy, if I was doin' all that, seein' the mountains and lakes and workin' in a fancy rest'rant and ridin' freight trains, I sure wouldn't leave out west just to be around here!"

Harry had to laugh at that, and he reached over to tousle

the boy's blond hair and squeeze his shoulder. "You really like all them things, don't you."

"Yeah, guess so. I want . . ." The kid was a little embarrassed at being made to confess his feelings. "I guess I wanna be like you, do all those things, go out west someday."

"Well, sure, you *can* when you're a little older. If a fella really wants to, he can do it."

"I might go out west and never come back."

"Don't be so sure. It ain't all roses out there, neither, or anyplace." He shifted and gently stabbed the air between them with a finger to give emphasis to the man-to-man advice that was just forming in his head: "The thing is, no one place has everything, and if you want more, why, you got to keep movin'."

Hearing his own words, knowing he himself would be moving along again before long, he added, "Yeah, that's it." He had never really thought about it before in exactly this way. To feel restless is not a matter of failure; it's just wanting more, sometimes, just trying to get ahead.

The boy had moved over right next to him now, and the two of them sat there awhile in silence. Red glow from the sunset deepened into blue and then night purple, and the brightening stars seemed to Harry lower than he'd ever seen them before. Funny, he thought; stars should have looked closer than this in the Rocky Mountains. Maybe he hadn't bothered to look up when he was there. Something to keep in mind for next time.

THE HUNTER

Sonny
1937

What made him look up was the sound—their mysterious calling to one another, the faint, intermittent chorus of
wild, barking cries. High against the distant blue autumn sky,
the big V-formation swept southward, late afternoon sunlight
reflecting the graceful motion of their undulating wings, light
and shadow alternating in every bird. Sonny stood motionless atop the corn stack, only his upturned face following the
movement of the flock, until the specks began to disappear.

"Geese," he said. "Not Canadian, maybe, but geese."

Since yesterday, the flocks had been flying, the migrating
birds coming from lake country far in the north, heading for
a winter of southern sun. These big brothers of the waterfowl
family, majestic in their movement and legendary in their wily
intelligence to escape the hunter, seldom stopped around the
Hidewood. The high-flying travelers were in too much of a
hurry to get to wherever geese go. Ducks, though, had no
such high-and-mighty pretensions. In fact, some mallards and
teals nested around Lake Poinsett, twenty miles away. Every

year about this time, different kinds of ducks would come by, sometimes highballing it in flying V's like the geese; and sometimes, maybe before stopping overnight at the lake, they would wing in, low and hesitant, looking for a good feeding place to land.

He scanned the open sky, west toward the lake where they'd be coming from at this feeding hour. Yes, over there, a small flock of ten or twenty, erratic in movement, was investigating the fields. And toward the cloud bank beginning to hide the late sun he could make out another, much larger flock, the random moving flecks like a huge swarm of summertime gnats, silhouetted against the blue and red clouds, golden rays shooting out like a colored picture from the Bible. Part of fall, he thought; made it the best time of year. Even though the chill reminds you that winter is coming, the cold also brings hunting season and pretty days. With threshing done and the corn mostly in, you could take time to enjoy it once in a while. Can't beat a day like this, so clear, so still. A while earlier he had spotted Pa out in the field picking corn, maybe a quarter-mile away, and he could even hear the regular pop of the hard ears, tossed one by one, every few seconds, hitting the bangboard of the wagon. He looked again and could not locate the high bangboard. Maybe Pa had reached the end of the row; he'd be coming in soon. A quick glance told him that the big flock of ducks had kept moving, still flying low, over toward Krauses', across the section.

Better get back to work, he knew. When he spotted the high-flying geese, he had just climbed up on the stack to get corn-fodder bundles to carry into the barn for the milk cows, already bunched at the gate, waiting to come in for food and warmth. Sniffling because of the cold air, he wiped his nose briefly on his soft cotton work glove and bent back down into the stack. The sweet, musty odor of cured fodder made him feel good. Hooking fingers into the twines that bound the dry cornstalks, he wrestled ten more of the unwieldy bundles out of the stack, made a game of throwing them to the ground, and then slid down himself and continued his chore. Images of flying fowl at sunset remained in his head. He could almost feel the shotgun stock braced steady at his shoulder, the beautiful wood of it caressing his cheek, the glint of the blue metal along the barrel, the bead right on those waving wings, ready for the kick as he pulled the trigger, prepared to see feathers fly and the bird drop—

No, he corrected himself, remembering what Pa had said. Getting ducks is not like shooting pheasants. You have to be ready to lead them more. They move fast, especially when they're flying downwind. May have to lead 'em three, four feet. You have to judge. "I can do it," he said aloud, addressing the stanchions as he dropped bundles into the mangers. "When the time comes for that first duck, I'll be ready." His mother would consider this talk "a little cocky," but she was not around to hear. Anyway, he felt strong in his confidence as a skilled hunter. He had proved himself during pheasant season, hadn't he?

Familiar sounds coming from outside interrupted his thoughts. The heavy, rattling clunk of loaded wagon wheels mixed with the tinkle of harness-tug chain links meant that Pa was home. Sonny hurried to lay out the last bundles and emerged from the barn in time to hear the husky "whoa." Pa had stopped the team halfway through the gate, and he sat at the front of the wagon, which was fully loaded with yellow ears, his legs dangling out over the faded green box, his heavy work shoes like weights pulling on the shafts of his overall pants. He had turned to look back toward the cornfield, and one hand pulled down the bill of his dark, sweat-stained cap as he peered against the sunlight. The twisted, long shape of his striped overalls, worn over his old blue denim jacket, gave him an unaccustomed look of graceful athletic action, like some dancer from a magazine picture.

"Whatcha doin', Pa?"

There was no immediate answer. His gaze followed his father's to the cornfield, and something surged inside him as he saw the attraction. A big flock—probably that same one he'd seen earlier—wheeled in lowering circles around one corner of their field.

"Ducks," Pa said. "Looks like they're gonna light." He seemed awful calm about it, the boy thought. Wasn't this about the first time ducks had ever come onto the farm? He ran to the wagon and climbed up for a better view.

"How many you spose there is?" he asked.

"Must be a couple hundred. Mallards."

"Ah." He hadn't been sure, mallards or teals. Pa seemed to know about ducks from his young days, even though he hunted only pheasants now. The duck stamp on your license would cost an extra four dollars, for one thing.

Some of the leaders out there fluttered just above the cornstalks, and after a changed flashing of wings they pulled up to drop out of sight in the dry brown field. By twos, tens, then fifties, the circling ducks followed their scouts. In a matter of seconds and hundreds of wing flashes, the entire flock disappeared. You would never know that right at this minute two hundred greenheads are out there eating our corn, he thought. The excitement made it hard to talk. He swallowed hard and watched his father's face. Pa still seemed to be looking into the distance.

Finally he got words out. "Pa—we goin' after 'em?"

"A fella should, I guess." It was more of a general observation than a reply to his question, as Pa turned back toward the horses and shook the lines. "G'dap." The team moved ahead. "We got this corn to shovel in the crib."

"But Pa, that can wait, can't it? Those ducks are right out there, and it'll be dark pretty soon!" There was a good chance that if he made enough fuss, he could bring Pa around.

"Well, we'll see. Shoulda got a duck stamp." Indecision, but maybe leaning in the right direction. If they did go, Pa might let him do the shooting. The wagon stopped alongside the corncrib, and they began to unhitch the horses. That much would have to be done, anyway.

Before the team finished drinking at the water tank, a swishing roar from the north road drew their attention to a car moving fast ahead of a long dust cloud that hung in the still air. The Dodge slowed for the driveway, and old Pup, barking and nipping at the front tires, escorted the visitor toward where they stood with the team at the tank.

"It's Vernon," the boy announced, unnecessarily. Vernon Schleuter was known as maybe the best hunter in the neighborhood. He not only hunted pheasants with the rest of the men, but he made special, early-morning trips to the lake for ducks and geese every year. He knew about hiding in blinds along the waterways, about calling ducks to come toward you.

The car door opened before the Dodge stopped, and Vernon's boot hit the ground. "Clarence," he called out, "there's a dandy flock of mallards out in your cornfield." Vernon was always saying things he assumed you didn't know, the boy thought, feeling the irritation of this intrusion, which might ruin everything.

Vernon had on his brown corduroy hunting cap and expensive tan canvas hunting jacket with big pockets in the back for game. He probably didn't even hear Pa's "Yup, big one, all right."

"Guess it's okay with you if I go after 'em, eh?"

"Sure, fine," he heard his father saying, and all at once, dismay gnawed at his stomach: was Pa going to give it all away, just like that?

"Why don't you come, too," added Vernon. "Better two than one, flock that size."

"Well, I got this corn to unload. But maybe the boy here . . ." New excitement in his belly. From under the hunting cap, scowling eyes looked him over. "Think you could do it?" Vernon put it to him directly.

"Sure." He wished he could make his voice sound more manly.

"You got a license and duck stamp?" It was obvious Mr. Experienced Duck Hunter didn't want a twelve-year-old kid tagging along.

Pa answered instead. "Ah, hell, on our own land it won't hurt none." He didn't usually speak out this strong. Good for Pa.

Vernon went along with it. "Well, fine, long as you take the responsibility. Let's go, then. Those ducks won't wait much longer."

Pa gave Sonny quick instructions. Run get the gun from the porch. Use the Peters shells, high brass, number four shot. The boy was already running. He grabbed the old Remington automatic from where it leaned in its corner behind the hanging coats and overalls, found the blue Peters box, and counted out ten shells. They weighed heavily in his jacket pocket as he hurried back to Vernon's Dodge. He laid the automatic gently against the back-seat cushion.

"That gun's not loaded, now, is it?" came the sharp question.

"No, no." Criminy, he thought, he must think I don't know anything.

"Well, you can never be too sure," Vernon said. "The other day, you know, Little Henry blew a hole right through the roof of his grandpa's Buick, carrying a loaded .410 in the front seat."

"Yeah, heard about that." In fact, he had seen the hole. Henry, a neighbor boy about Sonny's age, could have blown his fool head off. Vernon is right, he had to admit.

The Dodge rolled along the pasture fence toward a distant corner of the cornfield where the mallards had lit. Vernon shot him a sidelong glance. "Now, you've never hunted ducks before, eh?"

"Well, no. Hunted pheasants, though."

"Uh-huh." Vernon, silent, slowed down for rough spots and peered ahead on the grassy trail. Sonny knew what he might be thinking and felt again his awful opening-day embarrassment in front of the whole neighborhood group. Pa had let him handle the gun while walking their own cornfield, and he'd missed three easy shots, pulling the trigger too soon or something, before finally nailing a hen that flew up straight ahead at the end of the field. Vernon, who never missed, had watched it all. But neither Vernon nor any of the neighbors had been around to witness Sonny's good shooting since then, hunting by himself along the farm's ravines: five shells, four birds. He had experience with the shotgun now.

"All right, then." Vernon spoke again, while surveying the lay of the land to work out their approach. "Ducks are different, you'll see." He pointed his leather glove up ahead and to the left. "We can drive up to that clump of trees in the ravine without scaring 'em off. Sneak up on 'em from there."

After they stopped, he cautioned Sonny not to slam the car doors and continued laying out his plan in a more subdued, conspiratorial tone: "I'll go around to the right, up that little draw. That should be pretty close to where I seen 'em light. You can crawl along the weeds by the fence there till you get to the cornfield. Then you have got to be very, very careful: you don't make any noises; you move slow and careful. Understand?"

He nodded, intent.

"All right. Better load up now before we get too close, so they won't hear that metallic sound. They have good ears for whatever isn't natural to them. And only three shells. That's what the law allows for ducks."

He nodded again. "Right," he whispered.

"But be sure you leave your safety catch on, carrying the loaded gun," Vernon added, inserting with a deft touch three green Kleenbore shells into his twelve-gauge pump gun. Sonny clicked his safety on, shoved a Peters into the chamber of the Remington, then gently squeezed the button to allow the spring mechanism to close without noise. Two more for the magazine. Sunlight glinted on the high brass and bright blue as he fingered the heavy shells, and somehow his memory flashed back to earlier hunting times. As a little kid, he'd been crazy for it, running the corn rows with the men like a trained dog, spotting the birds racing low ahead of them, watching in fascination as pheasants rustled into flight, explosions all around, birds falling inert—then for his own trophies finding the empty shotgun shells—red Super-X, green Kleenbore, blue Peters—sniff the wonderful perfume of burnt powder, slip them over your fingers to make giant robot hands. Now the weight of loaded shells told him his days of kid games were long past. Time to hunt ducks.

Vernon spoke again. "All right. Let's go. Not too fast, now. Remember, if they get up over on my side and fly over you, they may be goin' pretty fast, so you'll have to lead 'em three, four feet." He smiled, man to man. "Let's go shoot ourselves some birds!"

Bent forward as low as possible at a rapid walk, he kept the pasture fence and its protective line of dry, grassy weeds between him and the slight side-hill of the cornfield, where the ducks should be. When he reached the edge of the cornfield, he crossed under the fence, laying the shotgun out ahead first as Pa had taught him. The sight of hardwood and glinting metal in the browned grass made him feel confident: just an old shotgun from Pa's mysterious past, but an automatic. Not everybody had an automatic. He crawled carefully on knees and elbows until well into the protection, once again, of the high, leafy stalks. Here the corn had yet to be picked, offering better cover than over a few rows, where Pa's picking and wagon axles had broken most of the stalks. That's probably where they're feeding, he figured—looking for nubbins left on the broken stalks, scooping up loose kernels shelled out here and there.

Crouching down as hunters must, gun ready to swing to his shoulder in an instant, he continued to pick his way carefully between the rows of dry tassels and leaves, some higher than his head. He knew that he must avoid stepping on a fallen leaf or stalk that would reveal his presence. It was impossible to see more than a few feet in any direction. He wondered whether Vernon was getting close to the flock. Methodically he made his eyes focus alternately on cornstalks to be avoided and, more intently, on the air ahead: they could be coming his way anytime now. He felt completely attuned to his surroundings, like a hunting dog intent upon the game scented ahead, like a lion in the forest stalking its prey, like the doughboys in the war who single-handed could wipe out a German machine-gun nest. He observed that a slight breeze had come up, providing a faint rustle of dry corn leaves that should help cover his stealthy approach.

He became suddenly aware of a new sound, and with every muscle tensing, he froze in position, weight suspended on one foot. He cocked an ear. Something there, barely discernible, like many small sticks from the school rhythm band clacking together. Listening more intently, he discovered over the clacking another unfamiliar sound—scattered, low-pitched, short, gruntlike animal noises: the ducks? Impossible—but it has to be them! The flock must be closer to here than to Vernon's side. Those little voices, they're talking to each other, and they're scooping up corn with their hard bills, that's the clacking, he reasoned. Keeping his body motionless, he allowed his eyes to squint sidewise, peering through the leafy cornstalks in the direction of the sounds. Nothing was revealed. All those rows of picked corn, dry stalks, and leaves broken here and there, unchanged in appearance since the wagon had passed over them hours ago. And yet—they were in there, some of them no more than thirty or forty feet away.

He was at the edge of something momentous. "Please, God," he silently mouthed the words, "let me do it right." Perhaps he should move in closer for a better shot. How different this from shooting gophers with a .22! There, you could just let them watch you, try to get close enough before scaring them down the hole. Here, you can't let these ducks know you're even here. What would Vernon do?

Cautiously shifting his weight ahead now, mindful of the need for absolute control, he slowly advanced his right foot to a spot in the soft earth that would not betray his movement. Tips of extended dry leaves brushed his face and arms as he inched by, but he made no sound—except for his heart pounding in his ears. A second step, successful. A third, fourth. Maybe close enough now. He could hear the ducks unmistakably nearby, still eating and talking. He felt actually among them, almost one of them. Their intimate, individual voices, like supper-table conversation—what would they have to say to one another? These creatures, so different from local birds that never leave the neighborhood—smarter, somehow. Equipped by nature with special sensitivities that let them find their way along thousands of miles between nesting places at northern lakes and vacationlands in the south, and they are talking among themselves all the way. His imagination would not stop. Are they talking now about places they've been? About the route they will fly tomorrow? About how glad they are to have found this cornfield with no danger in it?

He remained motionless for what seemed a very long

time, listening to their sounds. He began to wonder how long he could wait like this. Normal breathing became difficult. He knew without looking that his hands had begun to tremble—just slightly. What should the experienced hunter do at this point? Wait until Vernon scared them up, coming from the other side? Someone had once talked about getting close to a flock and yelling to make them all get up at once, and then just banging away into the mass to knock down two or three with each shell. Well, he would have to be ready for anything.

The safety catch, he remembered. It was still on. He slid his trigger finger up and around to ease the safety button, trying to make sure the light metallic click could not be heard.

A sudden hush came over the cornfield. For a second—two, three, four?—nothing happened. Then a startling flash of movement, just over to the left, and a whoofing, soft whistle of a single pair of pointed wings as the figure rose magically above the cornstalk level, light gray underside fully exposed, green head glistening in the sun's last rays. So close was he that for one fleeting instant of recognition, the drake seemed suspended, a portrait of flight pausing to etch itself into his mind, that bright, penetrating black eye in the center of luminescent green directed at him alone. For that instant, this representative of the wild and he seemed to look into each other's hearts.

But instinct, planning, and practice had tripped an impulse in his arms, and he swung the automatic up and over. The stock nestled perfectly inside his shoulder. By the time the rising duck began to wheel away, its wings were already in view over his sights. The bead at barrel end held steady on the bird, so pull over to lead him just a little. . . . NOW!

But for still another instant, he hesitated. He had a perfect shot, but his finger did not tighten on the trigger . . . how much longer? The question was not to be answered, for the scene suddenly became overwhelmed—to the right, center, and left—by an eerie, whooshing roar, and the air darkened with a hundred beating wings and rising shapes, some even closer than the first drake. Rattled now, he swung first to the right, then switched toward a still-better target, then more definitively toward a third—but a high cornstalk, caught on the barrel, obscured sighting. Desperately he lurched forward, jerking his head to seek the closest of the airborne birds, but by now all of them were fast moving out of range, the flock assembling together, rising high, fading silhouettes in the dim southern sky. They were gone. He slowly lowered the shotgun, clicking the safety catch back on. He bit down hard on his lower lip.

It had been the hunting opportunity of a lifetime. And he had goofed it up. The bad luck of it—no, his own failure—angered him. He relieved his tension with some grown-up cussing.

"Why didn't I nail that sonuvabitch when I had a bead on him?" he berated himself. But he knew the answer to his own question. He knew. The answer was in the image burned into his memory, and he saw again the shining green, the dark eye, the curve of the long neck, those orange webbed feet tucked into the soft gray underside, those long, fingerlike feathers spread right out to the tips of strong wings that could propel the traveling flyer straight up out of the corn row without touching a stalk and carry him far over the horizon.

"What the hell's the matter with you?"

Vernon's angry shout brought him back. The man trudged up the rows where the ducks had been. The tan canvas of his unbuttoned hunting jacket flapped with each step. He held his shotgun loosely over a shoulder, barrel pointing to the ground behind him, and he kept looking at the boy. "Eh?" he continued. "Why didn't you shoot? You must've been right in the middle of 'em, for Chrissake!"

There didn't seem to be any good answer. Finally he

came out with, "Well . . ." It didn't sound right, and he had to clear his throat. "Couldn't get this old gun to work, and then, uh, they were too far off."

Vernon stopped, two corn rows away. He pushed his hunting cap to the back of his head, but the scowl stayed on his face. He looked at Sonny again, took a deep breath, and exhaled very slowly.

"You probably forgot to take the damn thing off safety," he said, still looking at him and shaking his head, as if trying to believe all this had actually happened.

"Guess so."

"Yeah, well." He spit at a cornstalk, still shaking his head. "Bastards were all too far off for me, too, when they got up. 'Course they saw me and flew the other way. Damn shame you got to 'em in such a hurry."

"They were farther up this hill than you said," Sonny started to defend himself, "I tried to wait for you . . ." He heard his own voice rising, pleading, too much like a crybaby.

Vernon's mood softened. "Well," he shrugged, "I guess you'll learn, with more experience." He rebuttoned his coat against the growing chill in the breeze and started walking back toward the car. After a few moments he turned and, seeing his young companion still standing there, called out with a ring of impatience: "Let's go, it's gettin' dark!"

"You go ahead," Sonny called back. "I'm going to walk home."

The man shrugged again and turned, and the boy watched as distance grew between him and the tan hunting coat. He reached down to the chamber latch of the automatic and with three decisive movements ejected the blue Peters shells. He retrieved them from where they fell among the broken cornstalks and felt them add to the weight in his pockets. He hoisted the gun over his shoulder and started on his own way, directly across the fields.

OUTSIDE HELP

Bernice
1938

They had farmed on this new place for four seasons now, first enduring drought and crop failure and then, in spite of the grasshoppers, getting in some fairly decent harvests. With another winter coming on, Bernice and Clarence sat down at the kitchen table for a rare evening of assessment and planning.

Bernice recognized that they had not kept really careful track of the year's expenses and income, as she knew they should have. But their talk made a couple of things clear.

First, they would eventually need more land. A single quarter—one fourth of a mile-square section, the standard 160 acres of Homestead Act allocation—no longer let them keep up. Most of the neighbors, tractor farming now, worked more acreage. Second, they felt "sick and tired," in Bernice's words, of handing over one-third of each year's crop to the insurance company-landlord.

"We just got to own our own place, somehow," she repeated yet again. They sat alone in the bright glare of a mantled gas lamp that had replaced the yellow kerosene flame on the kitchen table. Bernice had one edge of the oilcloth folded over, face down, penciling on the canvaslike surface columns of figures in spaces where the kids had not already drawn pictures or played tic-tac-toe. "It won't add up," she added. "We'll never get ahead this way."

Clarence, seldom as intense as his wife about the need for progress, had set his newspaper aside. He fingered the scraps of bills and receipts before him on the table. "Yah, I spose so," he agreed after a moment, pale brow furrowing above ruddy face, "but I don't see how. Takes money."

She had no reply in the face of this undeniable truth, except quietly to strengthen her own resolve. They would first, in the following weeks, look around for ways to expand. Around the Hidewood, any smaller parcels that might conceivably be rented were already tied up by neighboring farmers. Clarence knew of another full quarter section available two miles away, but he figured he would never be able to handle that much more land alone, horse farming. He saw no way to acquire a tractor very soon, and it would be a while before Sonny, still twelve, would be of any real help farming. As for eventual ownership, of either the farm where they now lived or any other, they assumed that would probably have to wait a few years until they could save enough for some kind of down payment—maybe as much as two or three thousand dollars. "Takes money to make money." The old saying haunted them during those weeks, and they felt themselves confined to a hopeless circle.

Then Bernice began to consider seriously an idea that had been growing in her mind for a couple of years. What about Overhome? Last she'd heard, the farmland—a quarter and an eighty—was temporarily rented out, and the buildings stood empty. Maybe there was some way that place could become their own. She could not be certain in her own mind which motivation was the more compelling—the urge to reclaim some kind of symbolic family unity or the practical need for more land and ownership. In any case, she felt in her bones that this was the time to find out where things stood.

She sent a letter of inquiry to her cousin Amelia, who still lived in Hayti and served as executor of the family estate, which included the Overhome farm. In a few days Amelia's reply confirmed that the farm was still in the family name but "sliding toward legal limbo," as Amelia put it, "because there's $900 owed in back taxes." She reported that the neighboring farmer currently renting the land was in bad health and probably could not farm the whole place during the coming season. "The biggest worry, though, is those taxes. If they are not paid by October 15 they say the sheriff will have to hold another auction, sell the place to the highest bidder, just for taxes. Seems a shame, but the way things go these days, the Depression, I guess. Why don't you and Clarence come over and let's see what can be done?"

Clarence, too, felt the strong lure of possible land ownership combined with more acreage—all back in home territory, near his own brothers and countless friends from the old days. So one day in early March, he and Bernice drove the twenty miles to Hayti and stopped at Amelia's brick house. She was alone; her city-bred husband, Ed, one of Hayti's two barbers, usually stayed downtown all day. She seemed genuinely pleased that the old homestead and land of the grandfather she and Bernice remembered might remain in the family. "Ah, Bernice, Clarence," she exclaimed with intense emotion at one point, "this could be such a good opportunity for you, now we know you're interested!"

"Seems like it, we just hadn't heard about—"

"Oh, hardly anybody knows about it yet. We got until October 15. If you can come up with the nine hundred by then, this farm will be yours—clear title!"

Bernice wondered how anyone would want to pass up a chance like this. "I thought maybe you and Ed would want to take it over?"

"Us? Ho-ho-o-o!" Amelia threw back her marvelously marcelled head, so like a movie star's. She had always been the stylish one, Bernice remembered, going away to secretarial school in the city and coming home with new dresses and rouge on her cheeks—while others had stayed home to take care of baby brothers and sisters. "No," Amelia laughed, "'fraid not. We don't have that kind of money, and Ed's certainly no farmer. In fact," she became more serious now, "I agreed during that February blizzard we wouldn't go through another winter out here. So—Ca-li-fornya, here we come!" she sang out throatily and waggled her hands, fingers extended, in a Jolson imitation. They all laughed and then got to specifics. The Amersons would rent the Overhome eighty-acre parcel starting right away and farm it somehow, in spite of the twenty-mile distance. This would give them needed additional acreage and demonstrate their interest in the farm. During the spring and summer they would try to make the necessary arrangements for a loan.

"Seven hundred should do it," Clarence opined. "We should be able to save two hundred from the harvest, with this extra land now. All the papers and stuff, though—I don't know." He looked worried.

"Well, you'll need a smart lawyer, of course," Amelia said. "Go see this fella, here in town. If anybody can figure out a way to do it, he can." She wrote the name on a slip of paper.

A few minutes later, behind the "Attorney at Law" sign on the glass door panel, the man greeted them quietly and indicated two soft chairs facing his heavy wooden desk. "What can I do for you?" He became surprisingly short when he sat. His jowls jiggled as he talked, and the thinning dark hair, thick rimless glasses, and an unchanging, slightly smiling expression gave him an air of detached superiority. Bernice had never looked a lawyer in the eye before, and she wondered if they were all like this. As Clarence began to tell him what they had in mind, though, he became more interested and animated. No, he hadn't heard about this farm being up for public auction; he would look into it over at the courthouse. Yes, it should be possible for the Amersons to pay off the delinquent taxes and take possession of the deed. He agreed that farming some of the land this season might increase the chances of eventual ownership. Of course, he would be glad to coordinate with the local bank to facilitate a loan of the seven hundred dollars. "You leave it to me," he told them, grasping their hands as they departed. "We should be able to let you know within a few weeks." His polite smile widened in a friendly manner, and Bernice and Clarence left, feeling for the first time optimistic that this bold venture really might succeed.

Three miles out of town, they turned off the highway and into the familiar Overhome yard for a closer look at what was turning into the opportunity of their lives. They knew they had to be practical and that the euphoria of the moment might be making them just a little giddy. They stood together near the well, and Clarence leaned a callused hand on the upright steel beam of the windmill. "It would be nice, all right, not to have to start the gas engine every day." They regarded each other an instant, and both broke into little laughs of embarrassment, knowing they were foolish to jump to conclusions but enjoying the moment.

"Anyway," Clarence said, pointing at the gently rolling hills to the south, "over there's the eighty we'll farm this year, for sure."

"Good land, too. I remember Paw got some good crops off that eighty." After a pause, she added: "Going to be hard for you this year, though, twenty miles away, with the horses back and forth."

"Ah, not so bad. I can batch it here in the empty house, a few days at a time. Maybe get one of my brothers to help out on the plowin'. Might have to hire somebody for harvest, though."

"Well, Sonny's old enough to do more shocking this year," Bernice said, "and I can help, too. Maybe Bub and Bert could give us a few days." Bert had returned some months earlier from a difficult stay in Iowa to live briefly with his big sister. He was now working out on farms in the Hidewood.

"Oh, I don't know. They've both got their own jobs; they'll be needed all during harvest."

Bernice did not want practical concerns to ruin the heady mood. "We'll cross that bridge when we come to it," she said. "Now, these buildings, here, they'll need some work before long, but at least we have some experience now on how to do it. Good drinking water, highline for electricity right out there along the highway. This place really does have a lot of possibilities." She glanced back at her husband. "You know, if it was our own place, I mean."

He did not comment, and she went on, speaking as much to herself as to him. "Just imagine, being able to keep for ourselves the whole harvest instead of givin' away a third to the landlord. That extra money will go a long way toward making things nice around here. And you know, just three miles from town, the kids'll be able to ride the bus—to high school, even, when the time—"

She stopped because now she caught Clarence looking sidewise at her, a wide grin creasing his craggy cheeks. "Better hold your horses there. We got to find a way to buy it first."

In fact, neither of them had ever dealt before with financial matters involving so much money in one lump sum, and they felt uncertain about how to proceed. They had no relationship of any kind with bankers or banks, either in Hayti or back in Clear Lake, where they did the trading. But talking it over in the car driving back to the Hidewood, and over again, frequently, during the busy weeks that followed, the idea grew that maybe they could feel encouraged. The Overhome place was worth much more than seven hundred dollars—they figured maybe even ten times that, someday. With a smart lawyer on their side, surely the bankers would see that this was a good investment.

In the meantime, there was plenty to occupy their time and attention, with springswork upon them and the Overhome land to work in addition to the regular Hidewood fields. Providentially, Clarence had been able to do a good bit of fall plowing, which now permitted him to give extra effort to the distant acreage. He succeeded, as hoped, in getting two of his brothers to help out in the Overhome plowing, disking, and dragging. He and Sonny took most of one Sunday to drive four horses there, avoiding the highway and cutting through on direct routes that for part of the way were still the prairie roads he remembered from childhood. They pulled the old grain drill, with wagon in tow to haul seed plus oats and hay for the team they would stable in the musty barn. The rest of the family would arrive later, bringing enough food for a Sunday picnic besides the basic items for Clarence to "batch it" for several days of dawn-to-dusk work in the fields. Bub, who regularly spent Sundays with his sister's family, drove Bernice and the three little girls; he did not yet have a car of his own, and he liked getting behind the wheel of the Model A again. Bernice could see that the wiry, intense Bub had mixed feelings about their possibly taking over the home place. "So what do you think of this whole idea?" she asked as he steered down the wide, graveled highway.

"Oh, fine. You and Clarence ought to own your own land. You sure can't buy a farm cheaper than nine hundred dollars. I dunno, though."

"Don't know what?"

"Oh, those bankers and lawyers in town, I wouldn't trust any of 'em any further than you can throw a bull by the tail." Bub's experiences out west, she thought, maybe have made him feel this way, critical and doubtful about life.

"Ah, hell," he continued, "I'm just talkin' to myself." He threw her a sidewise glance and grinned. "I just wouldn't wanta farm back on that place for anything, I guess. Too many bad memories."

That's it, Bernice thought. The poor kid had such a rough time of it trying to keep things going, and then not being able to, with the drought and all. No wonder he feels so negative, he can't see it straight. Be different if he was older, had his own family, felt ready himself to own a farm. Someday he'll understand that there comes a time when you got to have faith in other people as well as in yourself.

Over the next days and weeks, the weather held. Clarence finished seeding the eighty, half in oats and half in flax as money crops, and right afterward a soaking, all-day rain assured ideal sprouting conditions and gave him a day off to return the horses and machinery to fieldwork at home. By the middle of May, only a few days behind the normal schedules of his neighbors, he had not only all his oats in the ground but most of the corn, too. Now the smallgrain, having stooled out nicely during the damp and cool April, shot up and turned expanses of black loam into growing green. Things were looking good.

The first letter from the lawyer arrived in early June. "This is merely an interim progress report," the typed line read. He said he had looked at the courthouse records and had "spoken preliminarily with representatives" of the bank in Hayti regarding their loan application. "While it is still too early to obtain a definitive response, I anticipate no difficulty." Bernice handed the opened letter to Clarence when he came in from corn cultivating. "I guess this means we are going along okay," she said. "Lawyers do say things in a funny way, though." Clarence read it twice and focused a third time on the word "progress." No doubt about the meaning there.

From that day they found themselves thinking more and more explicitly about Overhome ownership and what it would mean, immediately and in years to come. Clarence decided he should not fill the barn with too much hay this summer but stack some outside so it could be hauled Overhome in the move next March, if necessary. Bernice began to feel sentimental about this final season growing vegetables in her big garden, and she thought a lot about their good Hidewood neighbors and how she would miss them, even though both she and Clarence already knew folks back in the Overhome area who could eventually become good neighbors, too. Moving is sometimes part of the price for farm ownership, she figured.

The weather continued to cooperate. "One of the best growin' seasons I seen in a long time," Clarence observed one Sunday, viewing their dazzling Overhome forty-acre field of blue flax blossoms waving in the mild breeze. The blossoms developed into healthy seed balls; the oats fields turned from deep green to paler tones as the grain headed out; and on the southern side-hills lightened streaks of tan began to announce that milky kernels had begun to harden. With harvesttime coming fast, they still awaited that "definitive word" from the lawyer about the bank loan.

Finally, one day when Clarence was repairing grain binder canvas, a second letter from the lawyer came, but it was only another "progress report" telling them they would have to wait awhile longer. The bank was unable to make a decision on this loan until the harvest was in, the letter indicated, and there were references to "collateral" and "tight money." But in closing, the lawyer expressed continued optimism that by the end of August or so the loan could be nego-tiated. "Well, that will still give us better than six weeks before those taxes have to be paid," Clarence said when she showed him the letter. "Won't take us that long to cash the check."

Their main concern right now had to be getting the har-vest in. They would never be able to handle it alone, even with Bernice and Sonny doing some of the shocking on the home place while Clarence ran the binder. Bernice had to agree that Bub could not be expected to leave his regular job as hired man at Roeckers'. His good wages there were help-ing him get money ahead to buy a car. She liked having him come by on his Sundays off, using her place as home, keep-ing his savings carefully stowed in a covered bowl in Bernice's glass-window bureau. Maybe he would have been willing to quit his job and come to help if Bernice asked him to, but she could never do that.

So they would have to hire someone, but who? Asking around the neighborhood made it clear that any single men who might work out were already committed elsewhere for the harvest. Bernice and Clarence discussed the problem to no avail, and they began to feel desperate, picturing unshocked bundles of grain rotting on the ground in spite of what would have to be their own night-and-day efforts. Then, on the morning before Clarence planned to start cutting, Julius Schleuter came by with what seemed a miraculous solution: "Last night in town, I stopped at the pool hall for a beer," he told Clarence, "and I run into a coupla guys there from west of the river, said they was lookin' for harvest work. I told 'em they should drive out here to see you. They said they might."

Julius had always been the thoughtful neighbor. Clarence went into the house right away to tell Bernice. "What you think?" he asked. "Having strangers on the place, I don't know."

"Ah-h," she scoffed, "that's an old-fashioned idea. Just because people are strangers, that don't mean a person can't trust them."

"Guess so."

"Anyway, if they do come out here today like Julius said, we can look 'em over. Don't have to decide right away."

They both knew there wasn't much choice; they had to have help. It was a matter of hiring someone—with or without misgivings. As it turned out, their decision that day was both easy and pleasurable. Late in the afternoon, two young men climbed out of a new, gray Plymouth that had nosed tentatively into the driveway, and with relaxed smiles they introduced themselves. The amiable, sandy-haired one who spoke first called himself Johnny. He had a stocky build, wore a western hat and shirt, and sounded like a radio announcer. His tall partner, Ray, combed his wavy black hair straight back and wore a plain white dress shirt.

In apparent shyness, Ray let Johnny do most of the talking while he stood back, face tilted down, looking on through the tops of his dark eyes. Johnny referred to meeting Julius, said yes they were interested in harvest work, wondered about the job. After Clarence told them, Johnny nodded. They were both experienced harvest hands, having just finished the season out west of the river. The next two or three weeks sounded about right, and the pay seemed fair. Sure, they could wait until after threshing on both places for their money, and they would not mind batching it over there a few days at a time. Working together, the two of them could get the work done fast, and it would not cost any more to hire two than just one for the whole job. These principles having been quickly agreed upon, Johnny pushed his broad-brimmed hat to the back of his head, raising an eyebrow and a question. "There is one other thing, though," he said.

Oh-oh, Bernice told herself, I knew all this was too good to be true.

Johnny jerked his thumb toward the car and lowered his voice. "We got a neighbor boy with us from back home. Havin' a tough time with his dad so we let him come along. He could work for just board and room, wouldn't cost no money. If he could stay?"

Neither Bernice nor Clarence had noticed anyone else in the car. Now, as they watched, above the back seat rose a small head encased in a cloth cap pulled low. What little face showed wore the expression of a scared gopher. Johnny opened the car door. "This here's Chris. He can milk cows or shock grain or do anything, can'tcha, Chris?"

The boy's look changed from rodent to imp, and the little eyes sparkled. "I don't eat much, neither," a tiny voice said, traces of a grin starting on the pinched face. Bernice, amused and relieved, decided right then and there: this would be a good thing. These guys who are going out of their way to help a neighbor kid like this, they must be all right. And having this Chris around would be just fine, give Sonny somebody to work with and play with for a change. All of us will gain.

"Well," she said, regarding each of them separately to extend her private welcome, "it's about suppertime. Why don't you all come in, and we can talk about details, where to sleep and things like that."

Thus began a festive evening. Bernice decided to use the dining room to feed this expanded family and asked Clarice—home for a few days between summer jobs—to add boards to the round oak table. Ray's dark eyes had lingered on the blossoming, sixteen-year-old girl when they were first introduced, so it was no surprise when the tall visitor volunteered to help prepare the table.

Over supper, Johnny and Ray told them about cattle country; they described a recent visit to the Black Hills, where huge faces of George Washington and Lincoln and a couple of others were being carved out of a stone mountain. Young Chris, withdrawn at first, blossomed into a joke-telling comedian by the time they got to the pie. Afterward, Sonny referred to a song heard on the radio, and when he yodeled a sample chorus, Johnny and Ray exchanged glances. "You folks like music, we might have somethin' else to show you," Johnny announced with honeyed voice, looking mysterious and pulling car keys from his Levi's pocket. Outside, Clarence and Sonny watched him unlock the car doors and lift a guitar from the back seat and an accordion case from the trunk, then carefully turn the key in the latches again.

Clarence kidded him about the elaborate precautions. "You expecting Dillinger, or what?" he laughed. "Nobody locks doors around here."

The stocky visitor looked a little embarrassed. "Just old habits, I guess."

"Which one of you fellas plays the guitar?"

"Oh, I strum a little," Johnny grinned amiably again as they reentered the living room. "Ray, here, he's a real wizard on the squeeze box." His tall companion, looking modest, slipped the leather straps over his shoulders, and his long thumb and fingers spanned several of the pianolike keys to sound a melodic chord. They tuned up and began a number. "This is our theme song, 'Drifting and Dreaming,'" Johnny announced as if it were a real show, and he sang a verse against the harmonies of reeds and strings. They sounded professional. Bernice and Clarence could feel the glow of good times and good company. All three of these refreshing young strangers are nice guys, Bernice thought; going to be good to have them around. Things are working out.

During the next week, the three demonstrated that they were indeed reliable workers. From sunup until dark, those hot days with minimal dew, Clarence and his four-horse team moved his old Deering grain binder around the ripening fields, slats of the wide and spindly reel endlessly rotating, the binder wrapping and tying sheaves with lowest-cost, prison-made hemp twine. Clarence deposited the bundles in straight windrows for Johnny and Ray to set into shocks. The hired men not only kept up with Clarence but drove Overhome to shock in less than two days the entire forty-acre field of oats that Clarence's brother had cut for him with his tractor-pulled binder. At home, Sonny and Chris got on well together as they took care of the milking and other daily chores and some of the shocking, too. Bernice sent her three little girls with lunches and cold fruit nectar into the fields mornings and afternoons, prepared three big meals daily, and shuttled food and drink and bedding to Overhome when necessary.

"Say, we got some pretty good workers around here!" she exclaimed proudly one night when the entire group sat around the supper table.

"Aw, Ma, we're just afraid if we didn't work you might beat up on us," young Chris wisecracked. Everybody snorted and giggled.

The mood of hard work and growing satisfaction prevailed all through the harvest season. Every bundle of ripe grain was set into shocks in time, precious heads off the ground before any dampness could risk mold, and the long days brought excellent drying conditions. They began threshing on both places at about the same time. Clarence ran a bundle team for the Roecker ring at home while Johnny and Ray represented him with pitchfork and scoop shovel Overhome. Sonny and Chris, together most of the time, watched grain wagons and did chores; about the only time they did not seem to enjoy each other's company was when Clarence let Chris, not Sonny, drive the Model A to the neighbors' for drinking water or a social evening. Those two boys are like brothers, Bernice kept thinking. And Johnny and Ray, too, almost like brothers to us here, almost part of the family.

The way Ray kept eyeing Clarice was not exactly brotherly, though, and when he asked one evening if it would be okay for him to take her along to the picture show in town, Bernice worried a little about such a young girl going out with an older man. But Johnny suggested that Clarice's pal, Darlene Schleuter, and he make it a group. So Bernice said fine, and it seemed they all had innocent fun together whenever they went to town on "dates."

Even Bub had no complaints about "having these strangers around" anymore, not since the Sunday afternoon they played and sang his favorite popular cowboy tune, "Old Faithful." The two had harmonized, and Bub had joined in, his off-key tenor adding to the good times. That was the same Sunday Johnny and Ray overslept slightly and had to rush the thirty miles to Watertown to keep a date they'd made with the radio station to do their music. Sonny, riding along in the back seat to get in on the glamour, reported afterward on the roller-coaster race at eighty per over dusty graveled roads, and then on how the boys looked through the soundproof glass of a real radio studio, performing in front of live microphones just like Jack Benny, or George German on WNAX. The rest of them had tuned in at home. It was something to hear "Drifting and Dreaming" on the radio and to tell yourself that those guys actually lived right here in this house.

Grain prices remained surprisingly high for harvesttime, and the yield on both places turned out better than average. Threshing finished, Clarence sold local elevators enough of the harvest so that, in addition to the Rockefeller wad of cash he carried home in his overalls bib pocket, grain checks totaling $216 went into Bernice's writing desk, folded in with her newspaper clippings. It was time to pay off the hired men. Forcing himself to overcome reluctance at diminishing the rare handful of ten-dollar bills, Clarence fumbled each caressingly as he dealt first to Johnny, then Ray, and then found five ones, as Bernice had earlier suggested, to hand to a surprised Chris.

Their imminent departure—marking the end of a happy relationship that seemed to bring everyone good luck—made Bernice feel a little blue. She wrapped a dozen fresh cookies in waxed paper: "Here, you'll be getting hungry on the road." Sonny made a ceremony of getting all three travelers to write in his brand-new autograph book. After Johnny had packed their things and turned his key at the car trunk one final time, everyone shook hands. "Take care of yourselves, now," Bernice told them. The two men waved from the front windows and the Plymouth headed toward the road; Chris, his cloth cap again low over his eyes, slumped in the back. Poor kid, Bernice thought, seems so sad about leaving.

Everything seemed to start falling apart the following Sunday. Bub, in the process of adding to his savings hidden in the bureau bowl, exploded with sudden swearing. "What the hell . . . ?" A twenty-dollar bill was missing. No doubt about it, he asserted, the bill had been there the previous Sunday, and now it was gone. He wasted little time before pointing a finger of accusation. "Had to be one of them guys, or maybe all three of 'em in cahoots. No tellin' what might happen when strangers have the run of a place. That sneaky little Chris, I seen him watchin' me when I put the bowl back one time. He coulda easy swiped money out of there just before they took off." Bernice could understand Bub's bitter anger, and he seemed so sure that the twenty dollars really was stolen. It would take him another month to replace the money, postponing his buying the car that much longer. She felt the tug of conflicting feelings—shared anger with Bub, confusion on how anything could be stolen from her house, hope that some logical explanation could be found, fear that Bub's accusations could be true.

A second blow fell the next day. Needing other matters to occupy her mind, she got Clarence to drive them over to Hayti to talk with the lawyer, since the end of August had come and gone with no word about the loan. "Yah," Clarence agreed on the way, "he should know something by now." The lawyer did not seem pleased when they knocked on his door; he told them drily that he had planned to write that very day the discouraging news. The bank was not cooperating, he said. When Bernice suggested they themselves talk, right now, with the banker, the lawyer strode ahead of them across the street and escorted them past the brick and glass over the white-tiled floor to the varnished inner sanctum of the office, where the bank president confirmed to them, politely but firmly, that because "lending money is so tight right now" the bank could not at this time make a loan of this nature. He hoped they would understand, and he was very sorry, but this was final. Stunned, they tried to point to the good harvest, the two hundred dollars already saved toward ownership, the trust they had placed in the lawyer and in the bank. Yes, the banker was well aware of all that, but—"Sorry, nothing I can do." The lawyer told them later he had done all he could, and he was regretful, too; in view of the outcome, he would not charge them for his time and services. "We're much obliged to you," Clarence assured him.

For the next month, Clarence and Bernice desperately tried to find the needed seven hundred dollars. Bankers in Clear Lake and in Watertown were similarly regretful; loan money was difficult to obtain these days, or the farm in question was simply too far away for them, the bank could not possibly . . . Always, there was some reason why it could not be done. Clarence confided in his brothers and especially his brother-in-law, who, he thought, might have some knowledge of available money, but everyone's cash seemed to be tied up. "This damned Depression," as one of them explained it, throwing up his hands.

In the end, there was nowhere to turn. Dejected, they reported the situation to Amelia, whose remorse and disappointment matched their own. The October 15 deadline came upon them. They had to face the reality that they would not have the necessary funds to rescue Overhome from tax delinquency and the auctioneer's gavel. Farm ownership? They would have to forget about that, for another few years.

In late October, two pieces of news assailed them further.

First was a letter from Amelia, penned hurriedly in the midst of packing for the move to California:

> These lines are not easy to write, but I guess I have to, and maybe for me it's a kind of farewell to what Ed calls this lousy town. Anyway, about the farm, I was so sorry you couldn't get the loan, even with the help of our leading lawyer. I just found out from a girlfriend who's secretary at the courthouse that on October 14 somebody did pay money and took title to the farm. Guess who? None other than that fine lawyer I told you to see, may his soul rest in hell someday. And he didn't even pay the full $900, either. . . .

Shortly thereafter, as if coordinated by the devil himself, a second piece of news appeared in the *Argus Leader,* and Clarence spotted it purely by chance during his nightly perusal. "Car Thief Arrested," the little headline on page seventeen reported, over a dateline from the western part of the state. One John W——, wanted for a series of stolen automobiles in that area, was apprehended when he returned to his home county after more than a month of apparently hiding out. An unidentified companion had been released. There was no mention of a third person.

Dazed for weeks from the dizzying succession of events, Bernice tried to sort out fact from assumption. Their biggest loss had been this missed opportunity for farm ownership, and there seemed little doubt that the sneaky lawyer, with cooperation from bankers, had done them out of it for his own greedy gain. But deep down, this did not really surprise her. Those in power—strangers, really, people that ordinary folks never got to know—always could maneuver to keep the little guy down.

Harder to figure was the puzzle involving people she had come to know and to like, the missing money, the newspaper story. Could there be two men by that name? Surely our fun-loving Johnny could not be a crook. But thinking back on it, how come a farm worker could drive a new Plymouth? Why had he always kept it locked—other secrets to hide? Even if he was a car thief, would he be so low he'd steal twenty dollars from her bureau when he knew how much it meant to Bub? Or could the culprit actually be little Chris, who had found a real family here for that month? Bernice remembered uncomfortably how the kid had pulled his cap over his eyes and would not look directly at anyone when they were leaving. Had it been to cover boyish tears, as she'd supposed—or was this an admission of guilt? Frequently, with these questions tumbling in her mind, Bernice would bring herself up sharp with a reminder that they had no real proof of wrongdoing by the Johnny they knew, nor by Chris; she tried to dismiss her insistent suspicions without success.

One evening in November, Sonny brought his autograph book to her. "I still haven't got you to write in here, Ma. Saved the last page for you, okay?"

"Sure, afterwhile." Later, alone, she riffled through the small leaves of familiar rhymes and sayings reflecting timeless humor or wisdom. She ran across the page with Chris's penciled scrawl:

Don't kiss your girlfriend by the gate
Love is blind but the neighbors ain't.

Youngsters' teasing fun, typical of Chris at ease. She thumbed the pages and found what Ray had written, signed hurriedly by Johnny, too, just before they left:

Remember your Drifting and Dreaming friends
Ray   Johnny W.

Finally, in the quiet, Bernice chose a simple couplet she remembered from her own childhood:

Love many, trust few,
Always paddle your own canoe.

She had never before written that one as her own expression. Rereading the old lines, she saw that they contained for her a new truth, for somehow, she had trusted too many. The betrayals hurt. A defiling ugliness now occupied the place within her where innocence had lived before, and she could not be sure where to lay the blame.

CROSSROADS

Bernice
1938

All during that spring and summer of rising hopes and continuing uncertainty, Bernice had known that her other concern would not go away on its own. It hung around, like a cocklebur in the dog's tail, not something you had to get at right away but sticking there just the same, waiting for eventual attention. In the heat of August, she still kept turning over in her mind the pluses and minuses without coming up with a real answer to the basic question.

Should Sonny go on to high school or stay home and help his father become a modern farmer? Bernice had strongly supported more schooling for her Overhome sisters and her stepdaughters. All five of the sisters—except, oddly, Irene—had earned certificates. Marie would finish high school in Hayti the following spring; Clarice, with all the time lost in sickness and quarantine, had dropped out of school, preferring instead to start working out and earning money. It was her choice to make.

Now Bernice had to decide about Sonny, just out of the

eighth grade. Whenever she probed his easygoing father for an opinion, Clarence seemed to shrug off responsibility without taking a stand. He would go along with whatever decision she might make. She knew that if anything was going to happen, she would have to take the action, as she had before.

For her, two new realities made the situation with the boy different from the one she'd faced with his older sisters. At this point, in late summer, she couldn't decide to send him to the Hayti school—not yet, anyway. He could always transfer there next year if the loan came through to buy the Overhome place. Clear Lake, though still more than nine miles away, was much closer—"our home address," she kept telling herself, "where we belong for now, even if I don't know anybody there."

The other reality, harder to deal with, concerned gender. In her experience, boys simply did not continue school after the country school's eighth grade or age sixteen, whichever came first (she remembered several slow learners who had to repeat a couple of years and finally gave up on their sixteenth birthdays). None of her four brothers had even tried high school. Looking around this neighborhood, she could see that the old tradition continued in the Hidewood. Young Vernon Schleuter, farming with his dad. Young Clarence Roecker, the same. James Koppman, the same, and his brother, graduating with Sonny this year, seemed little inclined toward more schoolwork. No boys graduating from Plainview No. 41 had ever gone on to high school—with one exception. Early settlers Henry and Bertha Goldbeck had somehow arranged for their grandson Little Henry, who stayed with them, to attend Clear Lake high school last year. Bernice wondered how they did it.

She had been prepared to break with tradition and—somehow, whatever the cost—send *her* son off for a real education in high school. Now, to her own surprise, she felt less sure of the wisdom of this inclination, for it conflicted with another need maybe even more important than schooling. A family as large as theirs required more income than horse farming on a single quarter of land could generate. Sonny's help might be essential if they were ever to succeed in buying a farm of their own. Should their attempt to acquire the Overhome place fail, Clarence would need to rent more nearby land sometime soon and eventually acquire a tractor. Bernice privately felt in her bones that her good-natured, unaggressive husband would not likely take these initiatives by himself. But if his only son stayed home to start "farming with his dad," things might be different.

Back in late April, at the school picnic, Walter Thompson—the only male teacher the school had ever had and a former farm boy himself—had made an effort to speak privately with her about the issue.

"You know," he had confided as she spooned potato salad onto his plate, "Robert handles schoolwork well. I, ah . . ." The shy teacher became forthright. "I believe he should get a chance in high school, if you can arrange it."

"You think so?" Bernice always felt special pleasure when teachers praised her kids.

"Oh, absolutely! He reminds me of myself at that age— just *had* to leave the farm, see what the world is about."

"Well, I've always thought that way, too. No reason why boys shouldn't go on to school after eighth grade. But I don't know—"

"Believe me, I've been through that." He had looked about, making sure that no one else would hear what he had to say. "It's true, not every child is high school material. But Robert is. And those two little sisters of his will be too, when the time comes—such a joy to teach!" Elaine and Snooky, fifteen months apart in age, were now in fourth grade together, like twins, since Snooky's early start and precocious performance had let her skip a grade.

Bernice had smiled at Mr. Thompson's compliment, and their conversation had ended there, with others beginning to crowd around the picnic-serving platform. Later, during the improvised kitten-ball game, she overheard some of the men talking among themselves when the teacher took a turn at bat; the derision in their remarks implied that some of them saw him as a kind of freak who preferred books and lessons to real man's work. At one point, Harry Koppman, father of Sonny's classmate, spoke his mind to Clarence: "Hell, send a kid off to town and he's liable to stay away, turn into a teacher like this instead of bein' home to help with the springswork." The old-fashioned attitude only strengthened Bernice's resolve that day to follow Mr. Thompson's suggestion. But in the ensuing weeks, the very springswork Harry had referred to became a full-time concern, with two farms for them to work this season. She had to recognize that the neighbor men were not completely wrong. So she kept putting off any decision.

Haying and corn cultivating kept them busy in the first heat of summer. Then came the harvest—cutting, shocking, and threshing—which imposed additional tasks of providing daily food for the three hired men and two days of threshermen dinners. A midsummer letter from Mr. Thompson to Robert reminded her again of the unresolved question; an enclosed snapshot of himself, nattily dressed in a light, three-piece summer suit with a cocked fedora jaunty on his head, served to illustrate the choice. Walter Thompson, the educated, well-dressed teacher, had left the family farm behind him.

As to Sonny's attitude regarding high school, it was hard for Bernice to tell. He was barely thirteen, after all, and had practically no knowledge of town schools; he could hardly be expected to make grown-up judgments. On the one hand, he might be affected by the attitude of his pal and classmate, Craig, a strong and stubborn kid who never took to school. And Bert, Bernice's own car-crazy kid brother, exercised a greater influence. Five years older than his nephew and now working in the neighborhood, Bert had chosen not to attend any high school. He would rather earn money driving tractors and trucks. Sonny had always practically worshiped his playmate-uncle and probably would follow him anywhere. But on the other hand, the boy loved to read books, brought home good grades, and clearly saw teacher Thompson as a hero, too. He could be sent off in either direction. It was still up to Bernice to get him faced the right way.

By the end of August, with threshing done and the first day of Plainview school just ahead—Jeanie would be starting first grade, and all the girls needed school clothes, pencil boxes, tablets—Bernice knew she must not put the decision off much longer.

The next time she drove to Schleuters' to fill a can with drinking water, she decided to seek advice from her friendly, experienced neighbor. Two Schleuter girls, Lois and Darlene, this fall would be in their second and third years at the high school in town. An older sister, Laurel, had graduated some time ago.

By the time Bernice finished pumping the can full from the Schleuters' shallow well next to the house, the sociable Vera had come out, talking and smiling and rubbing her hands in her flowered apron. The two women exchanged greetings, and Bernice asked about Lois and Darlene getting ready again for school in town.

"Oh, they're already at it!" Vera reported matter-of-factly. "Took them in to Dad's Sunday night. I think high school started yesterday." Her easy smile and cheery manner showed Vera did not guess how this news affected Bernice's insides.

"Started so early?" Damn, her inner voice screamed. Maybe my foolish delaying has already decided the question. But maybe not. "I was wondering, we were thinking about sending Robert, you know, he's—"

"Well, I think it would be all right to get there a little late. Others have."

"You think so?" Bernice fingered the pump handle, uncertain of how to ask more personal questions.

"Oh sure," Vera said. "Just talk with the superintendent first, is all. You know, I said to Julius just the other day, I wonder whether Robert would be going this year, didn't want to ask. Walter Thompson certainly thought he should get to high school. Said so many times." Vera loved to chat.

Bernice nodded and took the plunge. "You sent all three of your girls."

"That's right. Having Dad and my sister Ol living right there in town made it easy, I suppose."

"But Vernon? He never went, did he?"

"Well, now." Vera looked at her neighbor, seemingly bemused. "That is an interesting question, all right." She leaned back against the chipped-paint siding of her house, removed her glasses slowly, exhaled on one lens, and used her apron gingerly between thumb and forefinger. "As I remember," she started slowly, "we talked about it some, and even sort of got him started with the idea, but then there was a lot of work that had to be done around the farm that fall. And so . . ." her voice trailed off.

Bernice understood well enough. "Yes, farm boys are usually expected to stay home and work."

Vera nodded, deep in thought. Bernice had never seen her look so serious. Vera kept nodding. "Always been that way, I guess. Far back as I can remember."

"Natural enough, I suppose," Bernice said after a moment. "School, learning—for farmers, it's almost the enemy, isn't it?"

Vera managed a wan smile. "'Fraid so, for some folks, anyway. Let the daughters and wives look after book learning—or piano lessons, or flowers. But the sons, they have better things to do!" There was something new in her eyes now. "And I guess we all get caught up in those old-fashioned ideas, right here in the Hidewood, too."

"Seems like it's one or the other," Bernice said. "Take your choice. School or farmin'. Too bad they can't go together."

"But they *can,* these days." Vera put her hand on Bernice's arm. "Look at my son-in-law—well, you know Fred Kaiser, Laurel's man?"

Bernice had seen big Fred a couple of times at club social evenings, always with a suit jacket, soft-spoken, refined, patient about playing cards with other husbands, though you could see his heart was not in it. "Yes, I remember."

"Well, Fred's not only been to high school. He's a *college* graduate! Studied agriculture. And he and his dad are the best farmers around Estelline."

"He went away to school, and college and everything—and came back to farm with his dad?"

Bernice exulted as she realized that she did not have to choose one over the other after all. She made her decision on the spot. "I guess we *will* try to get him into town school."

"Good for you. Let's change things around here!"

The two of them talked a few minutes more about how Bernice could contact the school superintendent for special permission to begin late. Bernice mentioned the need to find a place in town for the boy's board and room. "Well," Vera reminded her, "there's Little Henry Goldbeck, started last year. His grandma found someplace. Why don't you go see her?"

With the five-gallon can of drinking water sloshing in the back seat, Bernice, mindful of time already lost, drove the two miles to see Bertha Goldbeck. She was glad for this chance to ask the old pioneer woman for a favor; somehow the two of them got along well, really liked one another. Bertha had the screen door half-open even before she could knock and peered out over those round glasses. "You betcha," she beamed when Bernice made known her mission. "You come in, we'll talk over a cup of coffee." She said that Little Henry had started his second year rooming in town with the Kallemeyns, $3.50 a week. Maybe they had room for one more, she would telephone to find out. At the wall phone, Bertha had to listen several times before the line became free—"about twelve families on this party line, I think"—then finally got Central to connect her with the rooming home. She grunted "uh-huh" a couple of times while listening to the response, then hung up.

"She said she thought they could, but she'd like you to come by in person. You can do that, I spose?" The old lady's watery blue eyes squinted over her glasses.

"Sure. I guess so." Now would come the hard part of putting this decision into action. "If you tell me where to go."

"You prob'ly don't know your way around town too good. Me neither. But here's how to get there. You know where DeHope's bakery is on Main Street?"

Clarence had to use the car that afternoon to visit the Production Credit office in Watertown and see about loan payments, so Bernice went along to get in some shopping for school clothes. All four of the kids still at home came, too. She found nice dresses and shoes for each of the girls and a green sweater and dark pants suitable for Sonny to wear in town school. By the time they got home, it was chores time.

The next morning she drove to Clear Lake alone—Sonny had to help his father fix fence—and parked outside the three-story brick structure to see Mr. Froiland, as Vera had suggested. Taking the first steps past the heavy double doorway, she wondered whether she could really go through with all this, asking favors of strangers in such unfamiliar territory. But she pushed on, found the office, and was reassured by the down-to-earth manner of the heavyset, blond superintendent, who helped her feel at ease. "He's done this before, I bet," she told herself, and stated her case as best she could. The big head and pink jowls nodded. "That will be fine," said the metallic voice. "Have Robert come to this office on Monday."

Next she followed Bertha's directions, located the modest, gabled white house five blocks west of DeHope's bakery, knocked at the front-porch door. Mrs. Kallemeyn—gray hair pulled back, metal-rimmed hexagonal eyeglasses, kindly of face—greeted her with formal politeness and asked her in. They sat in the front room near the piano—a piano!—and what Bernice had to say seemed to persuade the lady after a few minutes. Yes, they could take him: "We have two double beds in the room, so he could sleep with the Goldbeck boy, if that's all right." Bernice nodded assent at this and also agreed to the price, $3.50 a week in advance, Monday noon through Friday noon. She had the egg money in her purse. When she stood to leave, she glanced through the double door into the dining room, where the lady said their family of four and the three boarders would take their meals. The wall telephone next to the square table caught her eye: in case of some emergency, these folks could always call Vera Schleuter. Bernice vowed that some day a telephone like that would be mounted on her own kitchen wall.

Driving back to the farm, Bernice felt a glow of satisfaction. She had risen to the challenge and come out successful in her purpose. Town school seemed ready for Sonny—if he was ready to face his own challenge.

She found him waiting for her when she drove into the driveway, eager to learn the results of her trip to town. His face brightened with excitement when she told him. Though Bernice detected a little apprehension, too, she knew he would be more than ready for town school, all right, now that the decision had been made.

She had planned to leave early the following Monday morning to take him in, but a heavy rain during the night threw the timing off a bit. The three girls, dressing for their own first day of school, worried about getting mud on their new school shoes. She finally found a paper bag they could carry the new ones in until reaching the schoolhouse. Then she herself worried about the road; once they got under way, she found that some of the low places did indeed require careful negotiation through pooled water and muddy ruts. Sonny, alongside her in the front seat, seemed to feel as tense as she did about getting there on time, and he asked her three times to repeat directions to the superintendent's office. Rolling on the graveled highway at nearly fifty miles an hour, she could not often turn to watch his face as they talked, but occasional glances both pleased and concerned her. He looked as good as he could, scrubbed clean, new sweater buttoned, blond strands of hair nicely combed, for once, out of his eyes. But he seemed so small, so young, so unprepared to be left by himself in a huge school, alone in a town strange to him—strange to all of us, she reminded herself.

"We won't have time to stop by the Kallemeyns' first," she said at the outskirts of town. "You leave the satchel, and I'll take it up there. You find Henry Goldbeck at noon; he can show you where the house is."

He said nothing but placed the bag he'd been holding on his lap down on the floorboards. His small face wore such a serious expression. It made her think of the look Clarence had when the doctor told them they had scarlet fever in the house.

By the time they pulled up in front of the big, brick high school, it was close to nine o'clock, but a few of the students were still rushing toward the double doors. She felt unsure, at the last moment, whether he could handle this without help, but he had the Ford door opened before the car stopped.

"You have your pencils, papers? Remember, up those two stairs to . . ." The sharp clank of the car door stopped her unnecessary reminders, and the boy stepped onto the curb, then moved briskly up the sidewalk. He did not look back. He mingled with two other figures, and then the green sweater disappeared. Sky again reflected in the glass of the big double doors after they closed.

Bernice stared at those doors for another moment. She had not prepared her son for all he would find within that building, she told herself, but she hoped she had done what she could. Now it was up to him. He will come out of those doors someday, she thought, a more educated person, better able than he would have been without any help from me to choose what he wants to do. Maybe he *will* come back and help his dad farm, become a really modern farmer himself, like Fred Kaiser. More likely he'll want to take up something else. Or maybe he'll be influenced by bad town kids, become a bum. Whatever happens behind those brick walls, he's on his own now. All we can give him from home is support.

The Model A, idling rough, nearly stopped. She felt for the footfeed and clutch and pulled the black gearshift knob into low. The girls would be coming home at noon, and she wanted to bake a batch of bread this morning. She looked forward to seeing the excitement in their eyes when they told of their first day in school.

TOWN SCHOOL

Bob
1938–1939

Things were not starting out so well. He sat at the rear of the big assembly hall, sneaking looks at the backs of unfamiliar heads, a hundred and forty of them laid out row after row like a field of checked corn. He had *expected* to feel a little out of place, but now an uncertainty he had not known before gnawed at him. He wondered if he would be able to stick it out.

The idea of going to high school had been exciting enough. When Ma had asked him a week ago if he wouldn't like to go to school in town, he'd just acted casual and matter-of-fact about it while inside admitting the thrill. Living in town! But no one had prepared him for what he would find inside this big brick building. His memory kept returning to those final school days last spring out in the Hidewood, when he and Craig, the other eighth-grader, were the undisputed big shots of the whole schoolroom. Here, instead, he temporarily occupied an empty desk in a rear corner of this huge hall, alone among a crowd of strangers who mostly seemed to know one another.

Why had he never found out more from his older sisters about high school? Marie was already in her fourth year, and Clarice had gone for a few months before she decided not to go back—today he could understand her feelings about *that!* Maybe they *had* told him of their experiences; he couldn't remember. For sure, this strange place had him bewildered.

He tried to spot any familiar heads from the neighborhood—especially that of Little Henry, the neighborhood boy whom he was following to town and would need to follow to the rooming house. There he was, seated way up at the front of the assembly. And the Schleuter girls must be around someplace. There would be no recess time here, though; and anyway, none of them was like him, a new "freshman"— fresh*boy*, more like it, fresh off the farm. Slumped in the back-row desk, he felt the pain of seeing himself as others must see him: just a thirteen-year-old country hick, and small for his age, at that. Everybody in this place, he thought, as his listless gaze wandered among the barber-haircuts and neatly brushed curls, *everybody* is older and bigger and probably smarter than I am.

Part of the problem, he knew, was having started a week late, the last straggling calf through the gate. Everybody else in this monster school had already had a chance to get acquainted last week. By the time Ma had finally talked with Mrs. Goldbeck about where Little Henry stayed, and then got to town to make the same arrangement with the Kallemeyns, things at the school had been under way for nearly a week. "Better late than never," she had said, but he was not so sure.

On the way into town that morning, in fact, he'd felt he should back out of the whole deal. Not only would he be starting a week later than the rest, but with Ma fooling around with the egg case and the girls' school clothes, and then the muddy spots in the road that slowed them down, he feared they wouldn't even make it on time. "A dillar a dollar, a ten-o'clock scholar"—town kids could make fun of him on his very first day. So when Ma began to stop in front of the big, square, red-brick building, he had grabbed his pencil box and loose-leaf notebook, opened the car door, and scrambled out. To his immense relief, a half-dozen figures hurried with him up the broad sidewalk toward the framed-glass double doors with the brass bars. A tall boy—one of the seniors?—made a big show of looking at his wristwatch and kidded with a girl rushing by, her blond pageboy flying: "Take it easy, Maisie, we still got two minutes!"

He followed them inside, moved with the chattering stream up the stairway, and found the superintendent's office where Ma said it would be at the stair landing. Standing in the doorway, he became aware of an antiseptic scent of varnish and cleansed floors. A sudden clanging all around startled him, and he made his presence known to the stout man busy at the desk. Blue eyes over the glasses regarded him for a moment, glanced at a paper on the desk; then the stiff, sandy pompadour nodded and the pink-jowled face smiled and spoke his name over the noise of the bell. Yes, he was expected. The man stood. He wore a dark blue suit. Even after the bell-ringing ended, the school sounds continued: a herd of shoes pounding up the stairway, agitated voices blending together. The man—it must be the superintendent himself—buttoned his suit coat and beckoned the new student to follow; they joined the others, moving up the stairway and along a hall lined with green metal lockers and into the rear of the vast assembly hall. The man's blond-haired heavy hand stopped him at an empty desk in the back row. "You can sit here for now," the hoarse whisper at his ear told him, adding something about alphabetical order in a few days.

The superintendent had left him then and walked briskly toward the front of the hall, his heels pounding heavy and authoritative on the wood floor as he passed by six grown-ups standing quietly near the long blackboard. "Must be the teachers," the boy figured. The superintendent looked over the mass of faces in the assembly and made notations in his book. Only after all that, when the flurry was over and there was a chance to breathe again, only then did the boy stop to realize that he'd rushed away from his mother in the car without saying good-bye or anything, without even looking back to wave. Such a dumb thing to do, this first time he'd ever been left alone with strangers. All so new, so dazzling. He felt a kind of tingling detachment, as if he were off to one side watching this happen to someone else.

He had to stop feeling sorry for himself when one of the teachers approached his desk, the superintendent's slip of paper in hand. "Hello, Robert, I'm Miss Steele," she began, and then explained how he would have to go to other rooms at certain times for the four freshman classes beginning later that day. He would take English I, algebra, and general science; and there was a choice between shop and Latin. "Do you think you'd like to learn Latin?" Miss Steele asked him. "Well, I already know some Pig Latin, will that help?" She fixed him with a steady glare, but when she decided he was not trying to be funny, she mumbled something about "probably enjoy woodworking more than Latin conjugations."

When the noon bell sounded, he ran to catch Little Henry. In the process, he corrected himself: I shouldn't call him that in high school, away from his grandpa, Big Henry. Henry was starting his sophomore year and knew his way around. Though the two boys had not been close pals during their Hidewood school days, Henry's dark, scowling face now was the friendliest thing in sight. Still, Mr. Experience didn't seem to have many insights to offer as they walked along. In answer to questions he would simply shrug and toss back, "Ahh, they're okay, I guess," or "not bad," or something equally noncommittal. Henry had always done things in his own way, even back in grade school.

He followed Henry up onto the porch of a white house larger than the one at home, and Mrs. Kallemeyn, gray and dignified, greeted him formally and handed him the satchel Ma had left with her. At midday dinner, Mr. Kallemeyn— small, dark, and equally dignified—sat at the end of the table and offered grace, while the newcomer remembered to keep his eyes down. Their son, Lawrence, a good-looking, demigod junior, according to Henry "played on the A-team for both football and basketball," games that country boys might have heard of but had never seen. Lawrence spoke little during dinner. Juniors and seniors did not talk much with freshmen, Henry had warned him. Lawrence's older sister, Ellen, already through high school, also came home for noon meals from the grocery store where she worked, and she seemed nice from the way she talked and welcomed the boarders.

"So, Bob," she said to him, "your first day at the big school!" He liked being called that, having resolved that "Bob" should be his high school name, rather than the formal "Robert" his teachers used in grade school. And certainly not the childish "Sonny" nickname still used around home. The third board-and-roomer turned out to be another farm boy from west of town, who, like Henry, was in his second year both at high school and here at the Kallemeyns; a shy and studious fellow, he was some kind of relative of theirs. Everyone at the table—over dinner, and again at supper that evening—seemed relaxed, used to everything. They belonged here.

The four boys would sleep in the upstairs bedroom.

Henry and Bob—"you two Hidewood guys," as the reserved, somber Mr. K put it after dinner with a surprising smile— would share one of the two double beds. (Doubling up was nothing new for Bob—back home it had sometimes been three in a bed, when Bert and Bub stayed overnight.) They would wash and brush teeth in the upstairs bathroom—running water!—though the only toilet stood outside, like back home. (Later that day, he discovered with utter fascination that at the high school, in the basement lavatories marked "Boys," the toilets flushed automatically when you got up from the spring seat.)

He had wondered about whether he should have acquired pajamas for this new life, and he observed with relief that night that the other boys, too, slept in their underwear. When Lawrence the athlete undressed, he carefully held his school pants cuff-up under his chin as he fingered the creases and hung them just so on a hanger in the closet alongside several other sets of trousers and jackets. Bob regarded his own new pants and sweater draped thoughtlessly over the back of a corner chair: "Better start taking better care of your clothes, Sonny-boy," came a voice from inside somewhere. Only a few of the older fellows wore a tie and jacket to school, but most of them at least dressed neatly, and their clothes looked new. Maybe later in the fall, he thought, when Pa sells a load of oats or some of the hogs, there will be money for a second pair of pants, new shoes and overshoes, even that leather jacket for winter.

Gradually, as one day blended with the next, it began to seem easier, more natural to him. Those strangers became familiar, and soon they were new friends. He could stop asking himself whether he belonged there.

He discovered that the town kids did not necessarily have the advantage. Familiarity with normal farm mechanics and an inclination toward drawing allowed him to hold his own, and then some, in shop; spelling and words and stories in English class came pleasurably. Even algebra offered an occasional opportunity to excel. One day the math teacher, in a superior pose, asked his students whether anyone could tell him what a monograph might be: "Yes, Bob?" at the upraised hand.

He remembered about monoplanes and biplanes. "Well, uh, mono means one, doesn't it?"

The teacher, visibly impressed, stared. "How did you know that?"

The object of class attention merely shrugged modestly, possibly implying a deep fund of comparable scholarly knowledge. After class was dismissed, he found himself looking into the lovely hazel eyes of Carol across the aisle. She sat there with an elbow on the desktop, her peaches-and-cream face resting on her open hand, and she said in tones of unmistakable admiration: "Gee, you're smart." He merely shrugged again and felt himself coloring in the direct glare of her glamorous gaze as the class dispersed.

Not that girls were beginning to occupy his mind much. He was painfully aware of being only thirteen, a year younger than most classmates and still immaturely small in stature. His surreptitious survey during those first days had determined that only one boy in the whole school was shorter. A few classmates—and even some of the town kids over in the grade-school building, younger than he—were said to be "going steady with" somebody, and a couple of the guys, bragging, hinted at even more intimate things. He did not feel ready for anything like that. He would limit himself to romantic fantasies about this or that pretty girl. Anyway, right now he was far too young to think about any girlfriend—or, more to the point, to have girls think of him as a boyfriend. As for the other, he laughed with the rest at standard dirty jokes, but doing it before you were married was wrong, wasn't it?

No, best just to be friends with both guys and girls, short or tall, farm kids and town kids. He would join with them, compete with any of them no matter where they came from, show them what he could do.

Music became a kind of equalizer. At home, singing in harmony—the old hymns taught by his aunts, Pa's fiddle tunes, or the radio's Hit Parade—was a frequent diversion. So he became a part of the school's mixed chorus and felt at home in the tenor section. Slowly he became acquainted with the way music is written, though he still didn't have the nerve to ask Miss Torgerson about the relationship between the A, D, G, or E on the sheet-music staff and the fiddle strings Pa called by those letters. In chorus performances, with everyone lined up on the risers according to height, he was placed second from the end. He became friends with the even-shorter kid who had thus saved him from the ignominy of the end of the line—Dwight, nicknamed "Tubby," a bright-eyed and witty farm boy who lived close enough to have attended town school all his life. Tubby even played trumpet in the band, and in generous response to queries about band music, he offered to sell his old cornet for three dollars. Ma would find the money somehow, and then Bob would join in harmonic sounds with other instruments never heard up close before—clarinets, trombones, the big bass horns. It was a long way from Plainview's little rhythm band of kazoos and clacking sticks.

So many new things to sample! But some of them would just be too complicated to learn quickly. School athletics made him bump against the reality of his small size and inexperience. Before coming to town, he had heard about football from only one source—the phonograph record on which the guy sang "You gotta be a football hero to get along with the beautiful girls." Back at Plainview they'd had a kitten ball and bat to play with, but no one had ever mentioned a foot-

ball or basketball, much less let him get his hands on one. If
only he'd had an older brother in high school to learn from,
to show how the games were played. But he would have to
break the ground himself.

There were uncomfortable moments. One came on the
first day of intramural athletics, in which everyone was
expected to participate. He had passed the preliminary test
admirably enough by convincing Ma that he needed an extra
three dollars for the required tennis shoes, sweat socks,
shorts, and athletic supporter. ("What's *that*?" "Well, just
something us guys are supposed to wear for sports." "Oh.
Supporter." He supposed it would have been even trickier to
try to explain jockstrap or slingshot.) So far so good, and he
appeared after school with designated others in the wonder-
fully smelly boys' locker room—only to discover that everybody was expected to change clothes right out in the open.
He delayed removing his underwear shorts as long as possible without attracting attention, all the while sneaking glances
at the others, and catching some of them doing the same
thing. He began to feel slightly shocked at the sight of a dozen
or so guys standing around chatting while stark naked; you
couldn't help but see everything. Back in the Hidewood, boys
might not aways cover up their wienie when they peed, but
nobody ever took off all his clothes with other people around.
At home, maybe the houseful of girls had something to do
with it, but when he or Pa took a bath, each did it in private.

Now more stolen peeks told him that the town kids obviously were relaxed about all this. They've probably been bare-
assed together ever since the first grade, he thought, and they
can laugh and joke with each other while sliding out of their
shorts just as easy as muscular James Koppman takes off his
shirt to get a tan at threshing time. Then came the worst part:
some of the snickering going on among the older town kids
seemed louder after they had looked over at him. And his fur-

ther visual inspection revealed that nearly all the boys had
some kind of fuzz growing down there; no wonder they want
to stand around and show off what men they had become.
Painful awareness of his own inadequacy made him turn to
face the wall, his back to the others, as he clawed to pull the
new jockstrap on right, first getting it backwards and having
to tug its clinging elastic down over his feet and then yank it
on again. His desperate act of modesty was to little avail; it
was too late for concealing secrets. A voice deep enough to
belong to one of the larger, overdeveloped athletes floated
over the conversational din: "Guess some of us leave it grow,
and some of us shave it clean every morning." Titters and
snorts around the room. He privately cursed the day he'd
been allowed to start country school at only five years old,
which made him end up with boys a year or more older. But
he caught himself: to hell with it. He was not going to let it
bother him. When he turned to face the others again, new
shorts in place, only one or two of them paid even passing
attention to him, and what he showed to anybody looking
now was, he hoped, a good-natured grin of shared, comradely
humor.

If school team sports were to be beyond his grasp, he
could sample athletics informally after hours when—luxury
of luxuries—the time was his to spend as he wished. Weeks
went by before he got over feeling guilty and giddy about not
having to do chores before supper. He found it delicious to
be out until dark learning to play touch football in the streets
or empty lots of the Kallemeyn neighborhood. Many of the
boys had bicycles, and five or six would cycle around town.
One evening he spotted among them the familiar figure of
a slightly younger boy who used to come out to stay at his
uncle George Roecker's Hidewood farm.

"Hey, Pete!"

The boy stood on his pedals to speed over, then swerved

and braked to a gravel-crunching stop. "Howya doin', Robert, I heard you was in town."

"Say, how d'ya do that?" Envy consumed him.

"Ah, just lean it and skid, I guess."

"I mean, balancing and everything—how do you ride a bicycle, anyway?"

"You ain't never rode a bike?"

"Well, you know, not many around the farm out there. How about showing me how?"

"Okay." Pete lifted a scrawny leg over the worn leather seat and offered the handlebars. "Main thing is, you have to turn the direction you're startin' to fall."

So he learned about bicycles, too, and began dreaming about the day he would have his own.

One night Henry introduced him to the delights of shooting pool in the back at Slough-foot's, where odors of stale smoke and unflushed urinals provided atmosphere for the clack of ivory against ivory on three green illuminated tables. Technically, it was illegal even to be in there, but as Henry said, "Ol' Slough lets us play pool, but he wouldn't letcha drink beer even if we had the money." A game of rotation cost only a nickel, and Bob usually had fifteen cents or more to spend each week. "And if you get good enough to win, you won't hafta pay a-tall," Henry advised him, sighting along his jabbing cue. Bob immediately loved the game. He blew the entire fifteen cents that night, and later, before falling asleep, he saw visions of colored balls on a field of green. He tended to spend more time there than he should have and felt vaguely guilty for not paying more attention to classroom homework. But he couldn't stop soaking up new experiences.

Schoolwork did, however, direct him to discover the town library—all those books under one roof. The assignment had to do with looking up works of Shakespeare and

Sinclair Lewis. On his first visit he ran across a Zane Grey shelf that offered not only *Riders of the Purple Sage,* the book at home that he'd read five or six times, but a dozen more he hadn't known about. Sorry, Shakespeare, old boy, I guess you lose, he thought as he took the orange-covered volume over to the librarian. Miss Kathryn Kreger regarded him over her pince-nez spectacles, and after what seemed an eternity, she finally stabbed at the borrowing card with her pencil and clamp-on stamp. He had almost expected her to scold him with something like, "Why do you want to read these cheap westerns when we have so many *good* books in this library?" His uncle Bert used to ride him that way for reading *Wild West Weekly* stories. Now he thought he'd have to answer the library lady that Zane Grey's characters, like Lassiter and Jane, had become such good friends that he wanted to meet some more like them, and in a way that was true. He figured that with all the chore-free time for himself, he could get the necessary homework done and read Zane Grey, too.

Time for himself. Freedom from those daily farm chores. The ease of town living, with electricity and running water. Plus all the new and really interesting people around, every day. Such a variety of experiences, trying things out, learning how things work, discovering his own abilities. At times, as the weeks and months of fall and winter rolled by, he felt himself in the middle of what seemed almost a miracle; he had become a vital, living part of scenes and events never even dreamed about before starting school in town.

He began to wish he did not have to face Friday afternoons, when this world of miracles would be suspended until the following Monday morning, like a Jack Armstrong radio serial whose images are shattered with a click of the dial, signaling time to get at the milking.

One cold Friday in early spring he found himself preparing for the inevitable. At four o'clock, the week's school activities over, he was saying so long to his contemporaries and one of the teachers as they flowed together through the heavy glass-framed doors onto the wide sidewalk. He glanced toward the graveled street out front, and there was the old family car, needing a wash job, Ma there behind the wheel waiting like some movie sheriff ready to take the paroled prisoner back to confinement. He was made uncomfortable by the conflicting emotions of the moment, natural affection for his mother and family overpowered by a new and growing resentment. He did not want her to take him away; he had come to hate the sight of the dirty, old farmer-Ford that, waiting alongside newer, shinier V-8's and Chevies and Nashes, seemed to symbolize the difference between the expanding horizons in town and the drab existence back home. Worse, deep down—he tried to ignore the feeling, but it was lurking there—he was actually ashamed to have his new friends see him getting into the rickety dirt-farmer car that would take him back to where he came from, backward to old-fashioned gas lamps and the smelly cow barn and the unending work with Ma and Pa and the little girls. None of them had ever known anything like what his new world allowed; they couldn't even understand when he tried to explain how it was to be surrounded by people and ideas, to have evenings without chores, to enjoy the festive fun of football games and singing tenor from written music, not to mention electric lights and flush toilets and the promise of untold adventures still to come. In this jumble of emotional conflict, he did not let his secret shame surface for very long, even in his own mind. By the time he opened the dry-muddied door of the Ford, he had pulled closed behind him that other door of his new world, which he reminded himself Ma had made possible for him, even if she could not understand it. He was ready to face the familiar confines of home.

Clambering onto the front seat beside his mother, he noticed for the first time that Jeanie, small and blond and pixie-faced, was sitting erect in the back seat next to the egg crate half-filled with grocery bags.

"Hi," he said, and swinging around, "How come this first grader's not in school today?"

"Oh, she had a cold this morning," his mother replied. "Thought I better keep her home. You all set to leave?"

"Yeah, got the laundry and everything here in the bag."

"Well, guess we can go, then. I already did the trading." The Ford started down the street, the loose front fender rattling conspicuously.

Before they reached the corner, Jeanie, still looking back at the big brick building, started firing questions at him: "Say, Sonny, was that Miss Torgerson, the music teacher you told us about? And where do they play basketball, right in school, or—"

Her mother interrupted her: "Say 'Bob,' now. Not Sonny anymore, we call him Bob."

He turned to reassure the little girl. "Yeah, that's right, that was Torgie coming out with us. And the gym, for basketball, is right underneath the high school, like a big room in the cellar."

After a while Jeanie ran out of questions. Ma mentioned that he could ride to town with the Schleuters Monday morning, and she talked a little bit about things at home, the good report cards for all three girls, Pa's getting ready for springswork. Bob sat mainly in silence, half-listening to Ma's remarks and amused and impressed by Jeanie's questions: how had she absorbed so much information about high school to ask questions like that? Then he realized that he and his littlest sister were really in similar boats—both still starting at a new school, both hungry for new experiences, reaching out. After eight more years of listening and learning, Jeanie would have her own first day in high school—surely, armed with more knowledge than he'd had. By then she'll know all about bicycles and basketball games and teachers' names, he thought. Elaine and Snooky, already in fifth grade, will remember even more about the stories he was bringing home and what they read in his school paper. He felt himself part of something larger, a pioneer adventurer carrying messages between two worlds, like Columbus or Marco Polo. He pictured his high school geography classroom, where the big globe stood next to a wall map of the county that showed Hidewood Township. In his mind, he drew the connecting line that must be traveled back and forth.

Out in the country, the wind seemed stronger. Blowing snow filled in the frozen ruts lined in the dirt road, and the Ford made its way only slowly across the miles.

ELMER'S BAD YEAR

Elmer
1939

"House burned down?"

The neighbors could hardly believe it when they heard about the fire. Elmer and Bessie Krause, over on the old Konold place, were just so careful about everything, so methodical about safety precautions. Elmer would never let anyone, even his own chain-smoking father, get near his barn with a lighted cigarette. He had often referred with open disdain to some of the less-cautious farmers around. So with shocked surprise, and perhaps a vague fear concerning the uncertainty of it all, people spread the news about the Krauses' bad luck.

Before long everyone had heard the details. Saturday night, warm for June, Elmer and Bessie were coming back from town, the two sleepy little girls crowded in the back seat of the Chevy with the grocery-filled egg crate. About a half-mile from home, Elmer wondered aloud about the strange glow discernible in the moonlight above the dark of their trees, and their alarm grew with the increased pounding of the old engine as Elmer gave it the gas. Both immediately thought of the barn—all that flammable dry straw, the possibility that the still-too-green alfalfa in the mow had created a spontaneous combustion, the calves and hogs that could be lost.

They thus felt unprepared for what they found when they passed the screening trees and careened into the driveway. As the Chevy coasted to a dusty stop, they gazed in numbing horror through eerie shadows at the origin of the glowing smoke. Where the house had stood remained only one jagged portion of a wall, charred and still smoldering; into the rectangular concrete of the basement had tumbled everything the house had been or contained, consumed and melted into useless remains, red-hot under graying ashes. Blackened pieces of twisted glass and metal—kitchenware, cast-iron pieces from stoves broken by the fall, aluminum frames from family photos that had hung on the dining-room wall, the flywheel and treadle of their sewing machine—only such things in silhouette remained identifiable in the awful glow and heat of those smoking embers. Nothing could be salvaged.

They could hardly bear to look yet could not pull themselves away from what had been theirs. Bessie's sobs became hysterical, and it took Elmer an hour to get her calmed down while the kids cowered back in the car, to where they had been ordered when Elmer feared that flying sparks or exploding mason jars still threatened danger. At least the breeze was not blowing toward the barn, but it could change. During another hour or two of dazed vigilance, unanswered questions tortured him: Why us? How could a fire start in *the house?* How come nobody else discovered it—maybe in time to save something?

Slowly, logical theories tentatively suggested themselves. From neighboring farms you can't really see this place, so

flames would not be noticeable to anyone not especially looking. On a Saturday night, almost everybody goes to town.
Strangers who might have been driving by on the highway
could have assumed that behind the trees a farmer had
torched an old straw-pile bottom. But how did the fire start?
No lamps had been left burning. No electrical connections,
like some of the more modern farms had. He was reasonably
sure no oily rags had been left lying about. The only possibility seemed to be the cookstove—some live embers from
the split wood burned to make supper, just before they'd
gone to town. An ordinary thing—but this time, somehow . . .
The kerosene jug, always kept a safe distance from the stove,
could it have broken or leaked in some way, the fumes eventually igniting from the stove? It would remain an unsolved
mystery.

"Well, gol blame it, don't make no difference now," he
comforted Bessie. "What's done is done. We just have to pick
up from here."

In truth, while stunned by the trauma of losing personal possessions, he began to feel at the same time, somewhat
secretly, a kind of spiritual exhilaration in this challenge. Old
Sunday school Bible lessons came to mind: perhaps he was
being tested. Men sometimes are, and they can emerge
stronger. If this fire was to be his personal trial, so be it; he
believed he could measure up. Indeed, he could feel lucki-
er than some, he concluded that night, as he turned away
from the charred ruins to join his family huddled tearfully
in the car. For while the house and all their living things were
gone, their source of livelihood and progress—the land, the
stock, the other buildings—remained intact. Compare that
with the tragedies of some families, when the barn filled with
livestock goes in fire or windstorm, or someone dies unexpectedly, or there's an accident. Just last year, Eldon Brandt
over by Clear Lake got his arm caught in his corn picker; left

the power take-off on when trying to clean out some wet stalks, and now he's running around with only one hand. Count your blessings.

So with determination and optimism, feeling almost cleansed by the experience, even as he stood watching the terrible ruin of what had been their home, Elmer immediately set about cheering his wife with plans for the future. By the time they'd driven over to his folks' place some five miles away—arriving nearly at dawn, red-eyed from fatigue and strain, shocking his parents and younger brothers with their news, grateful for the invitation to crawl into warm beds— the two of them had regained inner security and resolve. They would set up housekeeping in the garage for now while waiting for a new house. It would work out.

That Sunday morning all the Krauses forgot about church. Even before Elmer and Bessie had awakened, his two kid brothers had helped his father load their four-wheel trailer with basic items that would be needed: an old bed and cot that had been stored for years in the machine shed; motley dishes, pots and pans, boxes of sundry tools and materials that might help them get started again. The two families returned to the scene. Elmer rounded up the milk cows and began regular morning chores, while the others stood mute at the darkened foundation, taking in the awesome drama of ruin. In the stark morning light, lifeless ashes stared back at them, cold, gray, and offensive in odor.

"Hey, there's work to do!" Elmer tried to sound lighthearted as he called back to them from the barn door, and then the group set about in earnest to get at the milking and other chores. His father needed no reminder this time, he noted with satisfaction, to refrain from smoking cigarettes around the buildings. Together—even ten-year-old Lois and baby Audrey joining in—they removed from the garage lean-to accumulated pieces of junk, an old car engine Elmer had been saving to work on someday, some ancient harnesses that would need repair before being used again, several cans and barrels. They unloaded the furniture and utensils from the trailer and started opening some of the cardboard boxes of miscellaneous items his father and mother and brothers had included. In the large carton, resting on a collection of used work shirts and overalls, he was surprised to discover a familiar object: his old accordion, its rows of pearl buttons gleaming in the sunlight.

"What the heck?" He flashed glances at his family, lines of merriment crinkling around his eyes.

His brother Alvin smiled broadly. "We thought you might want some music in your new house!"

Elmer shook his head in bemusement, pleased by their thoughtfulness. "'Fraid there ain't gonna be much time for playing music around here, though." He carried the box from the trailer to the garage door, and the group turned again to the tasks at hand. They cleared the inside area as best they could. "Boy, a fella sure does pile up junk," Elmer observed at one point; no one else did much talking. They swept the dirt floor clean of loose dust. When the furniture from the trailer had been moved into the restricted space, Elmer paused at the wide-open doorway to assess the scene and its potential. It was not going to be easy.

But he said, standing at the doorway with arms akimbo, nodding affirmatively as he met each pair of eyes: "Yeah. I think we can make this darn thing work."

Bessie had been silent and sad-faced all morning. She lowered her short, chubby form onto the ancient kitchen chair she had been cleaning and blinked back tears as she looked about. One double bed, a folding army cot, two chairs, the crude table still showing the accumulated dust of ten years' storage, a chipped-varnish dresser with half its knobs missing, a few wooden apple boxes that might serve as chairs or shelves. "Oh, I don' know about dis," she murmured in the German accents of her family. "We are going to need so much." And she rubbed her soiled hands where her apron should have been until Elmer laughed and pointed out that she was ruining the only dress she had left to her name. Even Bessie was nudged to smile as they all realized they were still wearing their go-to-town clothes, and the mood lightened when the two little girls got into the conversation, talking about new dresses and shoes they would buy in town the next day.

Elmer's brave words, to his own surprise, began to seem prophetic. In the weeks following, it wasn't easy, but they did make it work. Good help came from the neighbors. Vera Schleuter organized a "shower" at her house so folks could bring gifts to get the Krause household started again. The tragedy made even closer the Krauses' relationship with the Amersons, across the section, whose daughters Elaine and Snooky were both in the same grade as Lois and her close pals. The Krauses and Amersons had visited frequently— dropping over without previous arrangement for talk and maybe cards and a cup of coffee. That first week after the fire, Bernice came over several times, bringing along items from her own family's closets, helping Bessie sew new "everyday" clothing for the Krause girls and curtains for the tiny single window in the garage. A borrowed kerosene stove heated their meals, a washtub served temporarily as the sink; wastewater got tossed into the weeds out in back. They added minor improvements, first laying flattened cardboard boxes and later pieces of linoleum over the dirt floor. They planted geraniums in window pots and hollyhocks outside the door to add homey color, and they scrubbed and painted. "Sure ain't a real house," Bessie said to her friend as they worked together, "but I spose dis will hafta do till dey build da new one."

A setback came a week later when they learned that the landlord would not accept this responsibility. Homesteader William Konold, now old and shaky, would never leave his town home to return to his land, and neither of his adopted sons would be farming here. So it wouldn't pay to make the investment in a new house, the Konolds said. The farm would just have to be rented without a house for a few years.

Elmer and Bessie could not think of themselves restricted indefinitely to living in the garage. Copious tears once again flowed from Bessie as this new uncertainty mixed salt into healing wounds. But Elmer would waste no time lamenting what might have been. The very next day he went back to town to trace a rumor that Clarence had heard from Julius Schleuter, that the Blake place, down below the hill near the Hidewood Creek, might be for rent. He found out that the report was true; the Blakes, who had been farming there for five or six years, would be moving on come March. Wasn't much of a place, Elmer knew. The upland acreage was pretty hilly and rocky, but the bottomland included sixty-eighty acres of good, black soil. Having to negotiate that steep, long driveway would be a problem, especially in rain and winter, but the place did have a house on it. And no other farm in the area, so far as he could find out, could be rented. He and Bessie agreed: they would do it.

The decision put them back on a positive track. Now they knew what to plan on, and they set about their summer work with renewed energy and purpose. Bessie helped out in the hay field. Together they took satisfaction in watching the growing fields develop into promising crops. Elmer did a valve job on the second-hand Farmall he'd bought the previous year; he wanted to be ready for the harvest and some early fall plowing on the future place. He felt good and believed that he had passed the test of adversity—that it had indeed made him a better farmer, a better man.

He began to take time to relax when the day's work was done, and one evening he delighted his daughters by pulling his accordion out of the storage carton. Since he had laid it aside before getting married, it had developed a leak in the bellows and two little-used keys seemed to stick; nevertheless, it still worked. He discovered that the old tunes he'd taught himself years ago soon came back. He also tried out other songs he'd heard on the family radio before it disappeared when the house burned. He practiced holding two and three buttons down together to make prolonged sounds of harmony, and he experimented tentatively with the left-hand chording keys.

On the tractor the next day, he surprised himself by thinking for hours about the accordion and its sounds, and that evening he picked it up again, this time taking it by himself away from the stifling heat of the garage to find a cooling breeze under the trees. Nearly every day he found some time for "the ol' squeeze box," as he called it in pretended denigration. It became a kind of private obsession that summer and fall. He never failed to find enjoyment in the music he made, mistakes and all, and in the memories of past carefree times that came to him as he rhythmically pushed and pulled on the instrument and listened to its soothing, melodic tones. For years his favorite song of all had been "Peggy O'Neil," and he softly sang the words—"If her eyes are blue as skies . . ." Strong recollections of past youthful follies often came back to him. A little music can put you on top of the world, he kept saying. He felt that the accordion helped him—the whole family—keep things going as they worked, through cutting and shocking the oats, then the threshing and the fodder corn, and starting the fall plowing on the new place before heavy frost came and with it the corn picking.

Living quarters in the garage had seemed adequate during mild weather. But as the temperature lowered, Bessie kept reminding him of the need to winterize the place. They could feel drafts entering around the big doors, and the thin, single-siding walls felt cold to the touch. The little kerosene stove they'd set up would never generate enough heat when real winter came. "How can we live here until March?" she kept repeating. Elmer acknowledged the need and spent a Sunday afternoon temporarily patching open cracks with old boards and bits of rag. "That'll do for now," he told his wife. "After I get the corn in, I can take two, three days and do it right."

By late October, Elmer, working by hand, had about half the corn picked, and it was running a better yield than he'd seen in years. Most important, the good big ears, hardened in the field, were bone-dry: the crop would keep in the crib indefinitely, with no need to worry about spoilage. At a farm auction, he bought extra cribbing—lengths of slat fence—to build additional storage space, and indulged himself with thoughts about selling some of his corn crop months from now, when the prices would be higher. There would be money for a tractor-mounted corn picker in the future. Yes, this was going to be a good year after all, he thought. He was passing the test, and then some.

It never occurred to him that a man might be severely tested twice in one year. Elmer's second disaster came late one evening after he had brought in a full load of his golden bounty. It seemed like just another day. His horses pulled the heavy wagon past the garage toward the two corncribs; Bessie heard the clonking wheels and leaned out to tell him she had finished the chores and to hurry in for his supper.

"All right," he called back. "I just have t'unload this first." In the day's fading light, he pulled the team close to the crib he'd built, already nearly full of ear corn, the second level of crib fence bulging with harvest as high as the wagon's bang-board. Most of this load could be piled on top, he figured. He opened the endgate, and for more than twenty minutes pushed and swung high his broad, tined fork to heave scoopful after heavy scoopful up onto the contained pile. Sweating, almost exhausted, he was cleaning up some of the last ears, bending low over the ground next to the crib, when it happened: suddenly, with a crack and roar he was never to forget, the crib fence above him broke under the added pressure, and an avalanche of several tons of corn poured down upon him, first hitting his head and shoulders, the weight of it doubling him over. He felt excruciating pain in his lower back and nearly lost consciousness. Within seconds, stillness again. His numbed brain told him he was alive, though buried. Hard corn crushed against his body. He could breathe, but any attempt to move sent agony through his spine and legs. He tried to call out, but he heard his own voice pathetically weak.

How long he remained there pinned and helpless he was never sure afterward. It seemed an eternity, but it must have been only a few minutes until Bessie's concern over his delay took her to the corncrib area. In shock and fear, she instinctively with bare hands tore at the mound of hard corn ears until she could try to pull him away. The pain of moving made them both realize he was badly hurt. Somehow she had the strength and presence of mind to lift him into the back seat of the Chevy and drive, faster than she had ever driven before, to the nearest hospital in Watertown. The doctors said he should be all right again eventually, but he would be a week in the hospital and would need a cast and back braces for months.

Immobilized on the hospital bed, Elmer could not escape a feeling of misery and depression. He became accustomed to the dull pain, but the antiseptic clinical surroundings suggesting injury, sickness, and human vulnerability seemed in nightmarish visions to press in upon him, just as the corn avalanche had. Over and over the questions ran through his mind: Why did it have to happen? Are accidents just that, random events—or part of some larger plan? Part of his being tested? Where had he failed? Had he been paying too much attention lately to frivolous memories and not enough to his real responsibilities? With no insurance, would hospital bills force them to give up their plans for the future? Would he be able to get through the winter and work again as before?

Though many torturing questions remained unanswered, arrangements had to be made quickly in response to immediate practical concerns. Bessie and Lois could handle the milking and other chores. Neighbors again pitched in. Vernon Schleuter and Clarence Roecker finished the Krause corn picking with their machines; Clarence Amerson fixed the cribs and did the shoveling, and weekends, when home from school, Bob came along to help with chores; Harry Koppman's two boys finished the fall plowing on the new fields that Elmer planned to sow next spring. Bessie had Bernice to rely on, and one day, before Elmer left the hospital, they discussed the problem that now dominated Bessie's worries—the drafty living quarters in the old garage.

"Elmer was going to fix it all up for winter, before . . ." Bessie shook her head in uncertainty.

Bernice noted daylight space showing between the large swinging doors, the bare wall still damp from the night's frost. "With him laid up, night and day, he'll have to be in a warm place." She did not mention colds and flu, which could be bad for Elmer in his condition. And a new notion came to her— a natural solution that any good neighbor might suggest.

"You folks can't stay here this winter. You come over and stay with us. We gen'rally close off the east room anyhow, so you might as well use it. That way Elmer can stay quiet and warm, and you won't have to worry about it."

Bessie found it difficult to reply. "But we can't—you have your own—"

"No, that's what we'll do. And you'd do the same for us if it was the other way 'round, you know it. We can start gettin' it ready, move this kerosene stove and a few things, and the east room'll be all set when Elmer gets out of the hospital."

They began to discuss the details. Bessie or others would make daily trips back to the Krause farm to take care of the milking and chores. Lois would have just thirty rods instead of two miles to walk to school in the tough winter months. The east room at the Amerson house was good-sized and even had a separate entrance, so the arrangement was clearly feasible. The two women made the decision; and as they expected, the men agreed—Clarence readily, Elmer after first resisting the idea of imposing on a neighbor.

The day they brought him back from the hospital a cold wind whipped snow flurries across the roads. By the time Clarence and Bessie helped him in his stiff back cast into the cozy east room and onto the bed, Elmer's feeling of helpless despair had given way to gratitude for this providential assistance.

Bessie fluffed his pillow. Bernice poured a cup of tea and set it on his bedside table. "Now here's what a good Dutchman needs to fix him up!"

"You folks . . ." Elmer had to stop and turn his head away so they wouldn't see the tears starting.

"Ahhh," Bernice shrugged in a gesture of self-deprecation, "it's what neighbors are for." Clarence nodded and smiled over his own teacup, Bessie beamed and hugged her smaller daughter; Lois played in the other room with her schoolmates. Fourteen-year-old Bob, remaining a little detached, sipped his tea and watched from the connecting doorway.

Thus began a new time for both families. During the

ensuing winter months, they maintained some semblance of privacy and independence—children on both sides of the connecting door learned early they were not to open it without permission. But for everyone, accustomed to living in isolation, the awareness of friendly neighbors so close changed daily living. Kids making too much noise got cautioned. Radios had to be kept lower. Bessie usually cooked for her family on the kerosene stove, but Bernice regularly found reasons to offer help, to enjoy being sociable—a larger pork roast to share, occasions to talk together over a cup of tea or coffee. Meanwhile, for Elmer it was a time for building. His back slowly began to improve, and—more important—he felt his confidence and optimism returning.

His biggest problem was dealing with enforced inactivity. When he was able to move into and out of bed by himself but still could not walk unassisted, time seemed to drag interminably. Bessie was often over at the other place doing chores, and the two children were away from the room a good part of the day. The new small radio they'd acquired provided only a partial solution: "Just blame foolishness, a lotta that stuff on there." He had never been much of a reader, and he tired of the farm magazines quickly. His thoughts turned again to his accordion, and he told himself that with all this time on his hands, it should be all right to indulge himself in the pleasure of the music he knew how to make. Maybe he had overdone it last summer, getting involved in all those old songs of his youth again, but . . .

"You wanna bring me the ol' squeeze box?" he asked Bessie one morning, and she was glad to oblige, pleased to provide him with time-occupying entertainment, said she wished she'd thought of it herself. The accordion rested between the bed and the soft chair at easy reach, and when Elmer was alone he would pick it up to spend a delicious hour or more every day. He avoided playing the songs with too many personal memories of times gone by, but he worked on the old standard waltzes and foxtrots.

Predictably, with the sound carrying into the next room, the Amerson children had to see just how he squeezed such marvelous sounds from the box. Bob, intensely interested, earnestly learned from him and before long began to replay simple versions of songs heard on the radio. One night during the Christmas holidays, with both families feeling festive, Clarence was induced to play his fiddle after the boy had brought it down from the attic for him. He adjusted the wooden pegs to tune the strings with the tones of the accordion. Elmer got comfortable in a wooden chair, and the two men delighted the others with duets of some of the old waltz tunes and a slow schottische.

During a lull, Bob asked something unexpected out of the blue: "Hey, can you guys play 'Peggy O'Neil'?" Elmer turned so quickly to look him in the eye that it hurt his stiff back a little; but the boy's question seemed innocent.

"You know, the song the Weisel kids tap-danced to in school that time?" Bob now directed his urging at Elmer, since Clarence had already picked up the old tune, still popular on the radio. The Amerson kids joined him in the words; they had sung it often.

Elmer made a quick decision and removed his thumb from the accordion's leather loop. "Here, you try," he told Bob, and handed over the instrument. The boy eagerly responded and soon found the note to join Clarence in the melody. There were some mistakes, but the two of them went through a version of "Peggy O'Neil" that permitted singing along and produced a round of applause at the end.

"He plays that blame thing better'n I do!" Elmer said.

"Like his pa, I guess," Bernice said. "Say, who wants some cake and ice cream?"

Their holiday spirit continued, and even into January they

would talk about the good music "the men" had made that night and how they'd have to do it again sometime, maybe work up a neighborhood party for dancing. Elmer thought back on the evening with vaguely mixed feelings of both pleasure and discomfort, and he was not sure why. It wasn't that he resented the kid's learning to play his accordion; that was fine. Maybe it bothered him to have Bob take over *that* song—one that Elmer himself had decided not to play anymore. If you are a grown-up, responsible man being tested by the Almighty to prove yourself once again, and if things are finally going pretty good, why, no sense in foolin' around. Let it stay in the past, all that foolishness and fun. There's too much at risk.

He found that as March approached he spent more time planning the move that they would have to make soon, and there seemed to be little occasion to sit around playing the accordion. Neighbors would help out again, as would his own folks and his brothers; and since he could not yet handle the heavy work, the least he could do was figure it all out beforehand. He listened to the radio more now, noting prices quoted for corn and hogs that he would sell, and reading more of the explanatory articles in the farm journals. Meanwhile, his physical condition improved steadily, and he even accompanied Bessie over to their place to take care of the light chores as she wrestled with the heavier bushels of feed. Before long, he knew, he would be back in shape.

On an above-freezing day in late March, it was time for the Krause family to leave their winter quarters in the east room. By now Bessie and others had moved the rest of their property to the new place below the Hidewood Hills, and the house there had been cleaned and stood ready for them. They had packed up their east-room belongings—the kerosene stove, bed, clothing, dishes—and Elmer, feeling almost normal in strength now, lifted the last cardboard box.

Bessie waited in the car. There had been no ceremony of departure, no moment for formal exchanges of expressions of gratitude or niceties. They all knew their feelings without having to put sentiments into words. But it didn't surprise him when Bernice called out just after he'd left the east-room door.

"Hey, ain't you forgot somethin'?" She held up in both hands Elmer's accordion.

"Naw, I thought we'd just leave that here for Bob."

"What for? You sure don't have to think you owe us anything for . . ."

"No, no, it ain't that! I just thought, he's got a good start on it now, might as well let him practice. And I ain't goin' to have much time for playing with that thing from now on, anyway."

"Well, we can keep it for a while, then, but you don't have to go givin' us anything."

"Sure. Well." He deposited the last box in the trailer and eased himself gingerly behind the wheel of the Chevy. Bessie called back and waved, "Seeya t'morrow, Bernice!" He nursed the rig along the muddy ruts of the driveway, satisfied he'd made the right decision in leaving the squeeze box behind. It was the only thing to do. Then he concentrated on the road ahead. If frost coming out of the ground meant more mud, that steep hill on the new place might have some bad spots. But he smiled out the windshield. Mud on the road. A nice, familiar problem to solve, on the way home.

HORSE FARMING

Bob
1940

The green sea of growing corn stood waist-high now. As the row he straddled came at him, each hill of broad green leaves first resisted his rigid cultivator, then gave way, brushing underneath his pantlegs with a steady, monotonous whoosh and a passing caress. His horses moved slowly in the moist July heat. Under sweat-stained fly blankets, both broad rumps undulated like a pair of clumsy, overweight dancers trying hour after hour to respond to the brushing leaves' vague rhythm. Sweat ran in dark rivulets down their bay flanks; with each plodding step, the rubbing motion against the heavy harness breeching deposited more foam that slithered and dripped along the broad leather strap. A faintly sour odor wafted in their wake and stung his nostrils.

Bob sat low in the metal seat, his pale blue shirttail dragging and rising upon each verdant cluster, then dropping again toward the freshly blackened earth. Long reins, dark with moisture where knots looped over his neck and one shoulder, sagged between him and the team, unneeded lines of communication: the horses had only to walk straight ahead between the rows. Feet firm against the steering stirrups, he kept both hands on the extended levers to strengthen his control of the plowing cultivator shovels down below.

In the tedium of the hot afternoon, thoughts had kept running through his head: strong control, that's what counts in this dumb job. If you want to give these cornstalks a chance to grow up, you *control* your working tools. Make those shovels eliminate the stifling weeds, even at the risk of getting too close, maybe killing a root or two. Every clump of arching green reacts the same: pointed leaves trembling at first touch, finally bending and accommodating to the willful force of progress. He was their liberator, his shining steel shovels flashing like underground Excaliburs. He let himself imagine that the whispery touches under him signaled sighing gratitude as the eager plants, like fair maidens, sprang back to a more fulfilled life for his having passed by. And the message repeated with another resilient clump under him. And another, in this slow, endless task. There must be a million leaves in this cornfield.

At last he reached the end of the row, where growing stalks dwindled into the grassy sod of turnaround space.

"Whoaaaa."

His own voice rang loud in the stillness. The horses, waiting for this signal, abruptly stopped. He pushed at the levers to raise the soil-polished shovels and slid backward off the low seat. It felt good to be on his feet again. A glance toward the blazing sun told him it was still too early for afternoon lunch—maybe one more round. He recalled Ma's breakfast-time prediction: "It's going to be a scorcher." She was right again. His arms looked red-brown through the film of moistened dust, and he rolled each sleeve still higher to keep the tan even. He'd had his shirt off earlier, but now the sun burned too hot, and the flies could be mean. He removed his

Frank Buck helmet, a distinct improvement over old-fashioned straw hats, with its suspended sweatband that let air
circulate around your head; he closed his eyes and turned his
face into the sun for a minute. Focusing again along the wave
of green, he saw that, across the field a few rods, Pa and the
four-horse team on the wide double-row had fallen farther
behind with each round. Seemed to be stopping a lot—
maybe a shovel that wasn't scouring, or morning-glory vines
plugging things up.

He knelt under his own single-row machine to pull away
strings of vines caught and trailing at the shovels, the white
blossoms wilting limp. Too bad how even some of the pretty things that grow can get in the way and have to be
destroyed.

Helmet back on, he started to mount his rig again when
a distant, unfamiliar sound stirred the quiet and drew his gaze
beyond the fence to another cornfield across the road.
Neighbor Adolph Knutson was trying out his new Allis-
Chalmers tractor with power-lift cultivator, and the crackling
of the powerful engine, at first barely audible, grew louder
and louder—like the crowd's excitement at last fall's homecoming game when the high school's star fullback surged
downfield toward the end zone. Adolph, mounted so proud
atop this bright orange vision, peered past a headlamp over
one side to guide the magnificent machine, its huge, black
rubber-tire lugs spinning up and around. He must be moving twice as fast as the best horses could ever pull a cultivator, the boy thought. Now already approaching the end turnaround grass, a touch at the gas lever to slow just a little, a
reach over to flick the hydraulic knob and—zip!—all those
shovels as if by magic came out of the ground at once. After
a sharp turn (you have to brake just one big wheel to do that)
and hardly slowing down, the complete marvel emerged from
the green cover, glittering orange and new and metallic in the

sun, bouncing on that rolling rubber, engine at controlled, haughty ease. Adolph waved a greeting to him just before swinging again into the new rows, and that wonderful roar of power came up automatically as the engine's governor fed more gas; then the exciting loudness began to recede once again. Bob found his hand still raised and felt foolish to realize that he had not even responded in time for Adolph to see him wave back.

He inhaled deeply, held it, and blew at length against the unmoving air. Perching again on the old metal seat, he picked up the loose lines and shook them sharply at the horses. "Giddap, hyah!" The team came to reluctant life; he pulled a line to turn them into the next weed-grown row and, this time without stopping first, yanked on the levers to drop the shovels to digging depth. The team, uncertain how to interpret this sudden change in burden, hesitated and almost halted. In flaring anger he shouted at them. "C'mon! Roxy, May, hyah!" The darker bay on the left pulled with renewed vigor against her tugs, but lazy May as usual delayed. With a hissing curse, he reached down to find a hard lump of loam and let fly point-blank at the lagging rump. "Dumb ox!" Both mares lurched ahead for three or four brisk steps, then settled into their normal plodding pace. Nothing was ever going to change them. "Can't teach an old nag new tricks, eh?" he snarled at their lumbering behinds. He settled into another hot, interminable round. The bending leaves began their repeated sighs: whoosh, whoosh. He was in no mood for any pretended gratitude. He listened for the Allis-Chalmers. Already too far away. Across the field and behind him, it looked like Pa had finished his rows and had started his slow turn into another round. The four-horse team must be even more cumbersome to maneuver than these two, he thought.

Horse farming. Why was Pa willing to put up with all this old-fashioned stuff? Nearly all the neighbors by now had some kind of tractor; Adolph's orange beauty was only the newest. The Schleuters had their old 10-20, the Roeckers had the big Minneapolis-Moline the neighborhood used for threshing, and the Krauses and Koppmans had their Farmalls.

It was so hard to talk about these things with Pa. He just didn't seem to want to face the fact that he was falling behind while others modernized. Every time the subject came up he would shrug it off with one of his noncommittal comments, like "good enough." Or he'd walk away to find some odd jobs to do, such as squatting at the barn door sill to repair aging harnesses. Just too easygoing, his father. Ma had been saying so for years.

Maybe, the boy knew, part of his own problem these days was having been away for two years in high school. Mixing with others—not only other country boys off modern farms but also town kids and educated teachers—it got you thinking about things that had never occurred to you back in the old one-room schoolhouse. The way people live, away from this backward neighborhood. Town guys having it so easy, no chores to worry about, and you can play touch football after school. When you want to read after dark, just flick a switch and the lights come on. And indoor bathrooms. Not just toilets, either, but *bath* rooms: right this minute, down there under the corn leaves, dust was stirring up and filtering right under the pantlegs of his bibless overalls, sticking to his sweaty legs. By tonight, they would be black. Without running water for a shower bath, like in town, tonight again before bedtime it'll be dip from the stove reservoir, take the basin out on the porch, and wash up to the knees, at least. Around here, those who really need electricity and running water are the last in line to get them. Unfair and just dumb. Such big changes going on all over the world—except here. In town they talk about Hitler making war in Europe and

Roosevelt running for a third term, Fred Astaire and Ginger Rogers. People buying new 1940 Packards, or flying airplanes coast to coast. And here we still sit in the dust behind a couple of plugs in a hot cornfield. Hell, maybe we can't expect fancy Hollywood stuff or new cars or electricity yet, but we don't have to poke long like *this* forever, either. Time to make some changes around here, too. There must be ways at least to *talk* about tractors, get Pa to plan ahead a little—

"Whoops! Damn!" Below his feet small, insistent muffled explosions interrupted his reverie. The wandering cultivator had just plowed up three hills of corn, and tentacles of uptorn roots lay behind him, exposed on the surface of the turned soil. Goners now, but what the hell, he shrugged, kicking a foot to correct the shovel's direction. "Quit your dreamin'," that's what Pa would say if he knew. But he wouldn't know. Pa didn't know about lots of things, and this might as well be one of them.

By the time he neared the end of the field again, he spotted the expected glimmer of light color amid the green. Jeanie, with his lunch, stood squinting and grinning at him as he pulled up. The little girl, so often excluded from the play of two older sisters, loved being a part of grown-up work.

"Your turn this afternoon, eh?"

She grinned more broadly and extended toward him her cargo: a syrup can for sandwiches and cookies and two pint mason jars of red fruit nectar (strawberry flavor, he hoped) held within an old silk stocking knotted as a carrying bag. In thirsty anticipation, he opened a jar and tipped it up: strawberry, all right, and good, satisfying—but almost warm. How much better it would have been with a few ice cubes floating in it! Boy, he thought, the things that others in the world take for granted, while the rest of us get along on "good enough." He lay his helmet on the ground beside him, felt both the evaporating cool and the sun's rays on his forehead, and bit into a bologna sandwich. Jeanie played among the corn leaves. Again, quiet heat, except for the Allis-Chalmers roaring along in the distance once more. One of the mares stamped a hind hoof to shake off a biting fly.

"Say, Sonny, why—"

He glared with mock ferocity at his little sister.

"I mean, *Bob,*" Jeanie amended her error. For two years he'd been campaigning to get his family to use his real name instead of that silly nickname left over from childhood, but they still had trouble remembering.

"Well, anyway," she went on in her little voice, "why's Pa stopping over there?"

Across the field, the four-horse team again stood motionless.

"You have to stop once in a while, to clean out the morning glories, stuff like that."

Strange, though, that Pa was standing out in front of the horses rather than bending under the cultivator. Maybe a nose-basket twine had broken—and you sure can't cultivate without nose baskets to keep the pesky nose flies away from the horses and to keep the horses from sampling the green corn and getting colic. Old Adolph didn't have problems like those anymore, with that Allis-Chalmers.

Pa finally came to the end, but instead of turning into new rows and waiting for Jeanie to run over with the lunch, he headed his four horses along the grassy area toward them. On the right were Tim and Diamond, the big, young bays, and next to them, black Beauty—named from the book: Pa had let him name each of the colts when they were born, and here they were, grown-up enough this year, these three brothers and sisters, to be hooked together, almost a family team. And on the near side, bony old Birdie, a brighter bay but smaller than the others, having a hard time keeping up.

Jeanie stood waiting, and when the big rig stopped, Pa

took a long swig of the nectar. "Ahhh, boy, that's good!" He smiled down at his daughter, his craggy face so dark from dust that his teeth and eyes looked too white, like some minstrel show actor. Jeanie beamed. Pa tied his lines and swung down from the high cultivator seat. The patches on his faded blue overalls stood out in the bright sun. With one hand he swept off his floppy, broad-brimmed straw hat, and with the other shirtsleeve he wiped his damp brow, where matted strands of dark hair contrasted with the whiteness of his forehead. Bob had discovered long ago that old men don't care anything at all about suntans.

"Say, Pa," he called out. "How come you're over here? Quittin' early?"

"Have to, I guess. Birdie—she's sick. Must be the heat." They all looked at the old horse then. Her head hung low— Pa had released the checkrein—and she was almost panting, like a dog on a hot day.

A few minutes later, Pa giddaped his team along the fence line toward home. Delighted Jeanie sat on his lap. "You make a few more rounds," he called back. "I'll get chores started early." Poor old Birdie tried to keep from lagging, but it looked as though even the weight of her bridle bothered her. With that harness on her, the ailing horse hardly seemed the same Birdie he sometimes rode Sunday afternoons, when one of the Koppman boys came by on Smoky, their riding pony. Old Birdie couldn't compare with Smoky, but—bones and all—she was the closest thing on this farm to a riding horse.

He made two more long and tiresome rounds, judged that the stubborn sun still hung too high to get by with quitting, and added a third before he levered his shovels high and tightened May's line to let the team head for home. Now the big mares moved along the grassway with real pep. "So," he sang out to them, sharing their joy at the workday's end. "You been saving your energy for the homestretch, huh?" Well, they would be thirsty and hungry, and there was May's colt, Tony—named after Tom Mix's cow pony—still only a few months old and kept in the barn while his ma worked in the fields.

He pulled past the water tank, where the popping gas engine pumped a fresh stream, and near the corncrib unhitched the team. Pa, watching from the barn, opened the lower door to release the roan foal, who skittered on spindly legs toward his mother. Unerringly, the colt's soft muzzle pushed under May's fly blanket and through the draping straps to find his supper, even as the freed mares themselves headed directly for the water tank. Both horses immediately plunged their bridled noses deep below the surface, the clear water level nearly up to their eyes as they pulled up long, deep drafts.

Pa walked over and stood by him at the tank. "They get pretty thirsty on a day like this," he said, as if to himself.

After a minute, Bob asked about Birdie.

"Played out, looks like." Pa's frown showed his concern.

"She going to be all right?"

"Don't know yet, see in the morning. Shouldn'ta made her work in this heat, I guess." Pa reached out absently with scratching strokes on the back of the suckling colt, and when Bob's horses finished drinking, Pa took over the job of unharnessing and getting them fed.

In the morning, old Birdie seemed no better. Pa decided he would use Roxy in his four-horse team, leaving Birdie to rest and May to stay with her colt. Thus unable to join his father in the field, Bob was assigned the task of cleaning the chicken coop. During the course of the day, he concluded that while cultivating corn may be one of the farm jobs highest in tedium, henhouse cleaning had to rate near the top in pure nastiness, and he invented epithets to mutter to himself: "Dumb clucks, smelly fowls, foul smells . . ." He tried to remember all he had ever read or imagined about modern chicken-raising, in which laying hens never touch the ground and their manure drops through cages onto moving conveyer belts. By evening he was in a combative mood and could barely contain the ideas that surged through him in condemnation of farming's primitive aspects.

At the supper table, it was his mother who asked about the old horse. Pa looked at her over his pork chop. "Pretty bad," he finally answered.

"Well, I hope she won't have to suffer, like poor old Jim did." Her reference to Birdie's mate in the old days recalled stories Bob had heard all his life about that handsome, high-stepping team in their leather-and-brass harnesses, hooked to a sporty buggy. Must have been back when the folks were first married. He remembered, too, that morning two years ago with Pa, when they had gone out to the big pasture to look for the weakened, ailing old Jim, who had failed to come around the barnyard for a couple of days. They'd found him where he'd stepped into a badger hole, and the agony of his last hours still showed in those rolled eyes and open mouth, the few yellow-stained teeth, his long black tongue out one side with ants crawling on it. Walking back toward the yard that morning, Pa got to telling him about Jim and Birdie in the old days, when their harnesses—the harnesses that today hung in the barn, the dry leather cracked and brass spots corroded—had been all new.

Now his father nodded as he poured gravy over a slice of bread. "I spose we should . . . ah, put her out of her mis'ry."

This piqued Bob's interest. "How would you do that?"

Pa did not respond, but his mother clarified: "Well, you know. Shooting's more merciful. They don't have to suffer."

Images of a cowboy out on the range, drawing a pistol in farewell to the faithful cayuse with a broken leg. In days of

King Arthur, they would call it the *coup de grace.*

"We'll sure miss old Birdie, though," his mother was saying. In the light of the gas lamp, Bob saw that she had stopped eating and was fussing with her fork.

"Yah." Pa looked resigned. "And when a fella needs six horses to get the cultivatin' done . . . I dunno, now anymore, where we can get a horse . . ."

"'GET A HORSE'!" Bob felt rising impatience explode within him. "Get a horse!" he shouted again. "For Pete's sake, you think this is 1923 or somethin'? Can't you see horses are . . . *obsolete?* If we'd have just ONE tractor instead of six horses, we'd be done cultivatin' long ago!"

His three younger sisters at the table looked in wide-eyed silence from one face to another. His mother glared at him sharply, but she spoke with calm.

"Horses may be . . . what you said, your fancy word. But tractors cost money."

"Sure. But it takes money to make money, you say so yourself. And tractors can work faster, save time, make money in the long run! At night you can just turn off the switch and that's it, no unharnessing, no oats, no stalls to clean. And"—now was the time to press the advantage—"tractors don't get old and die. When they start wearin' out, they can be repaired."

The silence around the table suggested that his argument was having some effect. After a minute, Ma shot a quick glance at her husband and spoke again.

"Maybe this would be a good time to start lookin' around. I got some cream and egg money saved up. We could get a loan from Production Credit."

Bob was quick to follow up. "I know a guy out east of town says his dad's gonna have their John Deere GP for sale this fall. Few years old, but good shape. Rubber tires, too. Only about four hundred dollars or so, he thought, with a plow thrown in."

He could see that the notion had taken hold. Pa still showed no signs of commitment, but Ma could always be relied on to see the benefit of new ideas, especially new ideas that might eventually help them save enough for a down-payment on their own farm. She spoke tentatively of additional land nearby that might be for rent next year, to help justify the investment in a tractor and plow. Heart pounding, he tried to put forth what he hoped would appear as objective, cold facts: their horse-drawn implements could easily be converted to be pulled as well by tractor. "That's what Schleuters are doin', just usin' their regular drill and drag and disk behind that 10-20. Even Adolph with that new Allis-Chalmers of his, he's usin' some horse machinery."

Pa cleaned gravy from his plate with a final crust of bread, savored it, drained his coffee, and set the cup down on the oilcloth. "Well, yah, I guess we could take a look at it. Maybe a fella should."

That was about as decisive a statement as Pa was ever going to make. As they left the supper table, Bob felt jubilant at the possibility of imminent change, and the subject was left there for the time being.

A heavy thunderstorm during the night meant no field-work the next morning. During chores and breakfast they agreed that, since this was Saturday, tonight in town it would be all right "at least to talk with" those people about the John Deere tractor.

Birdie was worse. When they'd opened the barn first thing for the morning milking, they'd found her lying down in the stall, fallen so far back that her halter rope, tied to the manger, stretched her neck out tight, giving her the shape of some grotesque creature from horror stories and not a horse at all. Even after they'd gotten her on her feet, she continued to wheeze; eerie groans and rumbles emanated from her insides.

"She ain't gonna make it," Pa said finally. "We might as

well get it over with this mornin'." They would take her out to the hog lot, he explained, and after they'd done the skinning—a horsehide was worth four or five dollars in Watertown—the carcass could be left there awhile for the pigs to feed on. Something about protein.

After breakfast Ma kept the girls in the house while the two men went to take care of what was necessary. Pa stopped on the porch to lift his Remington from the corner, and he slid two red Super-X shells into his overall pocket. Outside, he leaned the gun against the hog-lot fence, and they walked to the barn. Birdie was still standing but sounding bad. They tied an extra ten-foot length of rope onto her halter, and Pa coiled it over one arm and took a close hold on the leather straps, half-leading and half-supporting the weakened mare. They slowly made their way out the back door toward the hog lot. Bob followed behind, one hand on the bony rump to help get her started again whenever she hesitated.

Beyond the pigs' troughs Pa stopped and eased the old horse around so that behind her lay nothing but empty pasture, in case of an accidental miss. He stood there for a moment, lifting on the halter strap. Birdie held her head at a higher level now.

Bob felt uncertain of his role. "Should I hold the rope, or get the gun for you, or what?"

"You get the gun."

He loped over to the fence where the automatic leaned against the woven wire. Its weight and balance and the smooth hardwood felt good to him. The gun had always felt good, since that day when he was twelve and Pa had let him shoot it three times—once at a tin can on a fencepost, twice at cans tossed into the air—and he had hit the target every time. Long practice as a kid with the .22 rifle, maybe hundreds of gophers, some jackrabbits, a few pheasants, had all helped to sharpen his instinctive skill.

Pa had moved away from the horse, to the end of the long rope. He held in his hand the two red cartridges. "Here," he said.

Bob hesitated. He needed to make sure he'd understood. "Me?"

"Just be careful. Aim right between the eyes." The brass heads of the shells glistened in Pa's rough and callused fingers. "You can do it, can't you?"

"Damn right I can." He surprised himself by using a swear word, and a familiar wave of impatience made him continue: "I can do anything that needs to be done." He shifted the weight of the Remington to his left arm and reached over to nip just one of the shells from his father's hand. As he backed up for necessary distance, he slammed the red and brass into the chamber with an expert touch on the mechanism.

About fifteen feet away, Pa nodded. Bob brought the stock to his shoulder, felt the smooth cool of the wood on his cheek. He lowered the barrel toward the target. Birdie seemed to sense something. Her head remained high and steady as she looked at him. Beyond her alerted ears he discerned, out of focus, her dark mane along the rusty red of her arched neck, the curve of her small and bony back, which he had sat upon so many times, pretending that he bestrode not merely a workhorse but a real riding pony. To the task at hand, now: the bead held steady on that little patch of white between the eyes, and his finger tightened on the trigger.

Somehow, it all happened with more sudden finality than he had expected. Simultaneously with the explosion in his eardrums and the kick against his shoulder, the horse dropped to the ground as if impelled by a force stronger than mere gravity. Had he expected some lingering death scene from a Hopalong Cassidy movie? Or a simple plop of the rifle bullet exterminating a gopher crouched at his hole? This was

something else—something closer to reality. The instant
crumpling of all that height and weight into the brown carcass now before him—spasms still jerking the old hooves,
muscles and nerves exercising their last desperate claim to
life. Images flashed in his mind—what do they say about the
last lucid moments of drowning people?—his own remembered images of bony Birdie willing to play the pony of a
Sunday, even when old and tired, responsive to his urging
heels. He saw brighter scenes of an earlier Birdie with partner Jim, rigged in new harnesses that sparkled with brass
spots, clip-clopping along a prairie road, stylish heads high,
taut lines leading to the couple in a shiny black buggy. Now,
irrevocably, with just one squeeze on the trigger, all that she
ever was lay there on the ground, transformed into a horsehide to sell for four dollars and some protein for the hogs.

He lowered the gun barrel and glanced over at Pa. No
emotion could be read in that impassive, leathery, lined face;
his father simply stared down there. The long halter rope lay
where he had let it fall. Neither said anything.

He turned to carry the shotgun back, and he left it
propped against the hog-lot fence. When he looked again, Pa
had bent down to disconnect the halter from the shapeless
mass, from what had been a part of both their pasts. No use
watching anymore. He pulled his gaze away, beyond the barn
toward the fields of growing crops. He concentrated his
thoughts on the bright green and yellow of a John Deere tractor. He could only hope that the price would not come too
high.

IN TUNE

Clarence
1940

Clarence had not meant to eavesdrop like this. Coming home early from helping the Schleuters fill silo, he had stopped just inside the open barn door to tighten a shoelace, and during that moment became aware of talk between his son and his wife, there in the cow barn. They must be doing the milking together, he figured, since they expected him to be late. The anger in the boy's voice was what held Clarence riveted, one leg hoisted on a manger plank, listening to words he knew were not meant for his ears.

"Ahhh, it's just that Pa makes me so *mad* sometimes!" His high-pitched tones rose over the occasional rustles of the cows munching their fodder and the repeated, ringing, metallic squish of milk hitting the bottom of a near-empty pail. Bernice's reply, from farther down the line of stanchions, was barely audible.

". . . disappointing, not to buy that tractor . . . just have to wait awhile longer." Bob had been chafing ever since they'd had to decide, over a week ago, that a second-hand John

Deere he had located was still out of reach for them.

"But it's just so *typical!*" He was practically yelling. "We're about the only ones in the whole neighborhood still foolin' around with horses. Look at the old machinery Pa keeps tryin' to fix up with baling wire and twinestring. And that rattly Model A of ours, when everybody has a V-8 or a newer Chevy by now."

"Well, at least he lets you drive it all the time." In the quiet of the barn Clarence could hear their four hands softly milking into foam.

"Yeah, well, that's another thing, the way he drives a car himself. Racin' the motor, lettin' out the clutch too fast, sittin' there behind the wheel so stiff-backed and scared-lookin'. As if the car was the enemy or somethin'."

"Oh, come on, now. Your pa's sort of easygoin', sure, and maybe a little old-fashioned in his ways. But he's a good person, don't forget that."

After a moment: "I spose so. But you know, Ma—in school I see some kids whose fathers are really somebody, you know what I mean. Prosperous farmers or smart businessmen who just *know how to do things!* I just wish sometimes I had more to learn from Pa, is all."

Clarence did not wait to hear any more. As silently as he had entered, he stepped outside the barn. To escape facing the reality of the accusations? To keep Bernice and the boy from knowing he'd overheard and feeling embarrassed? A familiar melody began flowing through his head; he did not let it stay long enough even to identify it. Tunes often entered his private world at times when he felt especially relaxed or stressed, but now he had to clear his mind to think. He wandered past the well, and though the water tank was half-full, he decided to see if he could get the gas engine to start. The popping exhaust would be loud enough, even in the cow barn, to announce his return. He would make some kind of racket at the barn door, too, when he went back in, just to make sure.

"Wish I had more to learn from Pa." Clarence swallowed hard, watching for the first trickle beyond the noisy engine. That kid. Getting a little big for his britches, maybe, filled with new ideas, a couple years in high school bound to have its effect. Can't blame him, though, for wanting better things like some of the neighbors now—tractor, windmill instead of this worn-out gas engine, owning our own place. Maybe I am just not smart enough to see how we can do all those things. Maybe the kid is right, and his ma probably agrees with him. He ain't got much left to learn from his pa any-more, his pa who barely got through the sixth grade, who still drives horses better than he can drive a car, who tries to make up for what he can't do by working harder and longer at what he can.

Persistent feelings of inadequacy smoldered within him, nagging at his conscience during lonely hours, leaving him with an unresolved lump of burden he could not share. Several weeks later he still had not come up with any way to relieve his concern; and the realization of his impotence only compounded his mood.

Then an idea came to him one evening while he was play-ing his fiddle. The kids were sitting around with him; eight-year-old Snooky had asked him to play, then fetched from upstairs the old, black, peeling violin case, extracted the instrument from its protective red paisley bag, and handed him the bow and rosin. He fingered her requested "Three Little Fishies," learned from the radio, and did a bit of "Turkey in the Straw." Bob came in and picked up Elmer Krause's old button accordion and tried to join in playing "Peek-a-boo Waltz," but he couldn't seem to find the right notes. Clarence stopped.

"That's because I'm playing in A," he told the boy. "You

can only play in C on that accordion. Like a C mouth organ."

"Oh?"

"Here, I'll start again, in C this time." Clarence played another chorus of the song, and Bob's reedy melody line sounded right some of the time. He still had not really learned how to get much music out of that squeeze box. Seemed to be concentrating these days on singing in the high school chorus and starting to learn trumpet for the band.

"Pa," the boy said, looking puzzled during a pause, "I still don't really understand about keys. I should be able to play in A on this thing, shouldn't I?"

"Well, you don't have the sharps and flats, there."

"And when I play the scale on this, and then I play the C scale on my trumpet, they're different notes."

"Sure, the accordion scale is in the key of C, and your trumpet's a B-flat instrument, I spose. Any key but C, you have to play sharps or flats. You know, the black keys on the piano."

"I've never . . . it's pretty confusing."

"Well, if we had a piano I could show you."

They talked some more that night about musical concepts, but what stuck with Clarence was the implication of his own statement: "If we had a piano I could show you."

There was lots to show. Music had always been a part of Clarence's life, as natural as eating and sleeping. As a boy he had learned the keyboard from his mother—"Mor," she liked to be called in her native tongue—and she in turn had been taught by her mother back in Norway. His father had liked to fiddle and to dance the jig, and without ever offering individual instruction, he'd assumed his sons would follow suit. Each of the five Amerson boys had grown up learning to play something—piano, fiddle, occasionally a horn or guitar or drums—and before their marriages took them on separate ways, the brothers regularly played for house parties or barn dances. For Clarence, the melodic phrases that often kept running through his mind were reliable companions, always there when he wanted them. Sometimes he made them audible by humming, and occasionally when alone in the fields he might let them break out into full-voiced song. Without many chances anymore to play and sing with others, Clarence contented himself playing his fiddle solo from time to time— lost in his own world, sawing through the old favorites, trying out new melodies heard on the radio or things the kids might bring home. Now Bob seemed to be showing some interest in playing along.

The more Clarence thought about it, the more he felt the lack of a piano; he wanted to hear again its deep accompanying sounds of chords and rhythm; he wanted to demonstrate to his children how music works, how instruments can be played together. He remembered countless occasions of singing around the piano back home, Mor banging out the old hymns, a brother taking a turn at livelier numbers, the harmonizing, the dancing.

He thought of Bob's signs of restlessness. He remembered his own fifteenth year, his need to get out on his own, his brothers' breaking away, the temptations they all had faced. Singing around the piano can't substitute for everything, Mor had once told him, but it might help cut down on running around or too much boozing or chasing skirts. Maybe he was inventing excuses now, he recognized, but for whatever reasons, a piano in the house seemed a good idea.

Bernice agreed. While she seldom participated in homemade music, except for humming to babies in the rocking chair, she thoroughly enjoyed having Clarence limber up the fiddle; they had been avid dancers during the early years. Classified ads of the Watertown daily newspaper sometimes offered used musical instruments. Clarence and Bernice usually got there every month or two, for major trading and to see Clarice. For two weeks they carefully screened the columns of fine print, and finally they spotted what they were looking for:

"For Sale, Storey & Clark upright piano, fair condition, $30."

"Might as well go take a look at it," Bernice urged. "Might as well," Clarence agreed. "We could sell Old Anthrax, ought to bring around thirty dollars. That cow ain't been much for either milk or calves since she was sick."

The next day they drove the thirty miles, and the black-lacquered instrument stood before them tall and shiny in a corner of the strangers' carpeted house. A few ivories were missing and one of the higher keys sometimes stuck, but the piano seemed in tune, and it delivered a fine sound that almost made Clarence dizzy to listen to, thinking about all the beautiful chords waiting inside. They paid five dollars down and told the owner they would be back the following week with the rest of the money. Then they drove over to the big brick home where Clarice worked and walked around to knock at the back door. It was opened presently by a maid in a black dress and white apron—who turned out to be Clarice, her shy and self-conscious smile almost disguised behind that getup. The girl was obviously happy to see them, and there might have been a glistening in the big blue eyes when she looked pained and told them she couldn't come out right now: "We're gettin' ready for a cocktail party here." So they quickly gave her all the family news, including about the piano, which brightened her expression. Clarice declared right then and there that next week she would take a day or two off work so she might ride back home when they came to collect the piano.

Clarence's thoughts remained for hours on this growing-up daughter of his. Such a good girl always, never a complaint or criticism from her, content to learn the old ways through honest work instead of getting caught up in the smart-aleck ideas they seem to teach in high school. Or maybe, he wondered, raising a son is just different from raising a daughter.

A few days later they hooked the four-wheel trailer to the car and hauled bony Old Anthrax to the Swift plant near Watertown. While the check was being processed, they picked up Clarice, and before sundown the trailer was backed with its endgate snug against the east room porch, where Bob and the three little girls waited, eager to ogle this new acquisition.

Clarence gazed with the others for a moment after he opened the endgate. There it stood, erect and darkly mysterious in the fading light, seemingly aloof from the indignity of its temporary confinement within rough boards still streaked with drying cow manure. Clarice and Bob climbed behind Clarence into the box to help shove the heavy instrument along the straw-covered floor and onto the porch cement. Then all of them pushed and lifted and maneuvered its concentrated bulk through the doorway, which was barely wide enough. During one coordinated heave, the piano did get too close to the metal latch, but no one considered important the resulting gouge that chipped the finish. The smaller girls twirled the circular top of the accompanying stool: "Lookit, it goes up an' down!"

Once in place along the far wall, the instrument became a compelling attraction, and the girls had to try out the sound of every key, singly and in varied combinations. At one point Bernice laughed and called out, "Hey—Elaine, Snooky, Jeanie—one at a time!" Bob, more tolerant than usual of his kid sisters' foolishness, nevertheless reminded them that "pianos are for making music, not noise." Clarice, enjoying immersion in family affairs for a change, hung back in her shy manner awhile, then could wait no longer. "I can play 'Peter, Peter, Pumpkin Eater,'" she offered, and after Bob pulled the little girls back, she worked her index fingers on the black keys, right hand crossing over to finish the run.

"All sharps and flats," Bob observed. "Where'd you learn that?"

"They had a piano where I worked last year. I know the top part of 'Chopsticks,' too." Her two fingers went to work again, this time on the white keys.

Bob looked around at Clarence, still standing back. "Do you know the bottom part, Pa?"

"Oh, used to play it, years ago."

"Show us how!"

"Maybe after supper. We better get at the chores now." The stock would be getting hungry, true enough. But Clarence welcomed the delay. A little more time to savor the moment, to anticipate the pleasure. And then have the rest of the evening for making music. Through the next two hours or more—doing barn-cleaning that had been postponed from the morning, feeding all the stock, bedding them down; through the milking and getting skim milk back to the calves, then a hurried supper that everybody was too excited to do much more than nibble at—melodies and chords nearly forgotten came coursing through his consciousness. By the time he finished his piece of spice cake, only Bernice remained with him at the kitchen table. From the east room reverberated a cacophony of miscellaneous tinkles and bass bongs as small hands experimented at the keyboard. Presently Snooky poked her excited face around the door. "C'mon, Pa! Clarice's been practicin'. You can play the bottom part with her now!"

He let Snooky lead him by the hand into the east room. At the piano Clarice and Elaine were giving the beaming Jeanie her turn at the fun, twirling her around and around on the stool. They stopped and made way for him.

"Here, Pa, you sit down." Elaine, at ten, liked to take

charge of arrangements. "Clarice says she can stand up and play."

"Fine," he said. "Hafta turn the stool all the way down for me, I guess."

Clarice's luminescent blue eyes flashed at him. "I'll turn it down for you." Her voice and manner always reminded him of her mother, and also of Mor, whose brown-toned portrait had graced the piano back home. Clarence felt a wave of uncertainty: how many old memories could he handle? The room was quiet; eyes fastened upon him from all directions as he straddled the stool and seated himself. It was like a formal performance almost—like the time Mor had driven him and two brothers by horse and buggy the five miles into town to hear an itinerant piano player, the man in a long coat who came onto the school stage and made sounds of music he had never heard before or since.

But that was then, he brought himself up. "Let's see now, 'Chopsticks,' I b'lieve we play that in C, with these two chords, ain't it?" He tried them tentatively against Clarice's two-fingered notes. "Okay, let's go," he nodded at her, and he followed her steady waltz rhythm through the three versions she knew. Their audience applauded, and Clarice, less accustomed than he, even, to spotlight attention, wore a self-conscious smile as she retreated to a spot at the edge of the group. Bob came forward.

"Pa, can you show about different keys now, like you said once?"

The kid may be asking for more than I can give him, Clarence thought.

"Well, now, there's a lot about music I don't know, but I can tell you a few things, I guess."

"Okay. I know you can play the scale on these eight white keys, starting here." He laid his finger on middle C and an octave higher.

"Yah, that's right. Now here's the scale in G, with this one note sharp." He used all five fingers to run up and down the scale. "And here's F, with another black note, B-flat here. Or D, with two black notes, two sharps—see?"

Bob emulated his father's fingering, trying out the scales. "What about chords?" he asked then.

"Easy to learn," Clarence said. "For most songs you only have to know three chords in whatever key you play in. If you're in C, you have the C chord, these three notes; and the F chord here; then up to G chord, moving all three fingers up one key; and then back again to C, like this." He demonstrated chording for "Little Brown Jug," singing out the words, his left hand thumping bass, his right the three harmonizing notes for each chord. "See," he finished, "you change when it sounds right."

"Boy, that's really neat!" The boy was clearly impressed. "I can learn that! Show us some more stuff?"

Clarence turned to place both hands on the keyboard once again and without thinking about it fingered several warm-up chords to give himself time to decide what to play next. He could not help staring, as if mesmerized, at his big hands there at the end of his blue shirtsleeves—the heavy, scarred knuckles, those thick and callused fingers that never seemed to get clean anymore. For a moment he felt the sensation that the hands were almost detached, independent from the rest of him. He had not been quite sure, before, whether he would really be able to remember how to translate the melodies from his head into audible music, through his fingers and into the keys; but now it seemed that those clumsy-looking hands of his possessed memory and agility of their own. They moved on and up and around, seemingly remembering everything they had ever known.

As Clarence played, it was as if the last twenty years of piano abstinence had been magically wiped away, a mere rest stop between numbers. He went from "My Wild Irish Rose" to "Let Me Call You Sweetheart" to "Over the Waves" to "Red Wing." One piece recalled another, and for nearly an hour he worked the keyboard, immersed in the sounds, nearly oblivious to his enchanted audience, sometimes following the melody with his right hand, occasionally singing out the chorus and accompanying his voice with crashing chords and deep basses and then ending a piece with soft treble chimes. All his mother had ever tried to teach him, plus what he had later learned during youthful years with his brothers' band, seemed to have been waiting to come out; somehow those hard and grimy fingers of his knew where to look for that distant note, how to embellish a chord change with a provocative bass run, when to punch fortissimo, and when to let placid harmonies carry the mood. Finally, tiring, he became more aware again of the others, and gesturing to them with eyes and head, he beckoned them to gather around to sing along as he finished up with "Good Night Ladies" and "Show Me the Way to Go Home." Everybody laughed and cheered and clapped. "More, more!" Snooky shouted out.

"Naw," he protested, trying not to look too pleased, "that's about enough. It must be time for Cedric Adams, anyway." He and Bernice seldom missed the ten-o'clock news on WCCO. She hurried the three young girls out to get ready for bed. Clarice and Bob remained side-by-side on the couch. The girl wore that shy smile again—her grandmother's smile when she was showing pride and pleasure. Bob regarded him directly, unblinking: Clarence had not seen quite this expression before in the boy, and he had to look away. He rotated on the stool slightly to the left so he could pay attention to hoisting an ankle over one knee and untying the lace of his heavy shoe.

"Pa," the boy's subdued voice came from the side, "I

never knew you could play the piano like that."

Clarence dropped his shoe and pulled at his damp sock without looking up. "Well, we never had a piano before." And maybe, he told himself, I should have been better about teaching you kids things like this long before now.

"It's really interesting, how you can do a song in different keys. I don't know why they don't teach us that in high school chorus or band."

Clarice cocked an eye at her brother. "Maybe you can learn *some* things in high school, but not everything," she said.

Her remark struck Clarence as wise and clever, and he tried to hide his grin. He released his second shoe, and after the two youngsters left to join Bernice listening to the radio, he spent some time alone rubbing his foot gently, conscious of how good he felt. He thought again about his daughter's words, and of her grandmother. Mor might have put it her own way: a piano may not be everything, but it's something.

WATER WITCH

Bernice
1940

Bernice stood at the kitchen window, her fingertips pushing aside the red and green of her geraniums, watching the men work at the well. It seemed a strange sight. The high rigging of Pete Timmer's repair truck loomed like some prehistoric monster and blocked her view from the barnyard across green fields to the horizon of purple prairies to the west.

The men had said at the dinner table that they thought the new pipe and rods would be in by four or five, in time to pump enough water for the cows when they came home tonight from the dry pasture. Water had always been a problem on this place. They knew before they moved here six years ago that the well near the barn, 230 feet deep, would mean heavy pumping. Then they found what came trickling up at the stock tank unfit for human consumption. The bitter stuff would do for livestock, Bernice and Clarence agreed, but softer, sweeter water from somewhere else would be needed for household use.

They made do. Rainwater dipped from a deep cistern

under the house served for washing, but sometimes dead mice floated in the amber bucketful hauled up by rope from that dark place. Their early attempts to locate another vein for drinking water had produced nothing. Only one alternative remained: farms within a mile distant had shallow wells from which clear, good-tasting water came after a few strokes of the hand pumps. These neighbors had assured them right off that they were welcome to help themselves. The idea made Bernice uncomfortable—like borrowing money and never paying it back. But the task of hauling water had by now become another routine. Every couple of days year-round, someone went to fetch water, in the Model A when possible or on the stoneboat behind horses during blizzards. The old ten-gallon cream can stood there against the kitchen wall, side handles akimbo as if impatient for attention, reminding Bernice that again this afternoon somebody would have to run to the neighbors' for a fresh supply.

Water, she thought—so basic to every living thing. Every hill of corn, every blade of grass, all the birds in the air, the stock in the pasture—all of us in Nature's great scheme, we need water. But sometimes you have to help Nature along, to reach out beyond natural events to make things happen.

Abruptly, she shook her head and ran a hand through her short, curly brown hair. "I must have water on the brain," she said, half-aloud. She busied herself around the kitchen, but a growing notion in her head would not go away. Somehow, it seemed up to her to make something happen. Today. She wheeled away from the window and tossed her flour-dusted apron over the back of a chair on her way out the kitchen door.

At the well, Clarence had the ancient, greasy engine popping. She watched him ease the belt over the pulley. Pumpjack gears growled as parallel upright slats started the pump with a graceful, undulating movement. He hunched

288 From the Hidewood

over the engine's dark flywheels for a moment, ready to yank the belt off again should anything go wrong; his glances alternated between the pump and the well-digger. Big Pete Timmer—they had known the Timmer family years before the move—stood over the tank, his thick, rust-stained arms folded over the beer belly that strained the bib of his striped overalls. His small and unblinking eyes focused on the spout. He gave Bernice a quick sidewise glance, hardly moving the denim engineer's cap cocked on his sweating, oversized head. Clarence, his faded blue shirt and overalls and even his floppy straw hat similarly smeared with rust and grease, joined Pete and Bernice at the dry tank's rim. Engine fumes mixed with the musty odor of tank moss. The three of them stood there listening to the persistent staccato of the engine and a metallic groan of pumpjack gears. Nothing was coming out of the spout.

Afternoon sunshine reflected into Bernice's glasses, and the wind played with one of her short curls. She shaded her eyes and searched their faces. Clarence's Nordic features as usual revealed little; the intense way Pete watched the pipe probably meant he had his private doubts about the water.

"You think it's fixed all right?" She had to shout over the noise of the machines.

Pete lifted his glance to her again. When he finally spoke, it sounded like he didn't want to show any worry. "Ah well, y'know, sometimes it takes a while for the cylinder leathers to start drawin'. We put it together right. It's workin', she'll come, pretty sure." His reedy voice always sounded unexpectedly high-pitched, coming from such a big man.

Clarence nodded. "Yah, 230 feet. Long way to bring it up."

Then she saw that the flow had sneaked up on them under cover of the engine noise while they talked. Rusty liquid dribbled from the spout, splashed inaudibly on the dry tank bottom, and began to spread in a dark circle, as if wanting to make the point about its unpredictable nature, she thought.

Pete's big smile pushed into his round cheeks. He shared a triumphant nod with Clarence as they all moved away from the pump. "Okay, okay! That'll clear up in a few minutes. You'll have plenty water 'fore the cows come home!"

"We'd-a been in bad shape without it," Clarence said. The well had stopped working yesterday morning, and there had barely been enough water in the tank for the stock last night. Clarence had made three extra water-hauling trips to Schleuters' that morning to take care of the hogs and chickens, but with no water left in the pasture sloughs, the cattle and horses had so far gone without, and it was a warm day.

Bernice saw her opening, and jumped in.

"Y'know, what we really need around here is that *second* well—so there wouldn't be such an emergency every time something goes wrong with this one."

The men looked at each other, and Clarence started to say something, but Pete's loud tenor interrupted.

"Hell, Bernice, we been through all that before, ain't we?"

"Well, we been through it, all right. But maybe we should try again."

She could see that Pete was doing his best not to let exasperation show. He gestured with both huge hands, as if getting ready to brag about a fish that got away. "Now, you 'member, right after you moved on this place, I come over like you ast me, and we spent the better part of a day tryin' t'dig you a shallow well. Right?" He had moved closer to her, and his beefy six-foot-four frame blocked out half of the summer sky. He wasn't really trying to bully her, she knew, but Pete held strong opinions on most things and had his own way of expressing them.

"That's right, sure," she said. "But—"

"And then, you 'member, too, we talked to those old-timers around the neighborhood, and they told us that folks on this place over the past forty years been tryin' t'find good water, and none t'be had. Ain't that right, Clarence?"

"Well yah . . ." Arguments always made Clarence uncomfortable, especially if he had to choose sides for or against Bernice. But she knew that Pete had it right: old neighbors had told them that all efforts over the years had failed to find more water.

"Does seem funny, though," Bernice insisted. "Both Schleuters and Roeckers have good water from shallow wells." Her own words made her anger rise. "We been haulin' it from them for years. And they're uphill from here—those veins must run through this farm someplace!"

Pete glared. Plain to see, he did not like to have his expertise questioned by anybody, least of all a woman. "Well, the uphill business," he said, "that don't have nothin' t'do with how you find water. It's been tried on this place, over and over. Maybe you just oughta feel lucky you got yourselves one good well here, and workin' right, too." He gestured toward the filling tank and glanced around his truck at the tools to be loaded before he left. But Bernice's gaze held his bleary blue eyes for a last moment, and she said what had been on her mind all afternoon:

"Maybe you should try to witch it."

Pete did a double take: "What?"

"Witch for the water. People do."

He shot a wide-eyed look at Clarence, then at her. "You mean, walk around with a piece of willow branch or somethin'?"

"You never dug a well by witchin'?" She remained calm.

"Hell no, I ain't, and I ain't about t'start, neither. Don't believe in it." His voice rose still higher. "What's more, I don't ask the Sioux Indian medicine man t'beat the drums and make rain, and I don't pray for miracles at church Sundays." He turned to pick up two heavy pipe wrenches and tossed them into his truck with a ringing clang that hurt the ears. "Shit, Bernice," the big man said then. "I'm just a well-digger, not no goddam magician. Know what I mean?"

She took a breath. "Yeah," she said. "I guess."

Clarence's half-grin hinted at both amusement and relief, but he said no more. The two men finished loading the truck, and Bernice walked slowly back to the house.

She had seen it once, as a girl: a mysterious, dark-clad man who called himself a dowser, moving step by slow step across a neighbor's farmyard, the forked willow wand held before him in stiffly outstretched arms. Then the pointed end seemed to pull downward, so strongly that some bark twisted off the willow in the stranger's bony fists. And they found water there. No one seemed to have an explanation for it. She gave long thought to all this before falling asleep that night, and her startling conclusion made her sit up in bed. "I can do it, too," she told herself. "I can feel it in my bones."

She had no reason to suppose that magical powers might somehow be summoned. Even as a child she'd never believed in fairy tales. Nor would she look for biblical miracles, for she had never established such direct, personal ties to God. All she had were her hunches. She took occasional teasing from the family for basing decisions on "a little bird told me," or for feeling matters "in my bones," but never mind. When Sonny had those warts on his arm last year, he had snickered, too, as she rubbed a rotting potato on them, but after she buried the potato in the garden the warts went away—and the potato even grew a plant.

No willow trees were left on this farm anymore, she knew, and it might be hard to find one even along the Hidewood Creek. She had once heard of a dowser who used a metal rod, so she decided to try that, if she could locate something around the place. Next morning, her chickens fed and watered, she poked around in back of the henhouse and granary, where abandoned machinery rusted among the tall ragweeds. Some of the levers and angle irons might have served as divining rods, she thought, but they would be impossible to get at without the right wrenches. Loose pieces that she located in Clarence's pile of scrap metal seemed too long or too short or too spindly. She had nearly given up when, on her way back toward the house, she spotted the obvious, logical choice. Long and dark and strong, it leaned against the granary wall alongside some fencing tools: the crowbar. It was almost as long as she was tall. She took it in both hands, spread wide. Such weight concentrated in that dark steel! She found the balance point with her right hand, and raised her thumb to let the heavy bar hang level in the hook of her four fingers, the thicker wedged head of the rod pointing ahead of her. It resembled a giant needle on a compass, like those she'd been amused by in the kids' pencil sharpeners—simple, toylike, yet mysterious in the way it could find the north no matter which way the pencil sharpener might be turned. Could this huge metal needle, heavy in her hand, have the same kind of power? Would it find water only if pointing north?

Her first steps led her away from the granary toward the barn. She focused on the wedged tip of the bar, borne before her. At first, she noticed mainly a vague, slow movement, while the cracked gray leather of her shoe tips methodically pushed her ahead. Soon she became intensely aware of every detail that passed through her field of vision, bits of history from other times on this place: oat hulls that had spilled from grain sacks decayed in the dust next to the gray-and-white of chicken droppings; bits of corncobs from years gone by, fragmented into smaller pieces and returning to the soil, ashes to ashes; a variety of bent and rusted nails, all that remained from someone's building efforts; and odd pieces of metal from machines long since gone.

She kept moving in slow, even paces. She lost track of time, but it could have been only a few minutes so far, with no hint of reaction from the bar that hung in balance, heavy and inert. Her hand, her whole arm, began to ache. She passed over dried cornstalks from last year's fodder stack, through a patch of round-leaf weed-grass that grew wild everywhere. She made several methodical rounds to cover the area thoroughly, feeling uncertainty starting to gnaw at her. "Can't expect to find a needle in the haystack right away," she muttered, and kept concentrating on the big, black needle still lifeless in her hand. She wondered again whether she had to point north to make it work.

From where she stood, straight north would take her close to the house. She moved in that direction, and below her steady gaze ancient fragments of earth mixed with recent human throwaways—a short length of baling wire, a lost button, remnants of a bone left from the dog's table scraps. Nearing the kitchen window, she looked up just long enough to view her geraniums from the outside, and at first she thought that her forward motion must have caught the pointed tip of the rod in a high-growing weed. She instinctively stopped and jerked her eyes back to the rod. A split second later, she knew something was happening. No vine, nor anything visible, touched the rod tip, and yet it pulled down, down, in her hand. She felt her stomach knot, her scalp tingle. A backward step seemed to release the pull; reentering the spot, she again felt the forceful tug, and the wedged point dipped out of balance. She dug her shoe into the dust to mark the spot and approached it again from various directions. Her tingling sensation grew with the realization that pointing north had nothing to do with it. The power resided there in her hand, and it was completely different from the little spindly toy compass on a pencil sharpener.

She knelt to lay the heavy rod on the ground, its point at her shoe-mark. She felt a distinct stiffness in her arm. She wiped her forehead with the back of her hand. Her breathing returned to normal.

She did have the power. Not very mysterious, after all—nearly as simple as a rotten potato burying warts. Funny, she thought, how these things seem to work for some people and not for others. She marked the spot by pounding a short stick into the ground, and that evening, after Clarence got the horses unhitched from the cultivator, she told him about it.

"You sure?" he squinted at her from under his straw hat. "Right over there by the house?"

"Well, it drew down on the crowbar, good and strong."

"Never heard about anybody with a crowbar. I thought you was sposed to use a willow wand."

"Iron rods work too, they say. Did for me, anyway. I think we should dig there, see what happens."

Clarence was watching his thirsty horses, still at the half-filled water tank. "Think so? I could talk about it with Pete."

She knew he'd say something like that. "Oh—let's get somebody else," she said. "Pete prob'ly wouldn't come anyway; he already told us that."

"Yah, I spose." He started following his horses toward the barn and called over his shoulder, "Fella over by Kranzburg got a drillin' rig, maybe you could get him."

She did. Two weeks later, the man arrived with his machinery and stopped at the house to ask where they wanted him to set up. She walked him around the corner to the spot she'd marked with the wooden stake.

"Here? Right on this spot?" he had to ask. "What makes you think there might be a vein under here?"

She had never dealt directly with well-diggers outside of

Pete and couldn't be sure they didn't all feel the same about witching for water. No sense in getting him all riled up. "Our neighbors up the road," she said. "They have a good well next to the house. We thought we might try it here. To start with, anyhow."

He looked at her for a minute, and there might have been the trace of a little grin there. But he merely nodded and moved his truck into position. Bernice knew he would not object; the deeper he dug, the more he would charge.

She returned to her kitchen. At first she couldn't stay away from the window. After a few minutes, the fellow had his engine running to power the drill. She watched him standing over the revolving mechanism, one mud-stained, heavy shoe propped on the framework base as he leaned over to check what was coming up. For the first time since the crowbar pulled down, she felt doubts begin to assail her. What right did she have to risk hard-to-come-by cash for a notion as wild as this? Maybe something other than water had pulled on the crowbar. Even if there was a vein down there, what if he had to dig 230 feet and then found nothing but the same, awful-tasting stuff that came up at the other well? She turned away and, to keep herself occupied, began to mix dough for a batch of bread.

Halfway through the first kneading, she heard a shout over the racket of the drilling rig outside. She hurried back to the window. The fellow was yelling for her to come and look. He held wet mud in both hands.

He had hit it about forty feet down. By nightfall he had a sand pipe in, pipes tightened together, and a hand pump working. The water came up clear and sweet, as good as any they'd been hauling from the neighbors all these years.

The whole family celebrated for weeks. All the cold, fresh drinking water they could ever want, and right outside the door—no more hauling for anybody! An aura of mystery and power surrounded the well's discoverer: Clarence kept referring with rare public pride to "Bernice's well," and Bob seemed to do as he was told with a new willingness. Some of the neighbors teased her about "having our own witch right here in the Hidewood," but behind their remarks lay respect.

Bernice felt pleased with herself on the achievement, but her satisfaction seemed somehow incomplete. Then one day late that summer, while bent in her garden to select tomatoes and carrots for dinner, she watched Pete Timmer's rusty green truck turn into the driveway. Clarence and Bob were in the field, the three girls playing somewhere. She toted her vegetable basket back around to the front of the house, where dust was settling around Pete as he descended from the cab.

"Hullo there, Bernice," he rasped out, sounding cheerful. "Just in the neighborhood. Thought I'd stop by."

She nodded. "How're you? How's your ma?"

"Oh, fine. Say, uh, I hear you witched yourself a new well. Thought maybe I could have a look. Didja hafta go pretty deep?"

"No, just forty feet." They walked together to where the new black pump stood erect on its low platform.

"I'll be damned," the big man said. "Right next t'the house, too! Whatja use, twig from a willow?"

"Naw." She knew this was going to sound ridiculous to him, but she managed to say it without laughing. "A crowbar."

"Crowbar!" It took a while for this to sink in. Pete wagged his big head and mouthed the word to himself as he reached for the pump handle. "Easy pumpin', all right. An' good water, huh?"

"Try it out yourself," she said, releasing the tin cup from its hook. Pete let a couple of strokes splash, then caught a cupful and took a long swig.

He gave a reedy "ah-h-h" as he nodded at her. "Only thing better'n that is a cold glass of beer, and Bernice, I'll buy you one next time you come t'town." He replaced the tin cup and gave her one of his sidewise looks. "I never thought you could do it."

"You never know." Bernice knew she was smiling now.

"Say, listen." Pete bent toward her confidentially, almost whispering. "Tell me how . . . how you go at it, eh?" A kind of sparkle shone behind the bleariness of his eyes.

"What you want to know?"

"Well, I mean, d'ya hafta say some special magic words, or sort of pray, or what? You can tell me, I know how to keep secrets about findin' water."

"I thought you said you didn't believe in this stuff."

"Yeah, well, I did say that, and I don't, I didn't—I tried witchin' years ago with a willow wand and a iron rod, too, and nothin' happened. So I never thought there was much to it. Till now." His beefy hand gestured toward the pump.

"Well, Pete." She found all this hard to put into words. "There really *ain't* so much to it, at that. It's just . . . it's kind of like a talent. You know how some people can sing pretty, or draw pictures? Guess it turns out that I have this talent to witch water. Lots of other people prob'ly can, too."

The big man looked as sad as a scolded dog. After a moment he blinked at her twice, and his huge head wagged slowly, reluctant to accept the truth of it. "Not me, though. Not me. Sure wish I could." Then he straightened himself up. "Hell," he grinned, "I can't sing or draw pictures, neither."

"You sure know how to dig wells, though. Can't have everything."

"Spose not." Pete glanced up at the sun and moved toward his truck. "I better get back at it, I guess."

"Say hello to your mother for me."

His ruddy cheeks widened in the rusty green cab window. "Sure will."

She watched the rig disappear out the driveway. From

her garden basket she chose a small carrot and, working the pump handle, held it in the clear, cold stream. Then, one hand still resting on the wet spout, she crunched a first bite and took a moment to survey the panorama to the west, all the way from the purple horizon to the road just beyond the pasture, where Pete's dust cloud disappeared behind the hill. No carrot ever tasted better than this.

CAR-CRAZY

Bob
1941

It was a warm, June Saturday night in town. Along the one block of business district sidewalk, parked cars slanted, crowded nose-first into the curb. Dried mud on most of the fenders and wheels attested to farm families come to town for the trading and to take part in the main social event of the week.

This day, farmers had left their fields well before normal quitting time. The kids had lent extra energies to getting chores done early. Getting to town before others meant finding a good parking space where mothers, after the trading was done, could sit in front seats to tend small children. They might even enjoy a rare ice cream cone. They would have an hour or two to watch the people go by: farmers in new striped overalls and clean shirts and Sunday straw hats; other women, each with a baby on one hip and on the other a bag, perhaps of prized beauty notions from the drugstore; neighbors who seldom saw each other during the work week, stopping to chat. Other passing faces required guessing games. This was especially true for the two or three town ladies in the grandstand seats of their fancier, cleaner town cars, which their banker or store-owner husbands had driven downtown for them really early. But visible town people, except for those who worked in the stores, were few. On Saturday night, Main Street belonged to the folks from the country. Their street, their parade.

Teenage girls in light summer dresses did make a kind of circulating parade of it. Groups of them had banded together, giggling and trying to look sophisticated and charming as they kept surreptitious watch for boys along their endless sidewalk rounds. Small boys, too, sporting dress shirts and good pants, moved in clusters here and there. Boys in their teens loitered, dividing their attention between the girls on the sidewalks and the mechanized units of the procession on display in the street—actually, the widened block of Highway 77 that ran through town. That Saturday night, as all summer Saturday nights, six or eight shining, pampered vehicles of varying makes and ages had come to town—like their proud, young owners, all dressed up and washed behind the ears. They cruised slowly up the block. Their drivers, solitary or accompanied, expected to see and be seen. They made their U-turns at the intersection, purred their fine-tuned engines casually down the other side of the street to the end of the block, and repeated the maneuver.

Some of the cars, carrying young people with a more purposeful agenda, might stop eventually in front of Paulson's Drug. Good-time girls in the back laughed too loudly and exhibited lighted cigarettes as they waited for one of the guys to come out with a bottle-shaped brown bag. Then they took one more U-turn and headed north to the dance at Tunerville.

For Bob, about to turn sixteen and soon a senior in high school, Saturday nights like this brought confused frustration.

He felt caught between his two worlds—country ways versus the town life that he had known for three years now. Most of his friends from school were town boys, who didn't seem to figure in the Saturday night gatherings. Why should they, he reminded himself; they could get together anytime during the week. Sometimes he did recognize a face behind a steering wheel. This night, as he came out of the Gamble Store where he had bought a box of .22 shorts for gopher hunting with Bert, he took a closer look. He recognized both cars idling in front of the drug store across the street. The new '41 Ford with the spotlight belonged to those two good-looking farm boys from someplace east of town; they had a reputation as regular Tunerville dancers. The driver of the '39 Ford he identified as one of the Holt boys, graduated a couple years earlier. Girls were climbing into his car. "There'll be a hot time in the old town tonight," he heard the old song within his head. Then he walked on.

Ma and eight-year-old Jeanie occupied the front seat of the "new" family car. The '37 V-8 acquired the year before was a great improvement and certainly less embarrassing than the old rattletrap Model A. But it still was only another farmer car, needing a wash.

"Where's the rest?" he asked through the open window.

"Your father was looking for you," Ma said. "Took the kerosene can, maybe to Gamble's."

"Didn't see him in there." Bob fingered the concentrated weight of rifle cartridges in his pocket. "I didn't see Bert in town either, did you?" For Bob, Bert had always been more of a senior play partner than an uncle. Now twenty-one, he worked out at a farm across Hidewood Creek and had had his own car for a couple of years.

"No," Ma replied. "Maybe went to Estelline or Watertown." Bob nodded; when you're twenty-one you could do things that seemed impossible at fifteen or sixteen. She added: "The Koppman boys went to the show. I thought you was going, too."

"Naah. Hopalong Cassidy again. Tiresome." A glance at the Majestic showed its lights were off, the second show about over. The better movies came on Sunday nights, if you could get to town. "Guess I'll try a game of pool."

On the sidewalk he met Elaine and Snooky, on parade in the company of Lois Krause and Marjorie Jorvig, their two seventh-grade classmates from the one-room school. They gave him little attention and would keep orbiting until their mothers called them to the cars. Inside Rudy's, under the illuminated Grain Belt Beer sign, he was surprised when his eyes adjusted to see his father's lean figure at the bar. Pa looked younger with his hat pushed back on his head, gesturing with a cigar in one hand as he made a point to Elmer Krause, like an illustration of some politician in a *Saturday Evening Post* story. Bob paused, hesitating to interrupt. He and his father had never been in the pool hall at the same time before, and the moment seemed at first tender, then ironic. "Farmer Pa's weekly ten minutes of leisure time," he imagined a caption for the school paper. When Elmer spotted him, he joined them at the bar, aware that he was too young to be offered a beer. Right away Pa seemed in a hurry, downed his glass, tossed the cigar into a spitoon, and picked up the filled kerosene can he had set at his feet.

"Here," he said, "purt-near eleven. You take this to the car, I'll get the groceries from the Jew-store."

On the sidewalk again, Bob thought how strange, they got a sign painted on the store side a half-block long, "The *New* Store." Still everybody called it the Jew-store. Owners must be Jewish; did they name it New Store to rhyme on purpose? If they were the only people of that religion in town, did they feel any anti-Jewish prejudice, like you read about in big cities? How would the town react to a Negro family, like that carful he saw on the road to Watertown sometimes, the father wearing glasses and smoking a pipe like any farmer might? He wondered whether he should follow up on such questions in sociology class when school started again in the fall.

Pa had never cared much about cars, and Bob was by now the driver whenever the whole family went somewhere. On the graveled highway, he clicked on the radio Bert had found and installed for them; with the battered dial clamped to the steering post, it wasn't the same as a factory-built accessory, but it was a car radio. The Watertown station had a program of Glenn Miller records, and by the time the Ford splashed through the last puddle near Schleuters', "Elmer's Tune" was playing. It always made him think of the little button accordion that Elmer Krause had lent him. The others scrambled out, and Pa lifted from the trunk the double egg-case filled with groceries. "You bring in the kerosene when you come," he called back. "Careful you don't run the battery down."

Hands on the wheel, he luxuriated in isolation, listening to the music, appreciating the vastness of the starry sky, inhaling the car smells of oil fumes and dust and upholstery that since childhood had stimulated his imagination, satisfied his fantasy. A car. Driving a car. An absolute, basic necessity for a guy stuck out on a farm, to take you wherever you want to go. Like Bert, now that he had that neat Model A roadster, roaming all around the countryside. And the guys cruising up and down Main Street in their own personally adapted chariots, some of them attracting good-looking girls, too, taking them to the dance at Tunerville. Right this minute those guys were out on the dance floor holding sweater-girls in their arms like in the movies; and at intermission there'd be necking and maybe some boozing too and who knows what else going on out in the parked cars in the dark. Maybe he was not yet ready for all that stuff, he admitted. But something was wrong with the situation—nearly sixteen, and good little Sonny-boy went home from town Saturday night with mama and papa and his kid sisters.

There was only one answer, and Bert had led the way. A car of his own. Somehow.

He turned off the radio and left his sanctuary. While relieving himself against the lilac bush, he studied the glittering skies once again, trying to locate the North Star and settling on a brighter light that he thought might be Venus. In his head began another tune, and the words came clear: "When You Wish upon a Star . . ." Maybe that is what he had done, at that. The song was still there as he climbed the dark stairs and waited for sleep.

Bert drove in about midmorning the next day for his regular Sunday time with family. Ma made him some coffee and pancakes. Bob, as always, just enjoyed Bert's being around, with his knowledge and experience, his lanky frame and wavy red hair, his witty remarks when he was not being serious. Then the two guys drove both cars down to Vernon's slough, where deep rainwater was usually available for car washing. Bob eyed the roadster with envious eyes: the new tan paint job, already carefully waxed and buffed to a shine, the rumble seat and little round platforms on the rear fenders for passengers to step on, the sportiness of open sides and angled cloth top that folded down in a second. Bert had his rifle with him, and along with washing and painting gear they had tossed in an empty tin can for target practice later, in case gophers were uncooperative.

Since the roadster was already clean, they first washed the dried mud off the V-8, then worked at Bert's wheels with damp rags. He wanted to paint the black wire spokes and rims red, to "doll her up a little," as he put it. Bob, who had a steady hand with a paintbrush, was entrusted with the rubberized paint for white sidewall tires, where the outside edges had to be laid on sharp and even.

While working, they of course talked—about everything. About the movie Bert had just seen in Watertown; about his trip to Iowa the week before to visit Bub, newly married to a girl from across Hidewood Creek; about other relatives. Even, vaguely, about the war in Europe, always in the paper those days. And they got to speculating about various neighborhood girls. Bert had been a prime source of knowledge about the facts of life; his understanding of those things, like his knowledge about cars, seemed total, infinite. That afternoon, Bob confided his wish for a car of his own sometime soon.

The redheaded source did not fail him. Or maybe it was the lucky star he'd wished upon last night. Whatever, Bert came up with a valuable insight and a brilliant suggestion.

"You know," he said, pale blue eyes looking off into the distance, "when I was in Ioway last week, Bub told me he might be drafted pretty soon. If he leaves, he'll want to sell that Model A of his."

Bob's paintbrush stopped in mid-air, and white spots dribbled onto the bent grass near the tire. But he did not want to reveal too much excitement.

"No shit," he said to his uncle, man-to-man. "I didn't think he'd be drafted."

"Ain't surprisin'. I'm 1-A too, far as that goes."

"Well, guess we'll have to ask him about that Model A."

It worked out. Letters confirmed that Bub really was being drafted, like so many others, and he would sell his car for thirty-five dollars. Bob had no real savings of his own, but he made the case for a family investment. He shared his calculations one evening with his mother at the kitchen table.

"Look. Last year I drove the V-8 to school once in a while. Fine, but it left you without a car at home all day. If we"— first personal plural, more convincing—"had that Model A for me, I could drive in every day during good weather this fall, right?"

"I spose."

"Now, we pay three-fifty a week for my room and board at Kallemeyn's. If I drive just ten weeks, the car is paid for!"

His mother nodded. He gave her the clincher: "And I could help with the chores mornings and nights." It was almost painful to hear himself utter the words, but it would be worth it.

"Well, nights, anyway," his mother agreed. "You don't get up early enough to help much mornings, even on weekends."

This embarrassing truth did not keep the deal from going through, and two weeks later the Ford was on the place. Official regulations could be ignored, for the moment; they left the Iowa plates on instead of paying to register for new tags, and the state did not require a driver's license. Bob had a car of his own, and he was ready to go.

True, it was not much of a car. A '29 Model A coach, faded gray, could not compare with Bert's snappy roadster. But after a brief inspection, Bert pronounced the basics okay: "No knocks in the motor, tires good tread yet, runs smooth." And it would not look so ordinary once Bob added personal styling touches.

He started immediately with what he could afford. First, at the Montgomery Ward basement in Watertown, where he and Bert over the years had bought car stuff, he acquired enough paint to convert the dull gray to shiny black. The wheels became bright red, with white sidewall tires, like Bert's. Then he found a chromium mirror to clamp outside the driver's window and a marble green-and-white gearshift knob to substitute for the plain black ball from the factory. Small bolts with jeweled reflectors now held the old license plates—red jewels to the rear, green on the front. A pair of black rubber mudguards at the rear fenders added a lower, more powerful look. When he ran low on cash, he invented elegance, fastening with twisted wire a cast-iron, chromium-plated, streamlined greyhound sculpture broken off a '34 Ford radiator cap—Bert had found it somewhere and gave it to him—onto his Model A radiator cap. He frequently stood back to admire his work and was amazed at how his attentions had changed the car's character. And he was just getting started.

A few dollars earned from helping neighbor Knutson hay alfalfa went directly into the accessories fund. A steering knob, matching the color of the new gearshift, clamped to the upper right of the wheel, for turning fast corners. Chromium visors arched over each headlamp, with built-in, jeweled detectors to let you know when the lights were on. He applied more paint, silver this time, to effect a deluxe-model look around the windshield and back-window frames and to add an angled, streamlining design to the black side-ventilation slots on the hood. In Watertown he stimulated his imagination, wandering through Wexler's Auto Parts, a trea-sury maze of bits and pieces from hundreds of old or wrecked cars, some of them expensive models. He took home seven small auxiliary lamps. Two of them he bolted atop the front fenders (some expensive cars came from the factory thus equipped), another pair just below the windshield corners to serve as dressy parking lights that plain old '29 Model A coaches were never meant to wear. While he was at it, he installed the three smallest lamps on the windshield visor. He hooked all of these to a switch and a live wire, and if he want-ed to, he could light up brighter than the Majestic Theatre.

Then he started looking in stores and mail-order catalogs at illuminated fender guides that clamped above the front wheels, and elegant fog lamps for the front bumper, and a spotlight that would mount on the driver's side—all too costly just then. But he couldn't resist a set of blue trumpet horns that would look snazzy out front on the bar between the headlamps, and whose musical blast would command more respect than the old ah-ooga contraption Henry Ford put on at the factory.

In the process of all this personal restyling, his thoughts tended to linger on cars and on why he had always liked everything about them. One Sunday morning, alone at the slough—Bert was away, visiting friends in Iowa, he said— after washing and waxing the Model A, he tinkered with the carburetor idling jet, as Bert had often showed him, and tuned the motor so that with the spark and gas levers pushed all the way up, she idled just right: taTAtata, taTAtata, smooth and even. It was so satisfying that he backed away and sat on a grassy clump just to listen and look. The Model A had become a thing of beauty. Then the realization came to him that without the influence of his youngest uncle over the years—all his life, in fact—he really wouldn't have known much about cars, nor about the accessories that in Bert's car world added such style.

The even idling of his motor provided background music to his concentration, for the first time, on all he could remember about this person who had been so important to him. He recalled the car games the two of them played Overhome, Bert maybe ten, he tagging along about five, rolling buggy wheels and metal rims and discarded car tires around the yard. Each hoop would represent a specific, out-of-reach make—Packard, Auburn, Pierce-Arrow—and each tree-stop a gas station or a neighbor's place. Overhome, he and Bert could spend hours kneeling in the grasses of the nearby high-

way's shallow ditches, identifying cars as they approached—
"a '29 Essex! '31 Chevy! '27 Whippet!"—not minding the
inevitable clouds of dust. Bert knew them all. Those years,
whenever either of them could find fifteen cents, they'd get
to Kresge's five-and-dime in Watertown to buy another
miniature car or truck for their fleet. They'd played and pretended and painted those little vehicles year after year.
"Tootsietoys," Bert called them.

By the time Bert was fifteen, with the family broken up
and scattered, he'd been sent off to work for board and room
at the farm of some Iowa Hollander that Zee had come to
know from church. And by spring it had become clear that
the Christian spirit had passed by this obsessed farmer, who
worked the kid like a slave. After Zee finally rescued him,
Bob recalled with a glow of pleasure, Bert had come to stay
at his big sister's house in the Hidewood for a while. What a
dream come true it had been—a big brother for lonesome
Sonny to *do* things with! Bert and he and the Koppman boys,
riding workhorses of a Sunday afternoon. Bert's finally buying a single-shot, .22 rifle for them to use for gophers or rab-
bits or tin cans on fenceposts. They had even played with
their old collection of Tootsietoys once in a while, painting
one of the semi trucks to look like that of cattleman Elbert
Weisel, who lived in the neighborhood.

Then, in more recent years, needing to get out on his
own, Bert had started working out as a hired man for real
wages. Ma had encouraged him to start high school someplace, make up for lost time, but he just didn't want to do
that, didn't feel comfortable with the idea of school among
strangers. Anyway, he'd wanted to save money for a car. And
he'd found that roadster and fixed it up just the way he
wanted it.

Still relaxing on the grass, listening to the idling smooth-
ness of the Model A accompanying his memories of Bert,

Bob found himself feeling good. "No wonder his sisters think he's car-crazy," he said aloud. "I guess he's made me car-crazy, too."

Saturday nights in August, with the harvest taking precedence over everything else, activity in town seemed less intense than it had been in early summer. But there was always some action. Bob usually joined the procession for a while, taking a few cruises and U-turns along the main street. He did not, of course, stop at Paulson's Drug for those packages; he did not even drive to the Prairie Moon ballroom at Tunerville. But he made plans to learn about dancing and all that later in the year. The car gave him independence he had never known before—the folks didn't seem to mind if he stayed in town until midnight—and its dressed-up look attracted admiring glances now and then. Once when he was parked, idling, on a side street talking with Vance Ebert, a country-boy classmate, Vance's older brother who knew cars came up and paid him a compliment: "You must be a good mechanic," he said, "the way that Ford's idling, so smooth."

When school started in early September he began, as planned, to drive to town mornings, after rushing through morning milking (when he could) and breakfast so as to leave by eight-thirty. He sometimes arrived a little late. Every day the car provided private satisfaction, coming and going, though he was aware of its older vintage every time he pulled into the parking area alongside later models that other farm boys drove to school, most of them family cars. Not many of the classmates he liked to pal around with focused on cars much. Some took an interest in the fact that he now owned his own wheels and appreciated the special look he'd given the Ford. A friendly senior girl from north of town called out from the sidewalk one afternoon as he headed home, "Cute car, Bob!" Good taste, maybe wrong adjective. Sheriff Joe Staley, known as a good-natured man, from his jailhouse headquarters across from the school, had noticed, too, according to his freshman daughter. She said her dad hoped those seven lights didn't get turned on while the car was on the road.

Meanwhile, normal school activities increasingly absorbed Bob's time and attention. He became occupied with notebooks and texts for class work, mainstream after-hours obligations such as football games, and projects of personal involvement. He started writing a weekly rhyme for the school paper and felt the attraction of journalism. His voice had deepened, and he sang bass in the chorus. His trumpet playing for band had developed his interest in broader musical concepts of chords and arrangements.

Whenever school activities required cars to carry students to games or competitions, townspeople cooperated by lending their family sedans. Several classmates seemed to have no problem borrowing their parents' late models for occasional social purposes—dances in Watertown or Brookings, or even fooling around town evenings. One night, staying until after dark following a football game, parked at the dimly lit schoolgrounds with a mixed bunch in a friend's family's '39 Dodge, Bob found out how to play post office, an extracurricular activity he'd been hearing about for years. That night as they dropped him at the school parking lot to claim his car and drive home, someone in the Dodge announced, in what was probably meant as a simple, affectionate farewell: "Here you are, Bob, back to your jalopy— see ya tomorrow . . ."

Jalopy? Is that how others saw his car? Just a funny-papers flivver out of a Harold Teen comic strip? He mulled all this over during the dark miles home, and he came to realize that only country kids put much emphasis on personal car ownership—and not many of *them* were car-crazy enough to doll up their cars as he had the Ford. In his enthusiasm to follow Bert's lead, he had gone too far, outdoing his uncle, who at least seemed to know when to stop.

By late October a snowfall had covered the ground, and occasional flurries had begun to make the hard-rutted road unreliable. Pa and Bob had long since drained the radiators of both cars to make room for antifreeze. But the Model A's battery would have to be replaced before really cold winter weather set in. Bob had talked with his folks about schedules, and all agreed that he should start soon to stay in town again. Pa had most of the corn picked already, and Bob had been of some help, at least, to his father in the daily chores, though maybe not as much as he'd promised in his initial enthusiasm for buying Bub's car last summer. It was still great to have his own car, all right, but he wanted to turn his back on farm concerns for five days of the week and give more time to school-related matters.

Bert had let them know of his news: he had received his draft notice. The war headlines seemed to be hitting closer to home.

He drove in Sunday morning, the roadster's black isinglass curtains flapping in the raw wind. This would be his last Sunday with the family before leaving—the last Sunday he would drive the roadster before turning it over to James Koppman, down the road, who had been wanting to buy it for months. Bob wondered whether James would eventually become car-crazy, too.

Ma had cooked a terrific chicken dinner and had served it out on the dining room table to make a special occasion. She even had celery and olives, and a lemon chiffon pie. Afterward they all sat around and talked. Bert pulled out his

Camels and offered the pack to Pa, who rarely smoked. "They say everybody smokes in the army," Bert said, and this focused the conversation.

"You know," Ma said, "I was afraid you'd have to go pretty soon. Could feel it in my bones." Ma still felt protective about her youngest brother.

"Ah, well. You stand in the 1-A doorway, you're gonna feel the draft." Bert puffed again; he inhaled now, Bob saw. It was hard to make out the features of his face behind all that smoke, but he sounded relaxed. "It'll be someplace different, new."

"Where will they send you, you know yet?"

"First, Fort Snelling in Minnesota, they say. Then basic training somewhere else. After that—" The redhead hunched his wide, bony shoulders.

After a while Ma said, "You might be gone a long time."

"Or maybe only a year, like they say. Roosevelt might keep us out of the war yet."

"You all packed, have what you need ready to go?"

Bert took a final drag on the Camel and stubbed it into the saucer. He had a lopsided grin. "Yeah, just about. Except for one thing. I ordered a fog light from the catalog a couple weeks ago—then I got the draft notice. So I ain't even put it on."

This animated Bob. "You finally got that fog light you been talking about, and you don't get to see it on the roadster?"

Bert shrugged again, and the pale blue eyes focused on him. "You want it for your car? Let you have it for five bucks, less than it cost."

"Five bucks." Bob actually had that much cash put away, and a little more. But he had been looking through catalogs himself, and under musical instruments he had marked a page offering a white guitar, complete with instruction booklet, within his price range. With the knowledge he had accumulated through band and chorus, he had some ideas of his own about chords and harmonies.

The blue eyes were still on him, so he shook his head and looked away. "Guess not," he lied because it seemed the thing to do. "Can't afford it."

"Okay." His rejection didn't seem to bother Bert, who said James would probably want the fog lamp anyway, at full price, and he spoke of needing cash maybe to buy a motorcycle while in the army, if he could. Ma asked what he might want to do afterward, after getting out. Bob knew his mother well enough: she hadn't given up yet on more education for him, eventually.

"Oh, I dunno," Bert replied. His eyebrows rose quizzically, and he looked off to one side. "But I'd like to have a truck of my own someday."

"You mean, be a trucker? Around here?" Ma pursued.

"Sure. Grain to haul. Maybe a dump box for gravel . . ." Bert talked on about opportunities in trucking; he had it all figured out.

As he listened, Bob watched his young uncle, who'd always had so much to teach and to give, and a sense of sadness began to envelop him. Wherever the future would take them, from then on they would be traveling separate roads.

BIG LOAD

Bob
1941

Below treeless hills leading to the Hidewood Creek, behind the dark-red barn on Elmer Krause's bottomland place, the threshing rig all morning long had roared and groaned and bellowed, proclaiming its unquestioned primacy in the order of neighborhood life. From the extended nozzle of the pipelike blower a pale yellow plume streamed upward, tufts of straw and chaff first rushing into view against the sky, then seeming to think better of it, quickly losing momentum, wafting wide in gentle arcs onto the conical pile being carefully constructed. Thresherman George Roecker knew how to build a straw pile that would last, would shed inevitable rains and snow melt-off. He had learned his craft from his pioneer father forty years before, running the old steam-engine rigs.

Still, the shape of the straw pile could be only incidental to a thresherman's central responsibilities—to separate out the grain itself, to obtain the most from a farm's harvest. His stubby figure moved about restlessly, now stopping in the thin dust at the rear of the big machine to twist the blower gear-wheel and direct the flowing puff a few feet farther to one side; now lifting the galvanized metal door of his blower fan, increasing still more this sound of final harvest action, and inspecting a handful of straw for any signs of escaping precious kernels. He clambered up the metal ladder. Standing high atop the vibrating machine, he checked the half-bushel dump counter, caught grain in his palm, hefted it twice, and looked approvingly down at Elmer in the grain wagon attending the spout: "Good, heavy oats," his gestures meant, and the man who had planted it reciprocated with a grin of satisfaction that replied, "Yes, a farmer hopes all year for this."

The thresherman moved in short steps along the vibrating platform between rotating pulleys and chain gears, then paused, feet apart now, chubby hands splayed over his pot belly, bleary eyes squinting in the dust—taking a moment to survey, to monitor, to assess the tone of his noisy monster at work. Out at the far end of the wide power belt, his faithful old Minneapolis-Moline tractor, its yellow paint almost all faded away now, still had the stuff to handle eight bundle teams, two men at a time pitching steadily, one on either side of the feeder. He watched the feeder's relentless crossbars force the side-by-side sheaves below him into the chopping knives that cut the binding twine and pushed headed grain into the roaring teeth of the twenty-eight-inch cylinder. He listened again to the separation process itself: the pounding, shaking, sifting, blowing, the steady grind of gears and chains, the whine of belts and pulleys—sounds of a beautiful, well-oiled machine running smoothly under plenty of power. The sounds of threshing time.

One of the two pitchers at the feeder, Bob—just past his sixteenth birthday and running his own bundle team for the first time this year—kept half an eye on the thresherman. He should have felt good about finally being a real part of threshing. Not today. This was one of those crummy days when everything goes wrong. He knew they must be wondering if he could really handle a man's job.

It had started early that morning at home, after the milking. With the sun already up—Pa had said to hurry because with no dew, threshing could get an early start—Bob, moving fast, had been carrying the cream into the house. Maybe he had been rushing too much; all right, maybe he was a little careless and clumsy, too. Anyway, he had tripped on the porch step, and the whole damned can of cream had gone sloshing all over the cement steps and into Ma's hollyhocks. Great feast for the cats and dogs, but a lot less cream to sell this week. Coming in behind him, Pa had exploded in rare exasperation: "I don't see why the hell you can't be more careful!"

But worse had been the tip-over. Working on his second load of the morning, out where Krauses' oats field started running up the side-hill, he'd made the mistake of tossing too many bundles on one side of the wide rack before switching across the windrow to load from the other side. He had noticed the front corner of the rack sloping and teetering, and he worried as he turned the team up the incline. Then, sure as hell, there she went, the whole rack tipping off the bed and on its side, angled against the stubble ground. Nothing broke, but the few bundles that didn't spill out had to be pitched out anyway; bad enough to have the empty rack to lift back on. Worst of all was the humiliation. His partner, Vernon—and James Koppman, who was loading in a nearby windrow—had to come to his rescue, hoisting the rack up and over. With the time lost, he'd then had to hurry in with half a load in order not to miss his turn at the feeder. And it really hadn't helped much that Little Henry, in his second year at running a bundle team, had tipped, too, later that morning. Somehow, the men sort of expected Henry occasionally to get careless. The fact remained that good bundle haulers did not tip their racks.

Now, across the feeder, Bob saw that Vernon had nearly finished unloading. And he noticed that the thresherman, still atop his machine like a king of the mountaintop, took a quick squint at the sun, reached above where his striped overalls stretched tight over his belly, and pulled at a whang-leather thong anchored there. He briefly considered the heavy watch that slid from the bib pocket, then flipped up his greasy hand. Both pitchers immediately gave him full attention: the first rule of threshing demanded alertness at the dangerous work of pitching into the feeder. He looked straight at Vernon and held up his tethered watch. The man nodded responsively, gravely, and looked across the feeder at his partner.

"Robert!" Vernon's lusty voice, rising above the machine's noise level, had no equal among the other threshers. "Dinnertime. We'll need to clean up around the feeder."

The object of these instructions flicked one more glance toward the thresherman, who had now turned away to start back down the ladder. Bob simply gave a brusque nod across the feeder without looking up, and tried to repress the resentment that surged within him. He formulated words silently. This guy Vernon, just because he's ten years older, always thinks he has to explain everything to me: "Clean up around the feeder"—of course! Did he suppose I was going to drive away and leave him clean up by himself? Bob jabbed his long, three-tine fork into the last pile of bundles, swung them successively up onto the moving crossbars, and tossed up remnants of loose straw raked from the wide board floor of his rack. He unwound and jiggled the black leather lines, signaling the horses to move away from the machine; a slight pull was enough to stop them again. This team of Pa's, came the thought, he had trained them to be like he is himself, unexcitable and steady—most of the time. He recalled that first occasion, years ago, when Pa had Tim and Diamond, still colts, approach the noisy movement of the machine, and they had not become jumpy at all, like some horses might. James even had had a runaway two years ago.

Vernon was already working at the spilled bundles and loose stuff under the feeder. Bob found several forksful, then ran his tines perpendicular along the ground to rake in scattered spears with good heads still on them. Vernon's bellowed instructions again penetrated above the clacking of the feeder chain: "Some stones down here, Robert, be careful." Right, Vernon, without your guidance I might just toss one of these rocks up there into the cylinder, and bango, you'd really have something to talk about. But Bob only nodded at him again and continued skimming. The ground crawled and snapped with black crickets that had ridden in from the oats shocks. It made him feel like laughing out loud, remembering the time last year that Vernon, cleaning under the feeder just like right now, had a cricket crawl up his pantleg—just when the women were over by the tractor to pick up lunch pans, so he couldn't even take his overalls down to get at the invading cricket, and the thing must have been taking nips out of his hide in tender places, the way Vernon had grabbed and whooped as he hobbled out of sight behind the straw pile. Bob spoke silently now to his black insect brothers: "Come on, boys, let's do it again!" But in vain. Not even the damn crickets could do things right today.

He unhitched the team, let them drink from the tank, hooked their bridles over the hames, and tied halter ropes to the end of his rack. He found a half-bushel of Elmer's new oats so Tim and Diamond could enjoy their own threshing dinner, then turned toward where the small white house nestled against the barren foothill, the picture framed by dis-

tant thunderclouds on the southwest horizon. Only a few
straggling threshers were still in view: Vernon, just up ahead,
and the grain haulers, Pa and Julius Schleuter, in the shade
of the house getting ready to wash up. Far out in the oats
field, James Koppman and Clarence Roecker were just coming in with their loads from across the creek. Over near the
silenced tractor and separator, the rotund thresherman
finished writing in his notebook, slipped it into his overall
bib's wide pocket, and in quick steps also started toward the
house. Bob waited up. Funny, he thought, how the old farmers wear bib overalls and us young guys bibless; he glanced
down to admire the side buckle of his field boots, so distin-
guishable from typical farmer work shoes. Drawing nearer,
George untied the red kerchief from around his thick neck,
snapped dust from it once, and shoved his denim engineer's
cap to the back of his balding head. His friendly look made
a gold tooth glint in the sun. "Well, Bob, how's she goin'?"
At least old George knew what name to use these days;
Vernon kept calling him "Robert." At least he didn't hear
"Sonny" much anymore.

"Oh, pretty fair, I guess." Not much point in bringing up
the business about racks tipping, unless you have to.

"I guess you'll be goin' back to school next month. Your
last year, ain't it?"

"Yup, finally made it to the senior class."

"Well, that's good. I allus wished I'da gone to high school.
Tried to get Clarence to go, but he didn't want to. Little
Henry, he's quit now too, ain't he." The last was a stated fact;
Henry, a year ahead of Bob in high school, had dropped out
and was talking about joining the army after he'd finished
helping his grandpa with the threshing; Big Henry was getting too old to shovel grain.

"Yeah, quite a few of the farm boys who start don't seem
to finish."

"Sure, allus work to do at home. But lots to learn, too. Ever'thing is gettin' more complicated. What you goin' to do after—help your dad farm?" Old George and son Clarence had farmed together for years—two quarters and an eighty, with that powerful old MM tractor.

"Oh, I don't know yet." Bob shot a glance at his walking companion, and felt a sudden revelation: I am taller now than George Roecker. After a lifetime as the peewee of the Hidewood, Bob Amerson is no longer the shortest guy around. The notion emboldened him. "Don't know," he repeated. "Maybe farmin', if I could learn how to run a threshin' machine like you do."

"Heh!" George's gold tooth shone again. "'Fraid you're a little too late for that."

"Too late?"

"Yeah, hell, threshing machines, they're on the way out. It's all gonna be combines from now on; lots of farmers over by town use 'em already. So, no future anymore for threshers; this might be the last year we run this rig, you know."

He had stated it matter-of-factly, but Bob, scrutinizing, detected a kind of hardening in those watery eyes, and the corners of George's mouth seemed to crease down into his ruddy jowls.

They had reached the wash-up area at the north side of the house. The other men had already gone in. George rolled up the sleeves of his stained blue shirt, poured soft water from a pail into the basin set out on an old table, and leaned his face into what he dipped up in both hands. His arms and forehead glowed white, where the sun never got at him. His sudden exhaling into his hands sputtered in the water, and his stubby fingers extended the wet around his closed eyes and into his ears. Then he used soap briefly on his arms and greasy hands. "Well, that takes some of it off anyway," he said, using one of the already-damp towels.

"I'll get the basin," Bob offered, and splashed George's soapy gray water into the weeds.

"Fine," the thresherman nodded, and stepped briskly around the corner of the house. Bob took his time washing up. He had not considered before that this might be the last year of threshing. Not only for him, but for anybody.

On his way through the kitchen, he paused to talk with his mother, who was assisting Bessie Krause with the big meal. The two women every year exchanged help on thresher-dinner days. His three younger sisters and the two Krause girls scooted about like water bugs between kitchen and dining room to serve and clean the table—and get in on the event. In the dining room the lengthened table was set to accommodate the eleven threshers, including the two bundle haulers still coming in. Most of those at the table hunched over their plates in various stages of their meal. Large bowls and platters steamed with constantly replenished food: roast beef and fried chicken with mashed potatoes and gravy; corn, string beans, and asparagus; baking-powder biscuits and thick slices of bread; a variety of jams and jellies and relish and pickles; chocolate cake and apple pie. Bob found a place next to Little Henry and greeted his former schoolmate. "Howya doin', Henry? Looks like more grub than we used to get stayin' in town, eh?" Henry looked up, breaking concentration on his plate long enough to crowd an affirmative grin onto his bulging cheeks, and he took another drumstick from the platter that Bob handed him. Conversation around the table was subdued, maybe, Bob thought, waiting to hear from George, the leader—the leader who won't have anybody to lead, after the combines take over threshing.

"By golly, Elmer," the thresherman spoke up now, "these are some good oats we're thrashin' for you today, hey?"

"Yeah, looks like it," the farmer-of-the-day agreed. "This

first forty-acre field went pert-near fifty bushel, and the piece across the crick looks even better."

"Ohg, gyeah . . ." The thresherman responded through a mouthful of beef, lifting his fork like a bandmaster's baton to hold attention while he chewed and swallowed. "I been lookin' over at that field all mornin'. Pretty as a picture, those shocks out there so close together, somebody shoulda brought a Kodak. I bet that field will run sixty, seventy bushel."

"Goddam, Elmer," came Julius Schleuter's nasal assertion, "you boys're makin' us grain haulers work too hard, ain't that so, Clarence?" Julius cackled at his own effrontery; easygoing Pa only grinned, going along with the joke. But Vernon picked it up.

"Yeah, seems t'me any farmer with oats yieldin' like this oughta stand for the beer, shouldn't he?"

Through the good-natured laughter Elmer spoke up again. "Okay, you guys, I was goin' t'save this for a surprise, but I might as well tell you now—so neither the grain haulers or the beer guzzlers won't have nothin' t'complain about. I got Fred Wiswall comin' out from town this afternoon with his truck, and he's bringin' along some cold beer."

Hearty laughs and cheerful murmuring greeted this, but the news meant little to Bob. Last week Schleuters had had a tubful of iced beer out in the shade of the tractor to celebrate an exceptional wheat yield, but when Julius had queried Pa about whether Bob should be offered a bottle, Pa had hesitated—probably remembering how Ma felt about drinking—and mumbled back something about "pretty young yet." That was all right; learning how to drink beer or smoke cigarettes was not high on Bob's agenda. While shooting pool or fooling around in town, he had occasionally lit cigarettes experimentally, but he never inhaled, and he shared his mother's disdain for those who let themselves become influenced by alcohol. It could even be dangerous, as they'd seen with James Koppman over at Schleuters' last week. James was not much more experienced than Bob about beer, and the one bottle had made him so silly and wobbly up there on his load above the feeder that George had ordered him to come down and had taken over unloading James's bundles himself. Bob recalled George's story to them later about a guy years ago falling into the feeder, getting chopped to pieces by those knives, ending up as little bits of blood and guts inside the separator. The point about safety had been a somber one, but everybody had to laugh at the end of George's story when Vernon popped out with, "and I bet the worst of it was, George, that the fella plugged up the cylinder on yuh!"

Now, halfway through his meal, Bob became aware of a kind of conspiratorial silence around the table. Several of the threshers had finished eating and leaned back in their chairs, working toothpicks; as Bob watched, Vernon surreptitiously poked an elbow at his neighbor's ribs, and with a suppressed grin shot a glance in Bob's direction. But it was his school pal, alongside him, who was attracting their attention. Apparently when Henry finished with meat and potatoes, without bothering to look around the table and ask for cake or pie, he had reached out to grab what he took to be the nearest dessert, and he was now spooning up the last of a dish of strawberry jam—while everybody watched.

"Henry. Henny, Henny, Henny," Vernon finally intoned. "Bessie Krause's goin' t'charge you extra today for eatin' up all her best preserves."

Little Henry awoke to the reality and looked predictably sheepish. Guffaws around the table.

"I don't know about these high school boys," Vernon continued, loud and deliberate. "What do they teach 'em in that town school, anyway? First, how to tip bundle wagons, by the looks of things. And then to eat strawberry jam for dessert!"

Bob made a show of joining in their chuckling, but inside the familiar resentment rose again. So it happens that the two bundle haulers who tipped racks are also the only two who've been to high school, so what? And Vernon didn't have to lump him in with Henry about the jam.

The entrance of the two late bundle haulers now drew the group's notice. "Where you guys been?" George wanted to know. "I thought maybe you fell in the crick or somethin'."

Clarence Roecker, a taller version of his beefy father, raised an eyebrow and grimaced. "That ain't too far off, at that," he said, and looked half-accusingly at Elmer. "That's a pretty rough and rocky bottom, crossin' the crick."

"Yeh," James Koppman added, rolling a shirtsleeve still higher over his tanned Charles Atlas biceps. "When my steel wheels hit the rocks, the team got all nervous at the noise and the jolt. Couldn't hardly hold 'em."

"What happened?" Elmer asked in some alarm.

"Well, bounced the load too much comin' across, and I lost a whole back corner."

"Lost? How . . . ?"

"Oh, just a few bundles fell in the water," Clarence quickly put in, chagrined. "We fished 'em out, should be okay after they dry."

The thresherman pushed his chair back. "Yeh, well, pretty hard to build a good load that won't drop bundles in rough spots." He stood. "I got a little more greasin' to do. Machine time in about ten minutes." The threshers followed him out.

Standing at the front of his empty rack, Bob trotted his team behind Vernon's toward the waiting shocks of oats that thickly dotted the field, just visible over low willows lining the creek. Henry and Elmer had already hurried out there and were loading; beyond them, the gray and white billows in the southwest sky had become more pronounced. "Dark clouds on the horizon," he said aloud. "Miss Torgerson, in English 4 terms, would you say there's some kind of literary symbolism here?" He had to laugh, seeing himself weighing and sorting out his own feelings about his two worlds—farming and everything that had opened to him after three years of high school life.

So much of farming seemed just plain drudgery—dull, repetitive physical labor of routine chores, of obligatory work during hot, sweaty summers and bitter cold winters. Sure, pleasant weather came in the spring after the meadowlarks and mayflowers, but then a farmer had to be out there in the field twelve, fourteen hours a day, worrying about getting the crop in on time, eating dust behind machinery—horsepower or tractor power. Fall is maybe the best time of year, he thought, and not only because school starts in September and hunting season soon afterward. Something about the harvest really does satisfy; he was farmer enough to appreciate that. Living off the land, watching things grow, accepting the bounty of nature—they write poems and songs about such celebrations. "We gather together to ask the Lord's blessing . . ."

Tenor harmonies from the Thanksgiving music sung in school chorus last year ran through his mind, but it soon became crowded out by visions of harvest scenes: out in the stubble behind Pa's four-horse binder, acres of dropped bundles, all vulnerable to rain until set into drying shocks, heads up, one by one. Dawn to dusk, you had to be out there at those endless windrows of fallen sheaves, bending over all day long to set butts firmly on the ground, hoping the first two will balance until the next two can be added for support. The tall and slippery ones—oats sometimes and rye always—were nearly impossible to make stand. Barley and wheat beards penetrated gloves and shirtsleeves—and you'd better look out for your eyes. You had to take the heat and exhaustion and tedium of it all, with only occasional relief from the brown jug wrapped in wet burlap and left under a bundle out of the sun. You could tip the jug up on one elbow to take on needed water, by now tepid but at least wet, and then you might flop against a shock for five minutes of rest. Why would anybody choose to work like this if they didn't have to? he wondered. Drudgery was the only word for getting the harvest ready to thresh.

But threshing itself saved farm work from total tedium. He recalled early mornings, hearing exciting clanks and rattles over the steady exhaust of George Roecker's Minneapolis-Moline as he eased the big rig down the road and into the driveway, the thresherman standing to steer, waving as he passed by, wedge lugs on his tractor's heavy wheels leaving unaccustomed trails of power and glory across the yard, the monster machine following in its imperial metallic majesty. All the neighbors coming on the place, working together this one time of the year, talking and joking, glad to be freed from normal solitary work, enjoying each other's company and the big dinners, too.

For a kid, just watching all this was enough of a marvel, and gradually you could become a part of it, first tending the machine's grain spout at the wagons. There would always be plenty of sandwiches and cake in the covered dishpans the womenfolk set out in the shade of the tractor; you could kneel there and share lunchtime with the bundle haulers just in with a load. And when you were big enough to handle a fork, you could go out and spike-pitch, helping men load their racks, learning how to set the bundles butts-out above the sideboards, building the load until it got too high for you to reach. Some of the bundle haulers consistently made high, beautiful loads as a matter of pride. In this sense threshing seemed, in isolation, just the opposite of drudgery. It was, in fact, a kind of art that required skills and intelligence, working responsively as part of a team, achieving objectives shared by all.

And the whole thing was soon to disappear. George Roecker's words came back: "No future anymore for threshers; this might be the last year." One of those two-edged blades that they talk about in books, cutting both ways. You can't stand in the way of progress, including tractors and combines and all the other technology coming on. But no more threshing time? No George Roeckers running a threshing ring?

He became aware that Tim and Diamond had slowed. Ahead of them, Vernon had started his team into the creek crossing—a clearing about twenty feet wide, the murky water a foot or so deep. On this side of the cut, several new shocks of still-damp bundles testified to James's accident. Bob eased his horses down the incline and had them follow after Vernon. The hidden rock bottom jarred the rack, pinging against the metal wheels, but it didn't seem so bad if you took it easy.

He had tossed into his rack only a few shocks when he saw Henry, at the end of the next windrow, throw his fork atop a jag that sloped in on all sides—half a load, at best. Henry had to pull by him on the way in and obviously felt a little self-conscious about this pitiful appearance. "Runnin' outa time," he called out to Bob, "afraid I might be late at the feeder." It was a point, Bob had to concede; Henry and partner Elmer did have to hurry because they were first out after the dinner break, and Elmer as well had already started in. Bob only wished Henry's load looked as decent as Elmer's.

George Roecker had it right, this was a beautiful oats field—the shocks close together, the clean bundles tightly bound and well balanced between weighted heads and neat, flat-cut butts. Bob lost himself in the sheer esthetic pleasure of building his load above the rack boards—keeping the center level of bundles low enough so those he placed, butts-out, at the outside edge would incline heads downward. He had learned this technique early on, from George Roecker's homeless, unmarried brother Jack, who used to work as a spike-pitcher sometimes in George's threshing ring. He could hear the old hunchback's wheezy instructions: "See, you set each bundle in there hard, like this—ah!—an' then it's gonna stay put."

Remembering, Bob wielded his fork. Set the bundles into square corners and straight walls a foot wider than the rack—up, up, throw a few into the center, and up some more. The load was beginning to look good, and he did not feel like stopping as long as he could still make them stay up there. He peered past the corner of his load to check on his partner, and just as he watched, with a long swooping swing, Vernon tossed his fork high into the air, and it curved gracefully, tines down, to stick proudly atop his load, like the courthouse flagpole. Vernon's load was . . . well, respectable maybe, but not much more. Over at the next two windrows now, James and Clarence were back, starting new loads. Time was getting short.

Bob again appraised his own load. The outside edges of trim butts were built nearly straight up, just about as high as he could set them firmly. Vernon's noontime wisecrack came back to taunt him: "I don't know about these high school boys." He decided to lay in one more level row of bundles, shoving at the very end of the fork handle with the palm of his leather-gloved hand as he lifted and stretched; then he tossed up a few more into the center, to round it out. He stepped back to survey his work of art. If it wasn't a masterpiece, it was as close as he would ever come to it. Bigger than anyone else's load he'd seen all during threshing. He crouched for the fork swoop; it flew high, but the tines did not turn downward, and he had to jump out of the way when

the fork tumbled down off the high load. On the third try it
at least stayed up there, never mind the flagpole.

He laid a hand on Diamond's round rump, stepped upon
the evener, and reached up to where the lines were tied on
the standard, climbing the boards to rest a foot on the top-
most crossboard. The load level still loomed well above him.
For the first time a small voice inside intimated alarm: Did
I overdo it? Can I even make it to the top? He leaned heavily against the front wall of bundle butts, grasping tied twines
to pull himself up and make a kind of eagle's nest from which
he might drive the team. He found his uncooperative pitchfork and used it to rearrange the top of the load. It was his
highest ever—might even be dangerous, standing up this
high to pitch into the feeder; George would worry about balance and control, with or without the influence of any beer.

He clucked at the team, and the tugs tightened. James,
his boxer's torso again bared to the sun, paused as the big load
pulled by. "You're crazy, Bob!" he called out.

"Crazy? Nah, I just don't know my own strength."

"Anyhow, what don't fall off into the crick is gonna get
just as wet in the rain."

Bob looked around to the southwest. He hadn't noticed
how fast the thunderstorm was coming up. And—the crick.
The crossing. Maybe he had put it out of mind too much, letting other thoughts take over as he was building this load,
bundle by bundle. James is probably right. Nobody in his
right mind would try to cross with a load this high. What
makes me do these things—foolish pride? Misplaced enthusiasm of inexperience? Just plain careless, Pa might call it.
Well, what the hell. What was that Latin phrase he'd learned
from his teacher? *Quod erat faciendum*—we have done what
we had to do. Do it right while we've still got the chance.
Behind him, the blue cloud covered the sun and aimed gray
streaks at the earth, maybe a mile away. When it rains it

pours, just one of those days when things happen.

Up ahead, Vernon had long since crossed the creek, apparently without mishap, and was approaching the rig. Now: down the incline to the creek bed; he kept the lines tight, and the neck yoke pulled away from the horses as they tried to hold the weight back; hooves splashed. "Hoo-o-o— easy now," he called to them. The first submerged rocks clanged against his wheels, and the high load jiggled all around him. The horses seemed to understand that the next moments would not be easy, and they began to surge forward, building momentum to help carry the heavy load up the opposite incline. The entire rack wobbled and swayed but remained intact. Then, abruptly—clonk! Everything stopped. Tim and Diamond, uncertain, alternated in trying to move ahead, then backing against the rack front; panic was imminent. He held the lines steady and spoke to them, and they calmed. All became eerily quiet except for the babble of the flowing water. Now what?

He must have chosen a path this time to the left of where he had crossed behind Vernon before. He could see that just below the surface, a larger, solid rock blocked the left front wheel. Even if he could pull over it, the danger was that the high load would be shaken fatally, could even tip over right into the water. Only one maneuver seemed worth the risk. Softly talking to his team, he pulled them gently to the right, hoping that the blocked front wheel would somehow skid around the big rock; the risk included the possibility of breaking the long, wooden wagon tongue—and then they'd really have to send out a rescue mission. The horses strained to the right, the tongue bent . . . but did not snap, and with a grinding crunch the left wheel came up and over the blocking stone's slant, rocking the load dizzily this time, but the horses felt the motion now and leaned into their tugs. Then the front wheels were on dry land and the team, digging in, only had to pull up and safely over the incline. Bob looked back at the crossing. He had learned his early lessons well. Not a single bundle had fallen. "The Roecker Method comes through again!" he shouted, waving his fist at the creek.

Now he could turn his attention to the rig, still a quarter-mile distant. With everything in shadow, the details were hard to make out, but Vernon had parked his load alongside the faded yellow hump of tractor where he now stood with the thresherman. Henry and Elmer, at the feeder, had not yet finished unloading: he was on time for his turn, in spite of the extra minutes taken to build a load, in spite of the trouble at the crossing. Under the grain spout, Fred Wiswall's wide blue truck had replaced the wagons.

Small popping sounds on his straw hat reminded him of the weather, and a backward glance confirmed that the vertical gray shower was gaining on him. Occasional thunder began to growl. By the time he got close enough to hear the roar of the tractor and separator, splotching drops slanting down visibly had darkened his shirt. At the truck, Pa and Julius scrambled to help Fred spread a tarp over the box. Henry finished unloading before Elmer did—one of the advantages of a small rackful was less work at unloading, too—and then pulled up to start cleaning up under his side of the feeder. Some of the bundles there, already getting wet, produced loud groans of complaint from the whirring cylinder teeth deep inside. The machine seemed to know when it was time to stop.

George, standing on his tractor now, signaled with both arms and the bundle pitchers quit pitching in. The thresherman waited until after the bundles under the knives had passed through the angry grunts of the cylinder, and when nothing more wafted from the blower, he pulled back the hand-clutch lever, letting the separator coast to stillness. His short legs took him around in the rain to the front of his tractor to remove the big jack that had been braced against the wheel lug for belt tension. Then he bounced up again to inch the tractor ahead. Vernon was there to lift the heavy belt from the power pulley, roll it expertly, and stow the coil within the machine, safe from a soaking. Then George and Vernon together hurried— odd, seeing older men run like that—toward the nearby barn, where everyone else by now looked out from the shelter of its broad doorway. Bob tied the lines, climbed down from his load, and raced past the tractor, behind them.

"Dang," Elmer was saying in the huddled group, "And I was hopin' we could finish up today, too."

"Ah, hell," George said, watching the rain from the doorway and drying his round face with the red kerchief. "There's another day a-comin'. And if there ain't, we won't need t'thrash."

Some of the men standing around exchanged glances, letting traces of grins acknowledge the wisdom of their leader's words. But the thresherman remained silhouetted at the doorway, his back to the others, looking out into the slackening rain. Finally he turned to them, motioning with a stubby thumb back at the scene outside.

"Now there's a load of bundles," he said, and even in the obscure light that gold tooth gleamed. "Been a long time since I seen a load built like that, just so square and high, like a picture. That's pitchin' bundles."

Bob felt attention focus upon him, but his quick surreptitious glances revealed no one looking his way. Nor did anyone else speak. In the silence he imagined what some of them must be thinking: smart-ass kid, showing off, making the rest of us look bad. Even Henry might be sore, he thought, but I don't care. A guy has to do something right, for once.

"Say," Elmer's voice interrupted his uncomfortable quiet. "That case of Grain Belt's in ice water, in the tub over there. If we're just gonna stand around, might as well get at it now."

He nudged the truck driver. "C'mon, gimme a hand." Fred and Elmer hurried through the wet to where the shade of the tractor should have been, and they returned with the heavy washtub between them, brown bottles sloshing and clinking against ice chunks. They set it well inside on the barn floor. The threshers began to gather around it, picking out dripping bottles, prying caps off, and then passing the metal opener along.

Outside, past George's silhouette again at the doorway, the rain had almost stopped; the rumbling thunder each time became more distant. To the southwest Bob could see some blue sky showing through. But rainwater glistened shiny on the flat top of the threshing machine, and the slanting feeder dripped like . . . what? Like something out of a science textbook, the proboscis of some undiscovered metal dinosaur with a very bad cold. Threshing was over for today, all right—the sun would have to shine for hours before those darkened bundles on the two loads out there would be ready. He took another moment to appraise from this distance his square corners and high walls, rounded just right on top. Yessir. "Now there's a load of bundles."

A big hand grasping a wet bottle suddenly appeared before his eyes. "Here," Vernon was saying to him quietly. "Fella does a man's work should have a man's drink." Bob hesitated, then accepted the offer without further ceremony, without even looking around at Pa first; no need to worry today about anybody falling off a high load into the feeder. The opener worked the same as on pop bottles. Over at the doorway, George raised his beer briefly toward the others. "Well, boys, here's how." They tipped up; there were gurgles and scattered *ahs* of satisfaction. Light showed amber through his own bottle's neck above the diamond-shaped label. The froth tasted bitter at first, but he figured he could get used to it.

LOOKING OUT

Bob
1941–1942

In the high school that December morning, all eyes followed the superintendent, his strides heavy and purposeful as he crossed the front of the assembly hall. Under one arm he carried a domed, walnut-colored radio, its dangling cord grasped in his other hand. He set the radio carefully upon a corner of the raised stage and located an electrical outlet. He clicked the dial and then remained motionless, waiting for the tubes to warm up, one hand at the radio, his gaze concentrated toward the floor. Bob, seated halfway back in the hall, could hear the radio's faint hum break the dead silence around them. The superintendent—"Prof," the kids called him—turned up the volume, and over the humming and static came babbling murmurs of an excited crowd. Presently someone spoke out to introduce "the President of the United States."

Through the tinny speaker came the sound of applause and cheering that went on and on. Those people in Washington, Bob thought with a sudden insight that surprised him, they are just like us here today. They look to the president for leadership when a crisis comes along, the same way high school kids in this room are watching Prof, up there.

Over the cheers and applause and static, a gavel rapped. The familiar tenor voice, sounding stronger and angrier than in newsreels or Fireside Chats, began without ceremony: "Yesterday, December seventh, nineteen-forty-one—a date which will live in infamy—" (just what does *infamy* mean again?) "the United States of America was suddenly and deliberately attacked. . . ."

The president spoke of "severe damage" in Hawaii and "very many American lives" lost. Bob let his gaze wander from Prof, still immobile and staring downward at the radio, to Willard Carlson, across the aisle. Willard's dark eyebrows clouded the handsome face and disallowed his customary smirk; the two friends would have nothing to joke about this time.

Everyone had known, since yesterday, that they were living through a truly historic moment. Sunday's interrupted radio programs and subsequent reports and speculation from news commentators had made their impact in every home; he and Ma and Pa had huddled around the battery set half the afternoon and evening, even missing Charlie McCarthy. That morning he had heard lots of wild talk among the students before the nine-o'clock bell. "Boy, we're in the war now!" "I'm gonna join up, soon's school's over!" "Ahhh, we'll lick those little yellow bastards in six months." Bob could feel the agitation and shared some of the anger and bravado and even vengeful racial prejudice, but he still looked to the superintendent and the president for more explanation and some kind of guidance.

Now the president spoke of confidence and determination: "We will gain the inevitable triumph—so help us God." His words made everybody feel like clapping, but they did not explain very much. After Prof turned the radio off, he looked worried and said only, "We will be at war now, against both Japan and Germany, and we are all going to be affected, in one way or another." When he headed back toward his office, moving more slowly than before, he left the radio sitting on the stage. Bob wondered whether this was because he expected other announcements the whole school should hear, or what. Prof had been in the World War, he remembered; and he had two sons—one old enough to go right now. This wise, informed man probably doesn't know what's going to happen, Bob concluded, any more than the rest of us.

Uncertainty. Tremendous changes. Maybe danger or even dying, for some of us right in this room. Bob thought of Bub and Bert, already in uniform, and felt relief they had not been at that place in Hawaii. But they might see action before long. The Japs might bomb the United States itself, or send hordes of invading soldiers. Harry Koppman's Hidewood stories of the Great War—trench fighting, machine guns, mustard gas—took on new meaning. War. Hitler and now the Japs. All at once, we are in it. Exactly how are we all going to be affected? What about the future, for each of us in this senior class? In the tense excitement of the noon hour and over succeeding days, Bob asked such questions of himself and extended the discussion endlessly with Willard and with Vance Ebert, his other special friend and classmate. Big things were happening, they all agreed on that. The outside world was imposing a new agenda on the graduating class of Clear Lake High School.

When the intense emotional pitch of early December faded into workaday schedules around Christmas and into January, Bob felt a vague sense of disappointment. Being at war was not so different as he had thought it would be. Were people being patriotic enough, in the face of threats from Hitler and Tojo? Cedric Adams and H. V. Kaltenborn did speak daily on the radio of battles in the Pacific or over in North Africa; locally more of the guys were joining up or getting drafted; and people talked often about gas rationing or recapping tires. But for Bob, high school life went on almost as before, with basketball games, writing for the school paper, his role in the senior class play, musical performances with chorus and band, occasional dates with freshman girls—and, if not of the highest priority, the regular classwork. At home, things seemed as normal as usual. Occasional letters from Bub and Bert, in army training camps, speculated about whether they might get shipped overseas; other than that, folks around the Hidewood followed the same old routine. Pa did his winter chores and Ma took care of the house and the girls, and once in a while they all attended a gala evening with other neighbors in the Hidewood Club—really exciting stuff. Pearl Harbor had not brought vast transformation— at least not yet, though it might be a little early to judge. The war might last a lot longer than six months. Maybe he felt overly impatient for change, he conceded. The problem was, he could not decide what kind of change to hope for.

Graduation time approached all too quickly. For him, the senior year had been particularly fulfilling; he could feel himself changing physically, developing skills and interests on several fronts. Soon, all that "high school" implied would be over. Time for sentimental good-byes. And he wondered, penning witticisms and autographs in classmates' yearbooks, when will life be this good again?

School-related activities took on the special social quality that had always come with spring, but this year he lived with the sense that each of these final moments must be savored. He and Willard and Vance continued to pal around. The two of them now had steady girlfriends, and Bob sometimes managed to arrange dates as well, but girls were not always involved in their outings. There were regional competitions in Brookings, thirty miles south, for basketball or chorus. Or, often in Vance's family car (Bob's Model A served mainly to get him to town and back these days), they and other carloads of students might drive to Watertown's Lake Kampeska or to Lake Poinsett to take in dances or roller skating.

On a warm Sunday evening in April, Bob, Willard, and Vance lounged on a terrace of the roller-skating casino at Lake Poinsett. Still warm from the skating, the three of them sipped cherry Cokes and leaned against the terrace railing to catch the cooling breeze coming across the lake. Bob figured this might be the last time in a long while—maybe forever— when these two good friends and he could be together. He listened to water lapping at the casino's pilings down below; he took in the beauty of the moonlight dancing among the waves.

"Hard to believe," he said, pointing, "they used to fly planes right out there." He pictured the broad wings and yellow fuselage and the pilot's leather-gloved salute before the motor gunned and the plane roared skyward.

Vance, always interested in cars and airplanes, shifted his broad and muscular shape for a better look. "Really? On pontoons?" Like Bob, he was a farm boy who had come to high school without much organized sport experience, but his size and natural skills had made him a valuable lineman and pass receiver on the six-man football team.

"No, I mean during the dry years, regular biplanes, right on the lake bed—the shore line was a half-mile out there, then."

"The Old Man of the Hills, here, he's seen it all in his time." Tall, dark Willard had a sardonic streak, and he liked to kid Bob about being a year younger than others in his class. "But times have changed, old fella. You'd have to get the U.S. Navy to fly out there now."

"Listen, Carlson," Bob continued the banter, "you're not required to start bragging about the navy until you're actually in uniform." Willard had made it known weeks earlier that he had decided to join the navy rather than start at State College, where his two brothers had distinguished themselves.

"When do you go in, Willard?" Vance asked, an unusually serious expression on his good-natured face. "You know yet?"

"Yeh, June the twenty-third I trade in my tweed jacket for a sailor suit and a contract for one girl in every port." He cocked a dark eyebrow for emphasis.

"Then what?" Bob asked.

"You don't know what to do with a girl in every port? How young *are* you, anyway?"

"No, come on, I mean—training, and all that."

"Well, they tell me it'll be about thirteen weeks of boot camp, don't know where yet, then maybe some specialist training. You can come out with a rating."

"What kind of rating? Captain? Admiral?"

"No, that takes another thirteen weeks. Petty officer, third class, actually. Same as sergeant in the army. For instance," he turned more directly toward Bob, "with our experience working on the school paper, they might send me to a sort of journalism school and I'd come out a yeoman. Office work."

"That makes some sense," Bob said.

"Maybe too much. More likely, they'll turn me around the opposite direction, make a sonar man out of this silk purse. Anyway, Navy, here I come." He looked over at their companion. "What about you, Vance?"

"Oh, stay home and farm, I guess." Vance's broad smile faded and seemed to reflect slight discomfiture. "Maybe it's not the patriotic thing to do, but it's what the folks expect. They've already rented the land."

"Ah, hell," Willard punched him affectionately on a beefy shoulder. "Never mind the patriotism stuff. Farmers have to produce the food for our fighting forces!" Willard's long arm now rested at Bob's scrawny neck, and his brown eyes fixed on him, close-up. "Your turn. You still have a year to go before you can even register for the draft, eh?"

"I'll be seventeen in a couple of months."

"So what you gonna do with your extra year—become a country squire like Lord Vance, here? Get in some college? Or come along with me, Lucille, to join the merry navy and see the world?"

They both looked at him, awaiting his reply. All he had for them was a painful admission. "I don't know," he said. "I just don't know yet."

Planning ahead seemed beyond the abilities of his whole family, it seemed to him in the weeks around graduation time. "Just like his pa," neighbors might remark when, chording on the guitar, he would keep right up with Pa's old-time fiddle tune. Maybe the genes are similar in other ways, too, he thought. Pa going along day after day, year after year, without planning for real change. He still had no tractor, in spite of Bob's constant urgings and Ma's general agreement. There never seemed to be enough money. They were caught in a vicious circle: they needed money to buy a tractor to farm more land, but you need to farm more land to make enough money to buy a tractor. The folks ought to buy this farm, he knew. If they borrowed the money, it would pay in the long run. Make some improvements—windmill, electricity, indoor plumbing for the house, contour farming out in the fields. A little enlightenment. Planning ahead. Ma did manage to get me to high school, but now here we are again without a plan, at a crossroads where decisions are complicated. All I've got to my name is two cows and a calf and a beat-up bicycle, plus that Ford, and the whole kaboodle is worth maybe two hundred dollars; you couldn't buy a year at State College for that. Maybe some compromise. Graduating from high school doesn't necessarily mean leaving the farm—some farmers, somewhere, are even college graduates, after all. I've got to have that planning talk with the folks, he concluded, and soon.

The forces of nature intervened violently one late April morning to postpone any calm discussion about the future. He awoke to Pa's urgent call up the stairs—"Better get up, storm's comin'." Through his upstairs window came an eerie yellow light off the low clouds. He quickly threw on his clothes and clomped down the steep stairway for a look out the west windows, almost always the direction of summer storms. Beyond the tall barn, oddly orange in this yellow light, a dark and menacing mass of roiling weather loomed, coming at them fast. Ma—fearful of summer weather anyway—rushed about, pale and wide-eyed, getting the girls up. Within minutes a quickly rising wind drove heavy raindrops that splatted alarmingly against the west windowpanes as the family huddled around the kitchen table. Then both rain and wind attacked with frightening fury; puddles formed beneath windowsills; over the howling roar, as if from the inside of a gigantic popcorn kettle in a blast furnace, came sounds of debris slamming against outside walls. "Maybe shingles off the barn," Pa said, more alarmed now, his pronouncement punctuated by a tinkling crash as something burst through a pantry window. The storm had gained entry.

Pa rushed to find a quilt to hold against the window. Bob ran to the east room, picked up his guitar and accordion, and—feeling somewhat foolish—stowed them under the downstairs bed. When his gaze rose again above the bed level, he saw his mother kneeling on the other side of the bed, a look of agitated terror on her face and her hands clasped before her. He had never before seen her pray. Then he ran to join his father trying to keep the storm from coming in the broken window. The relentless roar around them seemed without end. In near-panic, Ma led the girls toward the pantry's cellar door, but at first she couldn't pull it open because of the inside pressure from the storm's wind. At one point the house shuddered, and they looked at one another in new alarm, but then the wind abated a bit and they summoned courage to peer through an unshattered watery pane. Through the distortion, Bob saw empty space where the high, dark barn had been. Within the bare foundation walls, wet shapes of terrified horses pulled tight on halter ropes still tied to the remaining timbers of their mangers. In the shiny wet yard, a sow without her piglets slowly wandered through the pelting rain as if demented, a splintered two-by-four still sticking in her side.

A half-hour later the storm had subsided. They discovered that the entire barn had sailed more than a hundred yards to make a direct hit on the front porch before crashing down in the house yard, creating tons of confusing wreckage. They gazed at the shambles, then looked at one another in the grim knowledge that it had been a near thing. "A little difference in direction of that wind," Ma said, "and you two, standing at that window . . ." As it was, in this battle only the injured sow figured on the casualty list. The tied horses, miraculously, had escaped without a scratch. "We have been lucky," Ma kept repeating. Bob wondered whether she gave some credit to her anguished praying.

It was going to take all summer to clean up the mess. Minor house damage demanded repair first. They quickly had to arrange a place in back of the granary where the cows could be herded for milking that very morning. Fence washouts needed fixing. In the next weeks, the broken remains of the old barn would have to be removed, board by jagged board, from the front yard. Carpenters sent by the insurance-company owners would do most of the work of clearing the ruins and constructing a new barn, but it would take weeks, and the men would have to be fed the noon dinner. Meanwhile, the normal farm work had to get done. And somehow it did—the planting, the cultivating, the mowing—until finally harvesttime approached.

For Bob, it was a summer of tedious obligation, of suspended decision. He went through the necessary paces of work during the week, looking forward to Saturday night breaks when he could see school friends in town. Occasionally he took in the dance at Tunerville, another ten miles away, really enjoying the dancing but skipping the standard boozing. Sometimes he hooked up with a girl to take home and got in a little necking. At an "Anchors Aweigh" party, he helped send Willard off to his navy destiny. Sundays Pa usually let him sleep in, and he would spend a delicious day of leisure, cleaning and washing his Model A and maybe the family V-8, too, down by Schleuters' soft-water slough. Later he might tighten and tune mechanical aspects of the cars, but he had stopped buying accessories. He read *Gone with the Wind* once again, seeing the movie scenes on every page, and he dog-eared a copy of *Esquire* magazine inherited from one of the guys at school, with its Petty Girl drawings that always produced tingling sensations. He kept the magazine under the seat in his own car to avoid questions from Ma or the girls. Once in a while he got to the movie in town, since Pa would let him get out of Sunday night chores. Then Monday morning, and the weekly work routine started over.

He gave up on the idea of getting both his parents together for a serious talk about the future. They just didn't operate that way. Instead, he awaited the right circumstance and mood for a discussion with his mother. It came one evening after supper, with the two of them at the kitchen table paging through the newspapers.

"Hm-m," Ma said, shaking her head slowly, "here's another list of boys getting called to the service."

"Yeah, I saw that too. James Koppman got his draft notice last week, Craig told me."

"Well, he wasn't on the farm anymore. Workin' in town. No reason he shouldn't get drafted." She paused. "There'll be some real fighting before long, you mark my words."

"Lots of the guys are in already. Little Henry, where'd he end up? Texas someplace, wasn't it? And you saw the card yesterday from Willard, in San Diego, California, the lucky stiff."

"I thought you said he might go to State College. Wasn't it one of his brothers played in the college band, we saw at the cornhusking contest?"

"That's right, but Willard, he wanted to join the navy. Some of the other guys from school, though, are going to State. One, I know, has already signed up for ROTC—that's Reserve Officer Training Corps. He'll be able to go to college and come out an officer."

"Pretty good, I spose. If you have to go in."

"Y'know—" He pushed the folded newspaper aside, leaned his elbows on the oilcloth, and looked at her more directly. "I've been trying to figure out what I should be doing, too."

She looked thoughtfully toward the kitchen wall, nervously chewing the inside of her cheek. "You're not even seventeen yet," she said to the wall.

He went on. "What would really be, uh, ideal, would be college, and ROTC to take care of the military part. But State College, that would cost three, four hundred dollars a year, at least. Old Slicko and her heifers wouldn't bring that. Out of the question, I guess."

She regarded him briefly and nodded agreement, but she said nothing. Bob mentally kicked himself: he didn't have to go talking that much about State College to her; he knew himself it was impossible. Had he done it to let her know he was having to make the Great Sacrifice? Had he expected her to come up with some miracle, the way she could make warts disappear or witch for water?

He rubbed his jawbone, coming back to reality. "So, I dunno. I guess I could always start farming, like Vernon or Clarence Roecker and everybody else around here." This time he was going to wait for her to say something.

"Well, ah," she cleared her throat. "Farmers help in the war, too, as far as that goes. That's why farmers are deferred. And there's lots of different ways of farming. A person can have it nice these days, if you work at it."

"You mean not just having a fence around the lawn but electric lights and running water and that famous bathroom right here in the house."

"Sure. A windmill for the well. He needs that. Maybe a milkin' machine, once you get electricity. All those things are easier, more natural, when you own your own place. If we farmed more land, we could get enough ahead to buy this place, I bet."

"But to farm more land, there'd have to be a tractor. When will Pa ever give up horse farming?"

She regarded him steadily. "If you was home to go into farmin', he'd be ready to get a loan for that tractor, all right."

There it was. She didn't come right out and say "Your Pa needs you to get ahead," or "Come help us get ready to buy our own farm." Nor would she ever suggest that a guy should dodge the draft by staying on the farm. She was only giving in to her natural, maternal instincts, he knew.

The conversation was left there, for the time being. Bob could feel himself inexorably swept along by circumstances and his own inertia. Maybe it was true that a farm boy could contribute to the war effort, raising food for those away from the home front. Certainly it was true that his hands around the farm could help carry his folks over the top—he paused, and had to laugh at himself, aware that the simile formed in his mind came directly from trench warfare stories. Well, if Destiny assigns me to fight the war on the farm, he concluded, so be it. He did not enjoy the idea, but soldiers like Bub, now in the cold, fogbound Aleutian Islands, or others on Wake Island or the deserts of North Africa—they could not enjoy their assignments, either. California, though, came the afterthought, that might be something else; Willard's postcards carried a message of glamour.

Whimsical weather once again intervened to make his assignment a questionable one. Late July had been particularly hot, and thunderstorm clouds gathered frequently. After noon dinner one day—ironically, on the very day Pa had finished repairing the binder canvases for the harvest—they stood together on the platform of what had been the front porch before the barn smashed it off, and they watched a dark blue rain cloud with white streaks sweep across their oats and cornfields less than a half-mile away. "Lot of hail in there, looks like," Pa said, in typical understatement. In a matter of minutes the hailstorm had effectively wiped out most of the crop for the year. There was no hail insurance; it had seemed too expensive in the spring.

Those next days, Bob could not throw off a feeling of dazed depression. Such a year of disaster for the family, demonstrating with staggering clarity the utter dependence of farmers upon the weather—weather over which they had absolutely no control. What was it—bad luck? Capricious fate? God punishing people for unidentified sins? Were these mysterious forces trying to tell him something? If so, they have succeeded, he told himself, mulling over the situation

constantly as he went about routine chores. High-risk farming could never be for him, not for a life's work. Once these
short-term obligations are done, he vowed, he would leave
the land for good. A quote from English class in high school
came back to mock him: "I am the Master of my Fate, I am
the Captain of my Soul." The concept festered, and twice
daily he took solace from a feed-store calendar tacked to the
inside door of the cream separator room in the new barn. Pa
used the numbered spaces as a breeding record for his cows;
Bob focused on the lettered quotation: "SELF-CONFI-
DENCE IS THE FIRST REQUISITE TO GREAT
UNDERTAKINGS." Mornings and nights, as he leaned and
pulled at the heavy separator crank, he repeated the quotation aloud, against the machine's growling whine. Once he
added, shouting: "I got enough of the first part for now; just
show me where the great undertakings are."

Then he learned that Destiny, Lady Luck, or whatever it
might be called could also show a happier face. The face,
quite literally, belonged to a smiling, distinguished-looking,
gray-haired man who drove a battered '34 Ford into the dusty
driveway one August afternoon and asked for Bob. "I heard
in town you might be interested in going to college," the tall
and elegant visitor said. "I represent the College of
Commerce in Minneapolis." A little strange, it seemed to
Bob, the guy coming around like the Watkins man, peddling
education instead of spices, but it won't hurt to listen. The
two of them started talking at the kitchen table, while Ma
fixed and served tea and her warm biscuits with chokecherry
jelly. Pictures and brochures came out of his case for their
inspection. The man spoke of preparing for a career in business, how useful office skills can be in many walks of life, even
in the military. Bob asked for more information about that,
and the visitor smilingly, convincingly, recounted how various graduates of the eight-month course had entered the

navy as qualified yeomen, third class, with opportunities to move quickly up the career ladder to become chief petty officers. What about cost? Just $150 tuition to cover the entire course, and there were many opportunities in Minneapolis to find jobs to pay for room and board. He would even be there personally to meet Bob at the bus station and take him to a boarding house near the school. "You don't have to decide now, of course," the man said, "just write me at this address."

A half-hour later Bob and his mother, by themselves, looked once more through the brochure on the kitchen table. "Not really a college, but just a hundred and fifty dollars," he said. Maybe he could get Vance to come along, just for the adventure. "It would be possible, you know."

She regarded him with uncertain suspicion. "What would be possible?"

"Listen. Here's my plan for a compromise." He heard himself proclaiming like a figure from Prof's history class—who was it, Henry Clay, the Great Compromiser? Maybe I can go him one better. He pulled his kitchen chair closer to the table and used both hands to describe the idea formulating in his head.

"Now, I got those cattle—little, runty Slicko and her roan heifer and now *her* calf. That's three generations, worth more'n the hundred fifty bucks. I could sell my car, too, for bus tickets and extra expenses. This course"—he waved the brochure—"runs about eight months, that's September through April. With the harvest wiped out now, there's not going to be much to do around here anyway this fall."

"What would you do all alone in the city?"

"Well, the studies, mostly. And I wouldn't be all alone, with Irene working right over in St. Paul." His mother's sister had just moved from Watertown to the Twin Cities.

"Oh, that's right." He could see this reassured her.

"And Pa's brother Oscar and them in Minneapolis, too."

She nodded, looking thoughtful. "Eight months, you say?"

"September to May. I could get back for springswork."

Now she got interested. "That would be before your eighteenth birthday," she said.

"Oh, sure, when I register for the draft, I'll do it here in town—like a good farm boy should."

"We could rent that quarter over by Koppmans', look for a tractor."

"You think Pa will go along with the idea?"

"He's never stood in your way before, has he? No, he'll be real glad to hear you're goin' to farm with him. I know it."

"Okay, I'll talk with him about it, then. But you think it's the right thing, going to the Cities for a while?"

She smiled, more confident now. "Long's you get back for springswork. And I'll tell you something else." She fixed him firmly in the eye, the bond almost tangible between them. "I'm glad you're going to get out and see the world a little bit. Sometimes I wish I'd done that when I was your age." She laughed, sharing certainties. "You know darn well I didn't go to all that fuss to get you through high school just to see you turn into another dirt farmer! If it wasn't for this war . . ." She threw up her hands and beseeched the ceiling in a gesture of frustrated surrender.

"Well, that's another thing, the war," he said. He conjured visions of himself amid city lights, taking first steps along a road leading . . . somewhere. He could almost see an eventual snapshot taken under a palm tree, a sailor in the navy uniform of yeoman, third class. "I mean, I don't know how *long* I'll want to stay farming. Let's plan to do this one year at a time, okay?"

"Seems fair."

"I wouldn't want to stay out of the war altogether.

Wouldn't feel right about it, and neither would you, once it's all over."

"Spose that's true. It's for you to decide."

He stood, feeling good about the cleared air. "Well," he said, "I guess I better get out and help with the chores, check on my cattle, if I want to look like a farmer around here."

She laughed again, and as he headed out she called: "And—say?"

"Yeah?"

"Don't figure on selling all your cows, or your car, either. I have some egg money you can use for the bus ticket. Leave Slicko here to get some more calves for you, like money in the bank." She hesitated a moment but had more to add: "You might need another escape plan someday."

"Right," he said, smiling back at her. At the door he turned to lift two fingers above his eye in the salute that elegant, leather-gloved pilots make just before taking off.

afterword

In the fall of 1942, a seventeen-year-old greenhorn eager for new experiences, I boarded a Greyhound bus bound for Minneapolis, two hundred miles distant. With that act I became part of a national population-shift statistic: another farm boy leaves, turning away from the tradition of father and grandfather. I did not even have to feel completely alone in the big town. Lovely Aunt Irene, then living in east St. Paul, was at the other end of the telephone line, if needed. The next few months provided excellent practical experience, if not much formal education, as I attended typing and shorthand classes at the College of Commerce and worked nights at a downtown hotel and a restaurant. Like many other rural teenagers—boys and girls, before me and since—I knew that my future awaited away from the family farm, and I gloried in making my own way in the city.

But I had a promise to keep. After eight months in Minneapolis, only slightly more enlightened about the world, I returned home to farm with my father. We rented another quarter section, doubling our acreage. I found a used John Deere tractor with a plow—not much of a tractor, but a big step above horse farming—and my father negotiated a four-hundred-dollar loan for it. We worked long days in the fields, as farmers must, and I tried not to dwell too much on the city life left behind. (Concentrating on accessible pleasures, I replaced my cherished Model A with Aunt Zee's 1934 Ford V-8, and realizing an old dream, I learned to fly light airplanes.) The weather cooperated, and wartime prices favored our cash crops. The Depression seemed over. Though the war limited production of farm equipment, after two years we managed to obtain a *brand-new* Ford tractor complete with plow and cultivator.

We made other improvements as well. My father persuaded the insurance-company landlord to put up a windmill: no more troublesome gasoline engine at the well. We bought an antiquated six-volt Wincharger electrical generator from a neighbor and bolted it to the peak of the house rooftop, where the wind could get at it. When a good breeze came up the whole house vibrated—but we had electric lights, via two wavering bulbs in the ceilings of our kitchen and living room, until the weakened glass batteries in the cellar ran down.

In those two years that we farmed together, my father continued to drive his beloved horses, leaving most of the tractor driving to me. But before I left for military service in 1945 (I agreed with the draft board, it was time to go), he had completed his personal conversion to tractor farming and felt confident that with the new Ford he could now work two quarters of land by himself. He probably had noticed that his daughters could also handle this tractor; "little" Jeanie eventually became especially adept.

While I was away in the army, my parents bought the home place. My father had always been a "good farmer," never showy, but in his quiet way willing to work unstintingly for his livestock and on the land. As a landowner, he began to take more interest in modern ways of doing things. He put up a silo for better use of corn fodder as feed for milk cows.

He became one of the first Hidewood farmers to combat erosion through contour farming, working with the county agent to plot graceful arcs that swooped across his tillable side-hills. He bought the right proteins for his hogs and became known for the excellence of a series of purebred Hereford bulls he acquired as yearlings.

Perhaps nothing meant more to my parents' life on the farm than the arrival of the REA—a spur line built to the Hidewood by the government's Rural Electrification Administration in 1946. Real 110-volt electricity illuminated every room in the house at the click of a switch; my mother could stow away the old kerosene and gas lamps, the smelly gas iron, and the gasoline-engine washer with its noise and fumes. She could consider a Mixmaster, an electric stove and refrigerator, a real toaster. Outside, a powerful bulb on a new yard-light pole facilitated after-dark chores, especially in winter. Current in the garage permitted power-tool options: grinders, drills, saws. The barn boasted a milking-machine system, making for a whole new style of dairy farming. I cannot imagine any American institution that needed or appreciated electrical power more than the family farm.

With ownership, the folks felt motivated to work at what they formerly considered nonessentials to enhance the quality of life on the farm. While I was home on a monthlong summer furlough, we landscaped the entire front yard, put a fence around the house and yards, and planted dozens of trees and shrubs. And a few years later they finally converted half of the downstairs bedroom into a bathroom, furthering my mother's longtime hope of "having it nice." My father, too, became fond of this handy utility that could give him the luxury of a bathtub filled with hot water after a dusty day in the fields. Other modern conveniences came into their lives: a dial telephone to replace the thirteen-party-line, hand-crank box so recently installed on the kitchen wall; a television set; a better car to drive over improved, graveled roads.

By the mid-1950s, Hidewood people talked of Social Security benefits becoming available to farmers as well as to wage-earning employees, and about possible enactment of some kind of national health insurance for older folks. Some farmers actually planned for retirement in town. My parents, too, began to think in terms of taking it easier someday; at my mother's urging, they even made an exploratory trip to agricultural zones around Los Angeles. One child still lived at home—Richard Terry, born in 1943, ten years younger than Jeanie—and his high-school education had to be considered in deciding where to reside. But some kind of easier living seemed in their future.

My father's unexpected death in 1957, at age sixty-six, cut short further speculation about retirement living on savings and Social Security benefits. My mother, only fifty-three, and fourteen-year-old Terry continued for a couple of years to live on the farm, renting out the land. Then they moved to the Twin Cities, where my sisters Elaine, Mavis, and Jean lived, for Terry's final two years at a big-city high school. For the first time in her life, my mother got herself on a payroll, working in the kitchen of a Chinese restaurant. She didn't like it. But she had finally taken her turn at being on her own.

And she continued on her own for another thirty years. After having offered her siblings a stable home for more than two decades, *she* became the wanderer. She lived for a few years near several of her sisters in southern California, baking pies and breads in a local restaurant and driving her sporty Chevrolet Corvair between the West Coast and the Midwest several times, occasionally alone. She lived for a while in the small town of Estelline, South Dakota, not far from her own roots and in the neighborhood of stepdaughters Marie and Clarice. Later she moved to Watertown, where she would be very near Clarice and her family, including their many children and grandchildren. She became the family matriarch. (Nearly everyone, including the grandchildren and Clarice's great-grandchildren, called her "Ma," a name applied to no one else in this extended family; even her sisters spoke of her as "Ma-Bernice.") Still later she moved once again to Minneapolis, and for nearly twenty years enjoyed having her own apartment in a complex built for seniors. When she died in 1993 at eighty-nine, she still had her memento-crowded apartment, her sharp mind, and her integrity. She had made her mark.

Marie and Clarice left South Dakota for a few years during the war, but both returned to the area where we all grew up, and they live there still. The other five of us, perhaps responding to our mother's push to seek education, all left South Dakota to obtain college degrees, and we have remained away. None of us ever questioned the need for higher education, even though our parents could not pay for it. In my case, the postwar GI Bill made all the difference.

But the continuing presence of our two sisters and their families in our home Dakota location has always offered solid family reasons to revisit our roots regularly. For my wife and two daughters and me, our home leave from Foreign Service posts in South America, Italy, and Spain was never complete without a visit to Marie's farm, and our daughters grew up thinking of the Midwest as home. They still do, although they live in the Northeast; moreover, they periodically take their own children back to experience our big family reunions on Marie's farm.

For me these return visits have always represented more than the simple pleasure of being with family and seeing old neighbors. There's something about the *place*, as well. From there emanates an almost mystical force—less compelling than the spawning salmon's urge to return to its origins, but, somehow, atavistically related. Every time we return to the area we have to drive by the home place for one more look at the rolling Hidewood Hills, at the long view Ma used to enjoy from her kitchen window, at the abandoned buildings themselves. It is useful to be reminded where we came from, and to remember the past, good and bad, symbolized in these sagging structures. In a sense, every time we note changes in the home place, we also mark the passage of our own years.

What we have seen in progressive stages has not all been pretty. After my mother and Terry left the farm about 1960, some attempts were made to continue it as a family farm. A young California couple, tired of the urban rat-race, tried but couldn't make it successful. Before long the house stood as abandoned as the privy and the chicken coop, though the granary remained useful to the new landowner, who also ran cattle in the pasture and occasionally made use of the barn's shelter. With the passing years, the empty house presented increasingly stark, evocative images. First broken windowpanes, then doors that sagged open and let in the harsh elements to start rotting the interior. Then gaping holes in the roof appeared, mercifully hastening the process.

One year, inspecting the place with my mother, then in her eighties, I peered through a dark hole in the east room wall and saw, among the shadows of peeling wallpaper and fallen plaster, what remained of our upright piano—the thirty-dollar marvel that had brought us so much joy. My mother had sold it with the farm, and the new owners never bothered to pick it up. At the north wall, through a decaying aperture that had been our folks' bedroom window before they converted that space to the long-awaited bathroom, a gloomy image awaited us. In the dim light I could make out vaguely familiar forms, like markers in some dusty tomb, under gray splatters of fallen plaster, caked dirt, and lifeless insects. Then in the dead silence these shapes suddenly came into focus as the very bathroom fixtures that my mother had once—not so long ago—proudly showed us in their glistening newness. In the intervening years, she had been stopping by the place every year or two, and she knew what the old house still contained; even so, the sight seemed almost too much for her. For any of us.

Eventually our house had a decent burial. The landowner sold the farmyard plot, separate from the productive land, as a home site. Today when we stop by the old farm and stand by the mailbox out on the road, we see only a mound of earth where the new owners finally bulldozed the old house in on itself.

Just south, an emptiness reminds us that the one-room schoolhouse, whose location was such a prize to us when we moved into the Hidewood, disappeared from its allocated acre years ago. After it had stood unused a while, a neighbor bought the building and moved it into the grove of his prosperous farm to use for grain storage. Now his farm buildings, too, long since abandoned, have all but disappeared. Local kids ride the bus the ten miles into Clear Lake, today the site of a county-wide educational system.

Consolidation has become the key concept in rural areas, including the Hidewood. Fewer farmers cultivate more acreage. Country schools and country churches disappear into centralized systems. Farmers and townspeople watch the same TV shows, make the same vacation trips, enjoy the same comforts at home. It is hard to find many pockets of isolation these days comparable to our neighborhood of sixty years ago.

With all these changes, some constants do remain in the Hidewood. The land itself continues to endure with a value of its own. The family-farm values that shaped those of us who grew up there a generation or two ago still predominate. I have wondered how much of the past is worth saving. My list—consolidated to match the rural trend—includes mostly lessons, sentiments, and values.

I learned early the importance of self-reliance and responsibility. Responsibility for chores at a young age, staying at a job until it's done, knowing you're expected to do your best, with or without a helping hand: farm kids just *know* about such things. And when such values become part of you as a kid, they tend to remain.

I saw what happened when people worked to make things better. And I certainly gained an appreciation for labor-saving devices of all kinds. I still find a good car—or a good wrench, for that matter—a thing of exquisite beauty and promise.

The Hidewood community taught me that you can trust people and expect them to help you. Out in the country, you can still assume your neighbor—or even a stranger—is a decent person, at least until proved otherwise. Although farmers in rural neighborhoods don't work together on common projects as much as we did many decades ago, this sense of community still prevails among folks who all know each other; if you request help, you'll likely receive it. This is a powerful force to carry within you: positive expectations tend to produce positive results.

More than anything, I value from the past the experience of not having had everything I wanted served up at once. I like having been obliged to figure out an objective and then to work to make it happen. This phenomenon translated into my generation's assumption that by pursuing a goal, with a little luck, one would eventually become "better off" than one's parents. The lives of our children and grandchildren are much more complicated.

To be sure, these values are hardly unique to yesteryear's family farm. Through the ages parents, rich and poor, from all walks of life, have sought to instill similar qualities in their offspring. Certainly many parents, favored by educational insights, financial means, or family connections, have succeeded in giving their children a better, more purposeful start than could most folks in the Hidewood sixty years ago. I suppose what makes our family's experience unique is that we had few options: kids were *expected* to work responsibly, to figure things out, to cooperate with the neighbors. Maybe we were lucky. What seemed at the time stifling limitation turned out, I think, to have had some long-term advantages.

Growing up on the family farm was not always easy for any of us, with the sheer burden of physical labor, the constricted enjoyment of the world at large, the sometimes formidable obstacles that faced us. Indeed, the negative factors compelled me to seek a future elsewhere. Nevertheless, these remembrances allow me to see more clearly that the fundamental value system inculcated during those formative years has stood us in good stead all our lives. Remembering what was, and looking about today, I am left mainly with a sense of gratitude for a life that began simply, presented opportunity along with huge challenges, and gradually brought rich rewards. I am glad I come from the Hidewood.

acknowledgments

Collaboration is an essential factor in most published works, and this personal memoir is no exception. I am deeply indebted, first, to the many members of my family who shared private insights and agreed that these historical realities—including hard times some might consider best forgotten—should be recalled here.

Among our Hidewood neighbors of yesteryear, Laurel S. Kaiser and Lois S. Stee deserve special thanks, notably for details regarding their mother Vera Weisel Schleuter. Likewise, my gratitude goes to Lois K. White and Audrey K. Dumke for their interest in telling the story of their parents, Elmer and Bessie Krause. On tales from our one-room school, Walter Thompson—the only "man-teacher" I ever saw at Plainview #41—offered enlightening personal background. And I only wish that Bessie Terry had lived long enough to read these words of appreciation—not only for her early skills that surely affected me fundamentally, but also for our latter-year conversations about her teaching experiences.

Finally, a doff of the authorial hat to two truly excellent practitioners of the written word—Minnesota Historical

Society Press managing editor Ann Regan and freelance editor Mary Russell Curran—whose thoughtful and sensitive thoroughness, far above the normal call of professional duty, it seems to me, helped to keep this work in sharp focus.